MUSEUMS
AND
AMERICAN
INTELLECTUAL
LIFE,
1876-1926

MUSEUMS

AND

AMERICAN

INTELLECTUAL

LIFE,

1876–1926

~

STEVEN CONN

The University of Chicago Press / Chicago and London

Steven Conn is assistant professor of history at The Ohio State University

The University of Chicago Press, Chicago 60637
The University of Chicago Press, Ltd., London
© 1998 by The University of Chicago
All rights reserved. Published 1998
Printed in the United States of America
07 06 05 04 03 02 01 00 99 98   5 4 3 2 1

ISBN (cloth) : 0-226-11492-9

A version of chapter 5 appeared as "Henry Mercer and the Search for American History," in *Pennsylvania Magazine of History and Biography* 116, no. 3 (July 1992). Portions of chapter 4 will appear in a forthcoming issue of *Diplomatic History.*

Library of Congress Cataloging-in-Publication Data

Conn, Steven.
   Museums and American intellectual life, 1876–1926 / Steven Conn.
      p.   cm.
   Includes bibliographical references and index.
   ISBN 0-226-11492-9 (cloth : alk. paper)
   1. Museums—United States—History.   2. United States—
Intellectual life—1865–1918.   3. United States—Intellectual
life—20th century   4. United States—History—1919–1933.   I. Title.
AM11.C64   1998
069'.0973—dc21   98-16850
                                                                        CIP

This book is printed on acid-free paper.

Contents

~

With Gratitude

~

Working on a project like this is a strange combination of isolation and collaboration. In the end, you stare at the blank page by yourself, but what eventually comes to fill it up results from the help, conversations, support, and good ideas of many others. I have been particularly lucky for the collaboration.

At one level, as an historian you are only as good as the archives in which you work. Thanks then to the splendid staffs in the libraries and archives at: The Academy of Natural Sciences; The American Museum of Natural History; The Bucks County Historical Society; The Henry Ford Museum and Greenfield Village; The Field Museum; The Philadelphia Museum of Art; The Pennsylvania Historical Society; The Franklin Institute; The City Archives, Philadelphia; The Metropolitan Museum of Art; Special Collections, Van Pelt Library at the University of Pennsylvania; and The University Museum at the University of Pennsylvania.

This book began—too long ago it seems—in the History Department at the University of Pennsylvania, where I was surrounded by the intellectual vitality and warm comradeship of a terrific collection of graduate students and faculty. Some, like Mike Zuckerman, Julie Sneeringer, Alison Isenberg, Drew Faust, Dana Baron, Walter Licht, and Beth Johns, made it possible to get through the first stage of this production. Others, especially Bruce Kuklick, Tom Sugrue, Sue Schulten, Sylvia Yount, and Andrew Walker, continued to hold my hand as I turned a dissertation into a book.

Since I have been at Ohio State, I have benefited mightily from the help and good advice of John Burnham, Claudio Fogu, Barbara Groseclose, Saul Cornell, Dave Madden, and Noriko Aso. Cicely Barker deserves a special thanks for her help. An Ohio State University Seed Grant sped this project along.

Anyone who has worked with Doug Mitchell at the University of Chicago Press knows what a gentleman and a scholar he is. He, and his assistant Matt Howard, have shepherded this book to fruition as gently and painlessly as could be imagined. Devorah Lissack came along at just the right moment to provide me with much needed help.

There is a deeper thanks I must give to those whose intellectual sustenance was eclipsed by the personal support they have given to me, generously and selflessly, on what has turned out to be a rougher road than I ever imagined. Those who understood what I needed and when include: Birgitte; David; Lisa; Marc; Margaret; Martien; Max; Trisha; Mike and Hannah (and Avital too); Ann and Arloc; Ann and Wendell (and Ellie too); Caprice and Mark (and Alex too); Mike and Cathy (and Rachel too); and Angela. Especially Angela. Thanks for your ears and your hearts and your shoulders.

I owe a debt not simply unpayable but incalculable to Abby. She and I both know why.

Finally, there is my family, Peter and Terry, Jennifer and Alison, David and Patrice, and more recently little Nolan. What an extraordinary, remarkable group of people. They have always reminded me that collaboration is more fun than isolation. I only hope that this and I prove worthy of the love and faith they have invested in it and me.

1   Thomas Eakins, *Frank Hamilton Cushing* (1895). Frank Hamilton Cushing
did ethnographic research among native groups in the American Southwest.
He became one of the foremost experts on the Zuni, and his work among
them led him to be initiated into a Zuni secret society. This full-length portrait
by Thomas Eakins portrays him surrounded by some of the objects associated
with this research. (From the Collection of Gilcrease Museum, Tulsa)

ONE

~

Museums and the Late Victorian World

Chaos was the law of nature; Order was the dream of man.

HENRY ADAMS

We begin with a visit.

In 1894, Frank Hamilton Cushing, head of the Smithsonian's Bureau of Ethnology, came to Philadelphia. He had come to visit the exhibits of the newly opened anthropological museum at the University of Pennsylvania. A reporter from the *Philadelphia Press* nipped at his heels as he toured the galleries.

Cushing was a minor celebrity in the world of anthropology and ethnology. The *Philadelphia Press* reporter wrote of him: "No one has done so much to read the every-day lives of the pre-historic people of America from the remains found and his skill in this direction is almost uncanny." To demonstrate this uncanny skill, the reporter asked Cushing to "read stories in pottery." Cushing responded by picking up a clay pot from Missouri:

> We can learn from this bowl more than the maker knew himself. We conclude that this Missouri people came from some forest country where the crested wood-duck was common. This handle is the conventionalized head of that bird. This pattern was originally carved from wood, or made from a gourd. The shape tells that. It was made in a part of the country where the wood was good for carving, and there was not fit bark for making vessels, probably therefore from

the northeast. Thus the maker of the clay bowl kept the same pattern
long after he perhaps knew why he put the head of a wood-duck for a
handle.[1]

This display of Holmesian deduction left the reporter, and presumably
his readers as well, dazzled and amazed.

The exhibits that Cushing came to see had been designed by his
friend Stewart Culin, who had already made a reputation for himself as a
student of folklore. He now directed the exhibits at Penn's new museum.
Cushing and Culin pursued the same goal in the work they did at their
respective institutions. As Cushing explained it to the *Philadelphia Press:*
"We have an idea in common—the making of stories out of all these
things, stories which will tell themselves to the untrained observer."[2]

We begin with this anecdote because it nicely encapsulates the way
in which many in the late nineteenth century looked at the world, and it
summarizes the way they set about to build the museums through which
they tried to reproduce that world. The intellectual architecture used to
build the museums of the late nineteenth century was predicated on
the assumption that objects could tell stories "to the untrained observer," an assumption I will call an "object-based epistemology." Late-
nineteenth-century Americans held a belief that objects, at least as much
as texts, were sources of knowledge and meaning. William Wilson, founder and director of Philadelphia's Commercial Museum, stated this belief
clearly to Edward Everett Ayer of Chicago's Field Museum: "All museum
material should speak for itself upon sight. It should be an open book
which tells a better story than any description will do."[3]

In this epistemology, objects are not precisely transparent, but neither are they hopelessly opaque. The meanings held within objects
would yield themselves up to anyone who studied and observed the objects carefully enough. Cushing only expressed a widely held assumption that, even for the "untrained observer," objects could tell stories.
A writer for the *Museum News* explained: "Museum specimens are not
merely objects to be looked at, they should be illustrations of facts or
exponents of ideas."[4] The books were open; the stories would reveal
themselves.

As illustrations of facts, museum objects functioned both as synecdoches, so that each butterfly or ceramic pot stood for the whole of the
category of butterflies or pots, and as metonyms, so that each stood for
part of the larger body of knowledge, for natural history or for anthropology. At the risk of stretching this linguistic analogy too far, let me

borrow some ideas from linguist Roman Jakobson to explain the way in which an object-based epistemology worked.

Jakobson imagined a two-part schema to help understand the structure of language. This schema, which Jakobson drew as vertical ("metaphoric") and horizontal ("metonymic") axes, describes a two-fold process of "selection and combination." Terence Hawkes writes that, according to Jakobson, "messages are constructed . . . by a combination of a 'horizontal' movement, which combines words together, and a 'vertical' movement, which selects the particular words from the available inventory or 'inner storehouse' of the language."[5]

The movement Jakobson sees as essential for constructing meaning in language might well describe a stroll through the galleries of a late-nineteenth-century museum. As visitors moved (horizontally) through the galleries, they saw objects which had meaning inherent in themselves. Combined together from case to case and exhibit to exhibit, the objects formed coherent visual "sentences." That coherence, however, was achieved only after those objects had been deliberately selected, quite literally from the basement storehouse, and ordered properly within the galleries. Meaning was thus constructed visually, with objects, like words in a text, as the fundamental building blocks of the museum language.

Almost without exception, the visual sentences that emerged from this process of combination and selection presented the metanarrative of evolutionary progress. A trip through the galleries followed a trajectory from simple to complex, from savage to civilized, from ancient to modern. The form that museums developed in the last half of the nineteenth century made this lesson inescapable to anyone who strolled their galleries. Museums functioned as the most widely accessible public fora to underscore a positivist, progressive and hierarchical view of the world, and they gave that view material form and scientific legitimacy.

The linguistic model can only be taken so far, however. Svetlana Alpers, borrowing from her own work on Netherlandish painting, has called the museum "a way of seeing," central, as Eilean Hooper-Greenhill puts it, to "the representation of the world as a view."[6] These observations remind us that the museum is an essentially visual undertaking. It was especially so in the late nineteenth century. Long before television and advertising turned us into a nation of gawkers, G. Stanley Hall observed: "It is very well made out that Americans, as a class, are rather more visual-minded than most other races."[7] A statement like this strikes us immediately as absurd, and yet it bears further considering.

American museums grew alongside American cities. Those cities, of course, became increasingly filled during the years of this study with immigrants from Southern and Eastern Europe whose cultural connections with the Anglo elite were tenuous at best. Indeed, it is probably the case that a majority of New Yorkers or Chicagoans at the turn of the twentieth century spoke only passing English. Some historians have noted how institutions, including museums, tried to instruct immigrants on the forms of proper behavior and functioned to turn what elites saw as unruly foreigners into well-mannered citizens of the United States. In this sense, museums functioned—and continue to function—as places of "civilizing rituals."[8] In the face of this daunting task of educating and/or controlling, how else other than visually to communicate in a world which had become confusingly polyglot, where verbal and written language had become through its diversity more complicated? Knowledge conveyed visually was not culturally or linguistically bound, or so the museum builders about whom this book is written believed. Museums, through the objects they displayed, were thus designed to communicate knowledge scientifically to people in the modern American city the way no other institution could.

To understand the museum as a way of seeing in a world where visual communication held as much importance as linguistic communication helps explain what many scholars and visitors now consider to be one of the most infamous, or at least tedious, features of the turn-of-the-century museum: the endless glass cases. Museum curators spent considerable time fretting about their cases and considerable resources trying to perfect them. They worried about proper size, about glare, and most of all about how to design cases that would keep dust off their objects. Finally, the exteriors of museums were designed so that the glass cases would be illuminated as completely as possible by natural light. Staff at the American Museum of Natural History proudly boasted of their "immense windows" through which "poured a flood of daylight that gave to the smallest object distinction and brilliancy."[9]

Specimen after specimen, case after case—this arrangement of museum objects seems now to be mind-numbingly dull. But the glass cases played a functional role in the development of an object-based epistemology. In the museums examined in this book, objects occupied center stage and museum designers, through the ways in which they organized and shaped museum spaces, encouraged visitors to observe these objects free from too much distracting text and context. The cases forced the visitor to stare at objects and to consider them first on their own

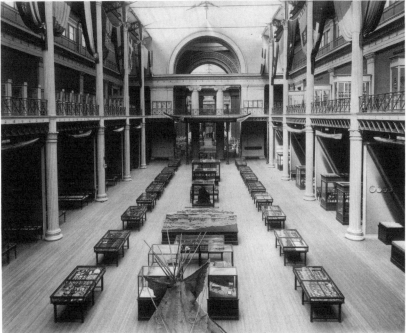

2, 3 *The form of the content.* Late-nineteenth-century museums, regardless of their focus, featured long galleries densely packed with glass cases full of specimens. The above photograph shows the main hall of the museum at Philadelphia's Academy of Natural Sciences; below, the gallery of American ethnology at Chicago's Field Museum, both from the 1890s. (Courtesy of the Ewell Sale Stewart Library, The Academy of Natural Sciences of Philadelphia, and The Field Museum, Neg. #8193, Chicago)

terms and then in relation to neighboring objects. Museum objects, and the relationships in which they were arranged, were intended to convey a narrative. The glass cases made sure nothing interfered with that. If the museum purported to represent the world metonymically through its objects, then the glass cases served as windows onto that world.

All of which is to say that the museums of the late nineteenth century developed a distinctive form, and that that form was connected importantly to the content of what museums presented. George Kubler some years ago made the obvious but critical point that before we can have meaning, we must have form.[10] The form that these museums took—galleries lined with glass cases behind which specimens would be placed without visual distraction—made it possible for the visiting public to understand the meaning of museum displays.

This form also served to distinguish museums of the late nineteenth century from their antebellum predecessors. Late-nineteenth-century museums embodied the Victorian rage for order.[11] Peale's Museum, founded in Philadelphia in the late eighteenth century, had made an admirable first effort to present the world in orderly fashion. But in the antebellum period, American museums degenerated into Barnumesque sideshows. Those who looked back at the museums of the pre-Civil War period from the vantage of the late nineteenth century saw only "mere miscellaneous lot[s] of objects brought together with no purpose," or worse, "monstrosities," "cheap theatricals," and "legerdemain."[12] The random clutter created a sensory overload which bored visitors and defeated the purposes of a museum in the first place. These museums, circuses, and sideshows—P. T. Barnum's enterprises exemplary among them—used objects to present a world of spectacle, disorder, and carnival. The objects displayed, genuine and fake, living and dead, accentuated the unusual, the bizarre, the grotesque. David Murray recognized as much when he wrote a history of museums in 1904. Museums had been "a collection of curiosities . . . there was generally implied in it the idea of strangeness or rarity."[13]

Museum builders after the Civil War found this presentation of the world unacceptable. The new museums of the post-war era distinguished themselves from their antebellum predecessors precisely because they strove for a rational, orderly, systematic ideal. In place of the freakish, these museums highlighted the representative and the ordinary. They replaced displays of a world turned upside down with one in which everything had its place. Specimens of exotic butterflies might well dazzle viewers in New York or Philadelphia, but their purpose, under that display glass, was to demonstrate that Nature—even her most peculiar creations—had an essential order, and more, that that design could be revealed, understood, and controlled by rational science and scientists. The museum of 1897, Murray assured his readers, "is far in advance of the museum of 1847."[14]

By creating this form, by putting specimens under glass, museum curators did not intend, as Alpers believes, to "turn cultural material into art objects."[15] That certainly did happen inadvertently, and increasingly throughout the twentieth century. Yet in the last quarter of the nineteenth century it was not art objects—objects whose value lay in some transcendent aesthetic—that these museum builders hoped to create, but objects invested with knowledge. This faith in objects as the source of knowledge lay at the center of how Americans of the late Victorian period understood the world, and it lay at the heart of the whole museum enterprise.

~

The years covered by this study mark a period of extraordinary institution building in this country. At one level a part of, at another a reaction to the dislocation brought about by rapid industrialization and urbanization, Americans erected imposing edifices of many kinds. New hospitals tried to deal rationally and scientifically with the disease and squalor of turn-of-the-century cities; colleges and universities became dynamic centers of learning in response to a world which more and more demanded command of information; libraries proliferated and developed new ways to keep their books in order.

None of these institutions better exemplifies the late-nineteenth-century impulse to order and rationality better than the museums that became prominent and central features of American cities as big as New York and as small as Youngstown, Ohio. Even an incomplete list of museums founded during this period is at once familiar and staggering: The Metropolitan and the American Museum of Natural History in New York; Harvard University's Peabody; the University of Pennsylvania's Museum of Archaeology and Anthropology; Detroit's Institute of Arts; the Carnegie Museum in Pittsburgh; Boston's Museum of Fine Arts; Chicago's Field Museum and its Art Institute; Philadelphia's Museum of Art. As many historians have noticed—Neil Harris, Morris Vogel, and Michael Kammen among them—the Victorians were "the great museum builders."[16] This much was clear as well to those who lived through the era. Writing in the Centennial year, Philadelphia paleontologist Edward Drinker Cope pronounced: "As the middle ages were the period of cathedrals, so the present age is one of colossal museums, and of an extensive development of knowledge of the sensible creation." [17]

Kammen has called the creation of museums "one of the most important trends in American cultural life ever since the 1870s." [18] And yet, though they continue to serve as central landmarks in our cultural geography, museums have received remarkably little historical treatment. A common historical view of museums was anticipated by J. A. Udden, writing in *Science* just before the First World War. In his opinion, "the growth of our museums is largely parallel with the growth of our national wealth." [19] More recently, George Stocking, discussing the accumulation of museum collections of anthropological objects, writes that for collectors made wealthy through robber barony, "palpable and visible objects could be seen as a return on investment." [20] Built as treasure houses which would both display and legitimate the vast fortunes of their founders, museums have been seen as perfect exemplars of Thorstein Veblen's culture of conspicuous consumption.

This analysis has proved remarkably persistent, and for good reason. One has only to think of the Frick Gallery or of the Isabella Stewart Gardner Museum to be reminded that museums in this country have served as grand personal monuments. Nor is this phenomenon confined to the past. In the 1970s, J. Paul Getty built a Pompeiian villa to hold his collection of paintings and antiquities, and even more recently Walter Annenberg helped fund renovation of the galleries at New York's Metropolitan Museum which feature the paintings from his own collection.[21] Museums and their collections still function to glorify the wealthy and their good taste.

Yet as long ago as 1962, Neil Harris called for a reevaluation of the Gilded Age museum. Pointing out that the accepted explanations of museum history "have rarely advanced beyond the economics of the situation," he looked at the early years of Boston's Museum of Fine Arts and discovered that "the Museum's founders did not intend it to be a treasure house of costly chefs-d'oeuvre." Further, Harris observed that, "in the forty years from 1870 to 1910 museum thought itself underwent a revolution." [22] Harris suggested that a more careful study of turn-of-the-century museums might yield a story more interesting than simply one of wealthy businessmen building monuments to their connoisseurship.

More recently, the critical analysis of museums has really amounted to critique of the contemporary. Less interested—sometimes interested not at all—in historical issues or questions, this newer scholarship has used a variety of theoretical tools to deconstruct, unpack, and otherwise expose museums. Gazing through the lens of post-structuralist theory, some have found museums to be part of the apparatus of a disciplinary society. The practices of collecting, classifying, and displaying must all be understood as exercises in power. Tony Bennett, attempting to mix a theoretical cocktail of Gramsci and Foucault, sees museums of the nineteenth century not as places that tried to "cow" visitors into submission but rather as places that "aimed to inveigh the general populace into complicity with power by placing them on this side of a power which it represented as its own." Museums do not coerce visitors into behaving properly, but they act as part of a larger, late Victorian, bourgeois hegemony. "The crowd," according to Bennett, "comes . . . to regulate itself." [23]

Museums derive this power, so this critical stance argues, through the reification of categories of knowledge. One of Foucault's central assertions has been that none of the categories and classifications into which human experience and understanding have been put represent natural, essential, or timeless truths. Knowledge about the world, according to the Foucauldian way of thinking, might well be divided into any number of different categories, and it is one job of museums to persuade visitors that the classifications they employ are the "correct" ones—that they do indeed represent self-evident truths about the world. Viewed this way, the claims to authoritative knowledge that museums make can be seen as contingent, socially conditioned, and the product of discursive formations. If, in the crude equation, knowledge equals power, then Eilean Hooper-Greenhill, applying Foucault's "epistemes" to the history of museums, is correct when she writes: "knowledge is *now* understood as the commodity that museums offer" (my emphasis). [24] Statements like these are at once critically insightful and historically shallow. Because many scholars of museums have not investigated thoroughly, or taken seriously, the intellectual foundations of museums, they seem to miss not only that knowledge was *always* understood to be what museums had to offer but also that knowledge was what they were charged to create and what they were obligated to provide to a visiting public.

Among the problems with a Foucauldian analysis, as I see it, is that it tends to deal only in terms of power. To see museum history only as a piece of the discursive formation of power leaves the historian careening from a conspiratorial view of this history on one side (who is doing what oppressive thing to whom in these museums), to an almost catachismic view of power on the other (where is power? power is everywhere). Further, this identification of categories of knowledge with power risks ignoring the necessary intellectual function that classification plays. The ways in which museums created, reified, and institutionalized categories of knowledge as unassailable truth does indeed reflect the operation of power. Museums were, and are, to borrow Paul Di Maggio's phrase, "ideological classifications embodied in organizational form." [25] But having said that, we must also acknowledge that understanding cannot happen and meaning cannot be constructed without some set of categories. George Kubler observed some years ago: "We can grasp the universe only by simplifying it with ideas of identity by classes, types, and categories. . . . It is the nature of being that no event ever repeats, but it is in the nature of thought that we understand events only by the identities we imagine among them." Or as anthropologist Igor Kopytoff similarly remarked, "the human mind has an inherent tendency to impose order upon the chaos of its environment by classifying its contents, and without the classification knowledge of the world . . . would not be possible." [26]

The categories into which these museums classed the world do not and did not represent truth in any essential sense. The knowledge they embodied might have been rearranged and reordered, understood and presented in any of a dozen different ways. But Kubler reminds us that knowledge can only exist within *some* framework of understanding. That is the dilemma with which museums wrestled. Critics in the Foucauldian vein, have only attended to one half of the oversimplified equation: they have analyzed power without understanding the knowledge that produces and is produced by it. Rather than accuse late-nineteenth-century museum builders either of naiveté or complicity, this book attempts to understand more completely how they constructed their categories of knowledge and what those categories meant.

The museums that are the subject of this book did indeed represent social constructs. They presented a view of the world in which humans, Western culture, and Western art are the crowning achievements of nature, civilization, and human creativity respectively, and they treated this view as if it were unarguable, natural, essential. With all this in mind, however, I want to explore more thoroughly the intellectual terrain that American museums tried to negotiate. By treating museums as the sites of intellectual and cultural debates, where the prevailing cultural ideas and assumptions of American society were put on display and where changes in those assumptions were reflected, I propose to examine how it was that museum builders arrived at the categories they did.

～

Grounding American museums more firmly in the intellectual history of the late nineteenth century also serves to bridge two of the era's most remarkable phenomena. The first, the energetic building of institutions, has already been mentioned. The second was the widespread Victorian fascination with "stuff" of all kinds. It is a commonplace to remark that late-nineteenth-century Americans surrounded themselves with things—Thomas Schlereth, for example, sees this "intrigue with the material world" as central to the everyday life of the turn of the twentieth century.[27] This fascination is obvious to a person who reads about any domestic interior, looks at any period photograph, or walks into any Victorian house museum. What remains less obvious are the reasons why people lived in the midst of such clutter.

One answer, a cousin of that which explains the rise of museums, might be labeled "bourgeois acquisitiveness." As members of the American middle class expanded in tandem with the industrial economy, they had increasing amounts of disposable income that they disposed of by buying the newly available products of that industrial economy— furniture, photographs, ceramics, an almost endless array of gewgaws. The objects that filled middle-class parlors gave physical and visual manifestation to the aspirations of this class. According to Miles Orvell, "individuals sought an elevation of status through the purchase and display of goods whose appearance counted more than their substance." Further, to make their purchases, the urban middle class patronized another of the great symbols of late-nineteenth-century materialism—the department store. As other historians have noted, the grand department stores of this era catered to and helped to define a new middle-class identity. When middle-class Americans worshipped in these "cathedrals of commerce," they performed a sacrament in which consumption became status.[28]

Museums, then, can be seen as a constituent piece of this culture of acquisitiveness. Linked to the industrial economy by the money that created them, museums stand with department stores as institutional embodiments of Veblen's culture of conspicuous consumption, though it would be some years until the museum became the site of actual purchasing through the proliferation of "museum stores." It is surely not coincidental that several of the country's retail giants—John Wana-maker in Philadelphia and Marshall Field in Chicago spring quickly to mind—also involved themselves heavily in museum work.

This explanation is persuasive, as far as it goes. Americans could not have stuffed their homes full of objects without an industrial economy to produce them, places to buy them, or the cash to complete the trans-action. But this explanation also misses much. It may explain a great deal about *how* the late nineteenth century became so crowded with things, but it does not explain fully why. Kenneth Ames suggests that the physi-cal environment of these late Victorians may provide the key to under-standing what he calls their psychological environment, while Orvell be-lieves that objects are so important for understanding the intellectual world of the late Victorians that he has written: "the most characteristic expression of the Victorian mind was *matter* in all its shapes and sizes, textures, surfaces, and substances." [29] Museums, department stores, and certainly world's fairs operated together to give shape to this world of objects. [30]

This is not to suggest that through an object-based epistemology all objects functioned in the same way for the late Victorians who sur-rounded themselves with them. We should consider several levels on which people related to objects. At one of these, meanings are per-sonal—keepsakes, heirlooms, mementos, old photographs. At another level, meanings derive from some kind of social transaction, such as buy-ing and selling. At a more abstract level, meaning results when individu-als engage in a deliberate, self-reflective act of symbolic interpretation. [31] It is on this level that museum objects, which are related to but not the same as department store purchases or grandma's china, functioned.

Objects in the late Victorian world must be seen, then, as invested with a meaning deeper than as signifiers of status. They were connected directly with ideas and with knowledge of the world, and nowhere more so than in museums. I want to suggest that museums provided the model for how Americans in the late nineteenth century used objects to order and understand their world. Mrs. Montiesor saw this connection quite clearly in her 1890 book on how to collect. She told her readers: "Every house ought to possess a 'museum.'" [32] Jane Addams did Mrs. Montiesor one better when she created a "Labor Museum" as an integral part of Hull House. When Addams wanted some examples of medieval textiles for her Hull House museum, she wrote to Frederic Skiff, director of the Field Museum, asking for them. [33] Addams thus made a seamless institu-tional equation between the socially redemptive power of domesticity and museums. In several senses, then, museums were centrally important places in the intellectual landscape at the turn of the century, and they are rich sources for us to understand that moment.

~

In 1866 the philosopher John Fiske identified "the whole duty" of a university as consisting of two parts. First, universities should train the "mental faculties" of students to pursue "varied and harmonious activity." Second, the university should provide its students with "the means of acquiring a thorough elementary knowledge of any given branch of science, art, or literature."[34] This description seems remote indeed from the current world of universities, where purpose and publication are synonymous—at least in the minds of many faculty. Fiske's assessment, however, reminds us not only that universities have changed a great deal since the end of the nineteenth century, but that our conception of how and where new knowledge will be generated has changed as well. For many intellectuals in the post-Civil War period, objects, not books, would yield new knowledge, and museums, not universities, were seen as the places where the work of producing that knowledge would take place. Prof. Udden, quoted earlier, saw the growth of museums as coincident with both national wealth and "the progress of higher education."[35]

Because objects, as I have suggested, were seen by late Victorians as the sites of meaning and knowledge, many intellectuals regarded museums as a primary place where new knowledge about the world could be created and given order. Miles Orvell has noticed a pervasive tendency in the late nineteenth century "to enclose reality in manageable forms."[36] Nothing exemplified that tendency, or undertook it on so large a scale, as the museums. As the world beyond the museum became to many Americans increasingly chaotic and incomprehensible, rationality and order could be maintained, at least within the museum.

That museums should be seen as the institutions charged with furthering knowledge and with creating order strikes us today as unlikely. Museums, for the most part, do not function in this way anymore. In the era after the Civil War, however, to see museums as the sites of knowledge production seemed completely sensible. American universities at that moment remained stagnant and sleepy places. Most functioned either as glorified finishing schools or as vocational centers, while the most prestigious remained rooted in theological studies. Besides, colleges and universities simply taught what we already knew—they did nothing, according to most commentators, to increase our total store of knowledge.

Museums, on the other hand, assumed intellectual leadership because they fostered original research through the careful and systematic way they dealt with objects. Edward Drinker Cope, a distinguished paleontologist who worked both at a university and at a museum, explained why museums were more important than universities for the production of knowledge. He reminded his readers in an essay for *The Penn Monthly* magazine that "the bulk and amount of material necessary for investigation in the natural sciences is so great, that very few universities can supply it, or the space in which to accommodate it."[37] Cope made what he thought was an obvious observation: research depended on objects. Museums had both the objects necessary for research and the facilities with which to conduct that work. Universities, simply, did not.

More importantly, museums made the fruits of their research available to a general public through exhibits, unlike colleges and universities, which were open only to a few. Many commentators complained bitterly about the fundamentally restricted access to higher education and extolled the virtues of democratically accessible, publicly funded museums by comparison. In the late-nineteenth-century version of the academic debate over teaching and research, the museum builders believed they had struck the balance. They would be places to produce new knowledge, and they would bring that knowledge, often for free, to the people. In a world understood through objects, and in a society wrestling with questions of citizenship and national identity, many hoped museums would assume a central and public role in the intellectual, and therefore moral, life of the age.

In the struggle between museums and universities for primacy in the production of knowledge, museums—with the exception perhaps of art museums—lost. Simply put, that is part of what the trajectory of my narrative charts. By the first quarter of the twentieth century, the business of producing new knowledge about the natural world, about anthropology, about commerce and business, and about history took place primarily at universities and colleges. This is not to say that the museums founded in the nineteenth century clutter our cultural landscape as grand, imposing failures. It goes almost without saying that the museums built during the period covered by this book continue to play an important role in American public life, especially for those who live in America's older cities and can enjoy them regularly. Though it is a quite common narrative strategy, I want to avoid here a "declension" argument—a "rise and fall" story about these museums.

Even though I do not argue that they rose and then fell, I do insist that they no longer fulfill the role of knowledge production that their founders anticipated. Eighteen seventy-six, the date which serves here as a symbolic marker of convenience for the great age of museum building, also marks the founding of The Johns Hopkins University. Johns Hopkins, with Harvard, Columbia, Pennsylvania, Chicago and others following, transformed the way in which knowledge was produced within the institutional framework of universities. These universities, along with the disciplinary associations that sprouted in the last quarter of the nineteenth century, professionalized knowledge. In so doing they struggled, in John Higham's phrase, for "authority in American intellectual life."[38]

I also want to insist that this shift in function has had important implications. As the production of knowledge moved from the museums to colleges and universities, the terms of access to that new knowledge changed dramatically. Museums, though their doors were not open to everyone all the time, and though they did demand that visitors behave themselves appropriately, were infinitely more accessible than colleges and universities. In this sense, the struggle over where knowledge would be produced was linked importantly to the question of for whom this new knowledge was intended. Historians have described the relationship between the growth of the new university and the increasing disciplinary specialization of knowledge, and they have lamented the ways in which that specialization made it harder and harder for scholars to communicate with each other and with the public. Historians might no longer understand sociologists, who no longer understood physicists, but almost none of them communicated the results of their research to the larger public. The museums of the late nineteenth century did make that attempt. A visitor to a museum in 1890 saw the latest knowledge about a given topic given visual, material form. That visitor's grandchild, going to the same museum thirty years later, did not. The struggle between museums and universities over the production of knowledge was not simply a contest over where knowledge would be produced, but over what kind of knowledge would be produced and who would have access to it.

As universities won this struggle for authority, they wrestled it away not simply from museums as competing institutions but from objects themselves. By the 1920s the metonymic language through which museum objects spoke could no longer carry the meaning of science or anthropology or history. Skeptical now of the stories museum objects once tried to tell, Americans by the mid-twentieth century no longer heard objects the way their predecessors had. As Curtis Hinsley has suggested, in the twentieth century "the lessons of artifacts were not at all as single or obvious as nineteenth-century museum presentations had suggested."[39] By the 1920s, I argue, an object-based epistemology had largely disappeared from the mainstream of American intellectual life. As I write this, American society has never been filled more with objects than it is right now, but, I would argue, those objects mean something very different for us than they did for our Victorian forebears.

The debate over where knowledge would be produced in late Victorian America hinged as well on differing and changing ideas about education. Both universities and museums in this country justified themselves in terms of the educational service they provided, but clearly education did not mean the same thing for each. Briefly, most museums defined two kinds of visitors, the general visitor and the specialist or student, and here museums were very much like the libraries of the period who divided their users into "casual visitors" and "serious readers." In the years surrounding the turn of the twentieth century, museums believed that they could be of educational use to both.[40] By the end of the period examined here, universities had assumed the primary responsibility for producing knowledge, made available only to a small and exclusive student/scholar constituency, and museums were left with the role of educating, and more and more of entertaining, a wider public, though not necessarily about up-to-date ideas.[41]

One result of this division of labor was that museums turned increasingly to educating school children. Though I will not examine the phenomenon in any great depth, I have been struck by the way almost all of the institutions I studied began to develop extensive outreach programs to schools in the early years of the twentieth century. They established casual and formal relationships with school boards, they hired staff especially to develop educational programs for children, and some even developed traveling museums designed to bring the museum to the school if the children could not be brought to the museum. Even at the University of Pennsylvania Museum, where a museum collection sat inside a dynamic university, management announced in 1911 bold plans for "systematic participation in the work of the schools of Philadelphia."[42]

Field trips to museums were certainly a staple and eagerly anticipated part of my public school education, and I suspect they remain so today. But the intellectual implications of the assumption that the primary educational role of museums is to work with third graders are enormous. This assumption underscores the perception that the knowledge available at museums is outdated and suitable only for children. It also suggests that we are content to offer our children knowledge which as adults we no longer trust. Either way, this shift to cultivating an audience of children is a symptom of the museum's loss of intellectual primacy.

The question of access raises another issue for this study, and I should be clear about what this book considers and what it does not. I am interested here in what museum visitors saw, but not in who actually saw these exhibits. This book studies those who built and shaped these institutions, and what it was that resulted from their work.

Museum audiences are elusive quarry for the historian. They left little trace of themselves and did not register with any specificity in the official records of most museums. Some museums kept attendance figures, some kept records of visitor comments, and occasionally individual visitors turn up in the record because they caused some kind of trouble. But beyond this museum visitors remain largely silent.

They can, of course, be found by diligent historians. David Brigham, for example, has shown us in more detail than we ever knew who did and did not come to see the exhibits at Peale's Museum in Philadelphia. His careful, creative work demonstrates how fruitful it can be to chase after those who came through the doors of America's museums.[43] I have chosen, however, not to pursue this kind of research. The audience will make brief, fleeting appearances in the following pages. When those who ran these museums worried about who was coming to tour their galleries, and when they tried to connect their didactic exhibits with a specific notion of who should see them, then I report those thoughts. Those thoughts demonstrate, if nothing else, that then as now the people charged with running museums fretted about who came.

The two competing critical approaches to museum history—institutions created by and for America's wealthy, and museums as the site of hegemonic control—present an intriguing contradiction for the consideration of the audience. On the one hand, these institutions seem to us the clubhouses of America's financial and social elite, restrictive, exclusive, and forbidding. On the other hand, they are places which exerted control over the "crowd," where the masses went for voluntary instruction. I am not convinced either of these views is correct. My re-searches suggest that museums did attract wide audiences, and that people came because museum exhibits spoke to them on a whole host of levels. It remains, however, for a very different kind of study (under-taken, I suspect, by a very different kind of historian) to elucidate the question of audience for turn of the century museums.

Finally, I do not want to suggest that the various and related changes that resulted as universities replaced museums in a privileged position in American intellectual life constitute a "paradigm shift" in the sense that Thomas Kuhn meant when he coined the phrase. Instead, it might be better to consider the victory of universities over museums in this debate as collateral to a set of intellectual shifts taking place at the turn of the twentieth century. As Orvell has pointed out, by the early twenti-eth century "long-held notions of order and stability" had dissolved, leaving a world that "no longer presented, on closer inspection, an as-pect of order and coherence, of solid forms and surfaces."[44] In that sense, the museums of this period stand as the institutional manifesta-tions of Kuhn's "normal science," where nature is forced "into the pre-formed and relatively inflexible box that the [old] paradigm supplies."[45] It was precisely that dissolving world that museums attempted to dis-play. By the 1920s museums became those boxes.

$\sim$

In a lecture delivered in 1888 to the new American Historical Asso-ciation, George Brown Goode, assistant secretary of the Smithsonian, ar-ticulated the connection between museums and ideas that was central to the late-nineteenth-century worldview. He told his audience that "the museum of the past must be set aside, reconstructed, transformed from a cemetery of bric-a-brac into a nursery of living thoughts." Later in the same speech, he described a museum as a "house full of ideas, arranged with the strictest attention to system." In this speech, Goode has met Mrs. Montiesor, thus demonstrating the interconnectedness of a world filled with objects: Mrs. Montiesor wanted each house to include a mu-seum, and Goode wanted to turn the museum into a house.

Goode also believed that, if museums were truly to be houses of ideas, then they must accurately reflect the ways in which knowledge was changing in the late nineteenth century. And changing it was. The rise of great museums coincided with an explosion in knowledge as new disciplines formed and others transformed themselves. The museum's central task therefore was doubly urgent. In an essay written in 1895,

Goode outlined how he thought different museums ought to divide their turf. The classification of museum types Goode proposed was his attempt to sketch the way changing categories of knowledge could be given institutional shape. His scheme included six classes: "A. museums of art; B. historical museums; C. anthropological museums; D. natural history museums; E. technological museums; F. commercial museums."[46] For Goode, these categories represented the sum of knowledge that could be displayed in museums. The categories represented as well the ideas which could be embodied in museum objects.

The outline of this book follows Goode's lead. In organizing the book this way I do not want to invest too much authority in his schema. It, and the thinking behind it, serve in this book not so much as a specific road map but instead as a rough guide to the intellectual and institutional terrain of this period. At the same time, of all those who wrote and lectured about the role of museums in late-nineteenth-century society, none proved more influential than George Brown Goode. From his post at the Smithsonian, Goode thought more thoroughly about museums than anyone else in this country, and his writings, directly or indirectly, set the terms of discussion about museum topics.

Goode's comment about the necessity of a system was a tacit admonition to those who ran museums. In order for visitors to absorb the knowledge inherent in objects—in order for visitors to understand the stories Frank Hamilton Cushing believed objects had to tell—those objects had to be collected, classified, and exhibited properly. Classification, and the systems through which objects were arranged and displayed, became the keys to unlocking the knowledge contained in museum collections. As metonyms, these objects only assumed their full significance through their proper arrangement. It was the way museums organized and displayed their objects that would turn them from "cemeteries," which killed ideas, into the "nurseries" which would help them grow.

This concern for classification, however, reveals a fundamental tension in the intellectual design of museums that appeared even as they proliferated and flourished. The ideal museum builders hoped to achieve was both to impose a stability and order on bodies of knowledge and to reflect and produce changes in that knowledge. Let me try to explain this tension further: The objects exhibited in museums functioned as synecdoches standing for bodies of knowledge. That knowledge could be obtained by anyone who visited a museum and studied the objects, provided the museum curators arranged the displays systematically. Goode wrote: "The museum cultivates the powers of observation, and the casual visitor even makes discoveries for himself and under the guidance of the labels forms his own impressions."[47] Further, the knowledge displayed by museums through their objects should be scientifically current—"living ideas" in Goode's terms.

However, the requirement that objects be systematically displayed made it difficult for museums to keep up with changes in the world of knowledge. Writing in the magazine *Nineteenth Century* in 1887, J. G. Wood complained to his readers about the "dulness" of American museums. More damningly, F. A. Bather told readers of *Science* that the way museums exhibited their collections served as a "potent agent for retarding the advance of science."[48] The problem, according to Bather, was that museum collections, classified and arranged in display cases, were not rearranged to keep up with changing knowledge: "By mere force of circumstances, lack of time, undermanning, and so forth, the arrangement of specimens in the show-case of a museum remains the same throughout many years. . . . Classifications come and classifications go, but the classification that was adopted when the museum was built, say fifty years ago, seems likely to go on forever."[49] How could museum classifications, after all, keep up with what Henry Adams called the "stupendous acceleration . . . before which the man of science stood at first as bewildered and helpless as, in the fourth century, a priest of Isis before the Cross of Christ?"[50]

In fairness, those who ran museums did spend a great deal of time reclassifying and rearranging their collections, but their attempts to get their exhibits just right merely underscores that the world was not as easily ordered as they had hoped. At some level, then, the story told here charts how one kind of understanding of the world was replaced by another. The intellectual architecture upon which museums were built collapsed by the first quarter of this century under the weight of its own contradiction. In short, and to borrow Goode's metaphor again, ideas had outgrown their museum nursery.

~

The object-based epistemology around which museums were organized had two parts: the objects themselves, and the systematics into which those objects were placed. Susan Stewart has made a similar observation about collections, noting that they function first as metonyms—"part for the whole, item for context"—and then through schemes of classification so that "the world is accounted for by the elements of the collection."[51] Objects had inherent meaning, but that meaning could only be revealed by the way they were presented in museum exhibits. Antebellum museums, after all, had plenty of objects, but they failed to treat those objects systematically, and thus they failed in a larger sense to extract meaning from them. As William Henry Flowers concluded, "it is not the objects placed in a museum that constitute its value, so much as the method in which they are displayed and the use made of them for the purpose of instruction."[52]

Flowers' use of the word 'value' is worth considering further. Many writers have observed that one outcome of placing objects in museums is to give them 'value.'[53] Usually this value is assumed to be monetary. We see this most readily in the world of fine art, but increasingly so in the world of decorative arts, photography, and the nebulous but endlessly expanding world of collectibles. Once an object of one type—an Impressionist painting, or a piece of Bauhaus furniture—finds its way into a museum, then the monetary value of like objects rises. Even after many museums have been priced out of the market by the astronomical rise in prices over the recent past, museums have and continue to play a major role in determining the monetary value of objects on the open market—from Mayan antiquities, to Ansel Adams photographs, to Benin brasses, to Hepplewhite furniture. 'Museum-quality' is, after all, a synonym for 'expensive.'

This is not, however, the value to which Flowers refers. Instead, he refers to a didactic value, an instructive value, with which objects have been invested. This value is the creation of an object-based epistemology. To explain this investiture, I want to explore ideas about value articulated by Georg Simmel and recently refined by Arjun Appadurai. Simmel's insight into the value of objects was to notice that objects do not have intrinsic value, but rather that objects achieve value through exchange. Appadurai summarizes this point: "In a word, exchange is not a by-product of the mutual valuation of objects, but its source."[54]

Simmel and Appadurai concern themselves with the way in which objects circulate through a cultural economy. Museum objects, by definition, have precisely been removed from circulation and divested of this kind of value. As Jean Baudrillard has noted, once an object has been removed from its original, functional context, "its meaning is entirely up to the subject" who has done the removing.[55] In place of functional or monetary value, absent now precisely because the objects no longer circulate, museum objects in the late nineteenth century were given an intellectual value through an exchange operating at two levels.

At one level, those who designed museum displays created value for their objects through the systematics around which those exhibits were organized. This value served to distinguish representative, metonymic objects on display at the new museums from the bizarre, extraordinary objects of the older museums and freak shows. Through an object-based epistemology, the systematics of museum displays gave an intellectual value to things like clamshells and potsherds, objects that had had little "value" before.

At another level, those objects only carried meaning insofar as visitors came to view them and walked away with the intended knowledge. Ultimately, for museum objects, this process of valuation was completed through the attention paid them by museum visitors. Just as Simmel and Appadurai see value as created through exchange, the intellectual value of objects created through an object-based epistemology depended on this relationship between viewer and exhibit. If no one came to the museum, or worse, if they derived nothing useful from the visit, then the objects in those museums became, essentially, worthless.

~

It is part of the convention of introductory chapters that they explain the parameters of the study, and this book surely requires such an explanation. The dates which bracket this work are approximations. Most obviously they mark a period that begins with the well-known Centennial Exposition and ends with the nearly forgotten Sesquicentennial. A small handful of major American museums date their founding to one end of this chronology, and Philadelphia's Academy of Natural Sciences, the most venerable of the museums considered here, underwent a significant transformation in 1876. Most of the museums I examine, however, came to life during this fifty year period. At the other end, 1926 marks several coincidental events: deaths of museum directors, shifts in museum operation, as well as the forgotten fair. But more importantly, the Sesquicentennial signals as conveniently as anything the change in the way museums functioned as purveyors of knowledge. As finally as anything, the Sesqui signaled the death of an object-based epistemology.

The table of contents also makes clear that this book is not about the history of a single museum, nor does it deal solely with one kind of museum. Instead I have chosen to examine a constellation of institutions of different kinds in different cities. The great advantage of this approach is that it enables us to see how various kinds of knowledge, embodied in museums, related to one another. My contention is that the museums of the late nineteenth century, taken together, represented an attempt to put the whole of the world's knowledge under glass. To look only at one museum, or only at a specific kind of museum, misses this larger point.

Having said that, however, I should quickly then make the reciprocal caveat. Because I have chosen a broad focus, I have undoubtedly sacrificed a certain depth. Specialists in the history of anthropology or natural science may find themselves frustrated that I have not treated these histories in sufficient detail. Likewise, art historians may bristle that I have ignored subtleties in the history of their discipline in my attempt to link art museums with museums of history and commercial museums. In my own defense, I can only claim that while I have tread on others' turf, I have tried to do so gently and respectfully. In so doing, I have taken up Sally Kohlstedt's challenge to do a comparative study of museum development which highlights "both the curious parallels that existed among museums and those characteristics that mark out individual institutions."[56]

The five central chapters of this book deal with five of the bodies of knowledge that could be given museum form sketched by George Brown Goode. The sixth I deal with epilogically. We begin with natural history. This chapter describes how the intellectual paradigms of natural history were central to the building of all these museums. Formulated by Bacon, and refined through the eighteenth and early nineteenth centuries, the method of natural history focused on the collection, description, and classification of objects. All knowledge merely awaited the patient work of the naturalist to be revealed. The carefully classified objects that lay at the center of natural history research also formed the basis for museum displays. Through these displays, the public saw a natural world arranged with taxonomic order and precision. When finally completed, the encyclopedia of knowledge created by natural scientists and displayed for the public in museums would faithfully reflect the Creator's plan of the universe.

The taxonomic stability of the world created by the natural historians began to crumble when Charles Darwin's *Origin of Species* reached this country in 1860. As American scientists wrestled with Darwin, it became increasingly clear that the natural world was not fixed and orderly. Rather, it shifted and changed often in unpredictable ways.

By looking at the Academy of Natural Sciences in Philadelphia, the oldest such institution in the country, and glancing as well at the National Museum in Washington and the American Museum of Natural History in New York, chapter two analyzes what I see as the two related ramifications of the demise of natural history. On the one hand, the focus of scientific inquiry drifted away from museums of natural history. Interested less and less in examining extensive collections of specimens and interested more and more in the theoretical, the microscopic, and finally the genetic, scientists left museums and located themselves and their work in university laboratories. As a consequence of this, they made the work of science a fully professional endeavor carried on by people specially trained for the task. Whereas natural history had been the purview of the interested and engaged amateur in the nineteenth century, by the end of the period covered in this study serious scientific research was no longer an amateur pursuit. This removal, as Robert Young writes, meant that "nature had withdrawn from the common intellectual culture." [57]

Chapter three examines the relationship between museums and the development of anthropology. American anthropology in the last quarter of the nineteenth century grew up in museums, but it did so largely attached to museums of natural history. Focusing primarily on the University of Pennsylvania Museum and secondarily on the American Museum in New York and the Field Museum in Chicago, this chapter will examine how anthropology developed in a museum context and how it tried to create an intellectual space for itself separate from the rest of natural history.

In separating themselves from natural historians, anthropologists during these years defined the scope of their discipline. This chapter analyzes how distinctions between New World and Old World civilizations were drawn, how an anthropological notion of "culture" was created in museums, and how some of the world's people were seen to have a history, while others were seen to have "cultures" that existed outside the boundaries of history.

While anthropologists in the late nineteenth century detached themselves from natural historians, they continued to borrow much of their intellectual framework from the older discipline. First and foremost they relied on collecting and classifying objects. This chapter will also examine how, by the first quarter of this century, anthropology no longer relied on objects but became more interested in such issues as social organization and linguistics. Just as the new natural scientists needed microscopes and not museum collections, anthropologists shifted the focus of their interests as they moved out of museums and into university departments. This shift was most dramatically illustrated when Franz Boas, America's most influential anthropologist at the turn of the century, left the staff of the American Museum to join the faculty of

Columbia University. By the end of the period covered in this book, museums no longer played a primary role in creating anthropological knowledge. They might serve to educate the public about the world's cultures, but what they displayed was no longer considered up-to-date by academic anthropologists.

The fourth chapter constitutes an act of historical recovery. In it I examine the Philadelphia Commercial Museum, the only such museum in the country. Defunct and now largely forgotten, the Commercial Museum was once an enormous and important operation. Founded in 1893 by University of Pennsylvania botanist William Wilson, the Philadelphia Commercial Museum was designed to be the semi-official repository for much of the material displayed at the International Expositions between 1893 and 1926—a permanent world's fair. By the First World War, the Museum had grown to include a complex of exhibit buildings, thousands of displays, its own press, and a monthly journal, *Commercial America*, printed in both English and Spanish. Through its exhibits and through its associated Bureau of Information, the Commercial Museum served as a forerunner of the Federal Department of Commerce.

The purposes of the Commercial Museum were two-fold. On the one hand, its founders hoped its displays would convince the public about the possibilities for American commercial expansion overseas. On the other hand, the museum put itself at the service of American business-men, providing them with the information and advice necessary to com-pete with European firms in foreign markets. By enthusiastically advo-cating American commercial expansion overseas, those who built the Commercial Museum promoted commerce as a way for Americans to enjoy the benefits of empire without the troubles of colonial rule. In this way, the museum was an important actor in debates over American im-perialism. This chapter examines how the Commercial Museum, through its exhibits and publications, tried to create an intellectual architecture for American expansion.

By the 1920s, the Commercial Museum no longer enjoyed the promi-nence it once did. Its function of facilitating American business growth in foreign markets was superseded by the dynamic new Department of Commerce in Washington. This eclipse, however, represented more than one institution triumphing over another. Instead, it signaled that by the first quarter of this century, objects in museum displays were no longer relevant to the business of business. Objects in exhibits for the general public had been replaced by data collected by experts.

Chapter five looks at the way American history could be embodied in museum objects. The end of the nineteenth century witnessed the birth of the historical profession. The American Historical Association's founding in 1880 is as good a marker as any of the emergence of a professional discipline. Borrowing the seminar methods developed in Germany, American historians at universities including Johns Hopkins, Pennsylvania, and Harvard created the rigorous study of history. If the universities won at the turn of the century, then they defeated museums as the place where history could best be learned. This chapter, by looking at the extraordinary museums founded by Henry Mercer and Henry Ford, will examine how American history was presented through objects rather than through books.

Trained as an archaeologist of ancient America, Henry Mercer left the University of Pennsylvania Museum because he decided he had been pursuing archaeology "from the wrong end." Instead he devoted the rest of his life to the collection of objects related to the labor of pre-industrial America. By the time of his death his museum, a bizarre seven-story pile of his own design made entirely of poured concrete, housed over 25,000 objects. Mercer brought his archaeological understanding of objects to the creation of his history museum. The objects are exhibited—the museum has not been changed much since his death—without interpretive signs and without being situated in contextual displays. Each object is identified by a number painted on it in the manner of an archaeological artifact. Mercer believed that these objects, more than anything historians wrote in books, told the story of American history from the founding of the nation to the dawn of the industrial age.

Mercer's museum, north of Philadelphia, was the only one Henry Ford ever visited, or so he claimed. It became the inspiration for what would become Greenfield Village. Like Mercer, Ford had no use for history as it appeared in books, but his oft-quoted statement that "history is bunk" is only half of what he said. He went on to say that the only history that was valuable was that which could be seen. Though Ford was inspired by the scientific collecting that Mercer used, when Ford amassed his collection in the 1920s, he had a different agenda than Mercer. This chapter will conclude with a discussion of how by the 1920s objects had failed to communicate serious historical knowledge and became at Greenfield Village a refuge for nostalgia.

Chapter six starts from the observation that while art museums sit today atop our cultural hierarchy, they did not arrive there without contest. This chapter examines the reasons for their triumph. When the Philadelphia Museum of Art and the Boston Museum of Fine Art were founded in the 1870s, for example, they were designed to be both displays of, and schools for, industrial design. These were precisely not to be palaces of fine art but functional places instead where art would be put to the service of industry. The Metropolitan Museum, on the other hand, was established to exhibit the objets d'art collected by its wealthy benefactors.

These three institutions struggled symbolically to define what fell into the category of 'art' and how it was to be displayed for, and used by, the American public. Initially Boston and Philadelphia looked to London, to the South Kensington complex specifically, for inspiration. At South Kensington useful museums had been established where art informed industry and vice versus. New York looked instead to Paris's Louvre for its model.

When the Philadelphia Museum opened its new building in the late 1920s, Paris had become more influential. Sited at the end of a broad new boulevard that was designed by French-trained architects and intended to be the Champs Élysées of the United States, the new building no longer had much to do with the school of industrial arts. Like the Metropolitan, it now displayed the European fine art treasures gathered by wealthy patrons. Beyond telling the story of how the category of fine art was debated and ultimately defined, this chapter argues that the reason art museums are regarded as premier in the cultural hierarchy is not simply that they are supported by the wealthiest, most influential elite. In addition, I will suggest that the fine art objects in these museums, more so than the specimens in natural history museums or the artifacts in anthropological collections, continue to function successfully as objects. Natural science and anthropology may no longer reside in museums the way they did in the last quarter of the nineteenth century, but art history and art museums still enjoy a close intellectual relationship.

This book concludes in 1926 by resurrecting that year's Sesquicentennial celebration. Of all the world's fairs that delighted millions between 1876 and 1939, Philadelphia's Sesquicentennial has been almost entirely forgotten. Even Robert Rydell, who has written two volumes on world's fairs, mentions the Sesqui only briefly. It fell between one era and another.

By most accounts, the fair was a disaster. Much of the construction was not completed on time, and it rained more than half of the days the fair was open. The failure of the Sesqui to excite the public the way the

Centennial or the Columbian Exposition once did, however, had more to do with changes in American culture and in the way Americans understood the world than it did with the weather.

This chapter explains the flop that was the Sesquicentennial by asserting that its promoters continued to rely on an object-based epistemology to present the world to visitors at the moment when that epistemology had largely collapsed. The understanding of the world based on objects no longer resonated with people the way it had in the late nineteenth and early twentieth centuries. Subsequent fairs—in 1933 and 1939 in particular—were organized along different intellectual principles. The Sesquicentennial marks as well as any event the close of an era when Americans understood the world through objects.

This chapter also looks at the most successful of the Sesquicentennial's exhibits: High Street. Under the direction of groups like the Daughters of the American Revolution and the Colonial Dames, a completely fabricated version of Philadelphia's High Street circa 1776 was built on the fairgrounds. High Street's appeal lay in its sentimentalized view of a bygone age, and I discuss how it symbolized a new relationship between art, history, and objects.

Readers will notice from this review of chapters a decided emphasis on Philadelphia in this book. Some will be surprised by this focus—as a friend once told me, all books that are not about New York require justification. This project began as a study of Philadelphia institutions. It is an obvious observation to make that, with the founding of Peale's Museum, Philadelphia has had the longest museum history of any city in the nation. As I broadened my focus, however, I discovered that it may well have the richest and most instructive history as well.

Philadelphians in the late nineteenth century, for a variety of reasons, did not build on the vast and opulent scale that New Yorkers and Chicagoans did; there was no Marshall Field or J. P. Morgan in Philadelphia prepared to issue almost blank checks to museums. But Philadelphians were at the forefront of using museums to organize knowledge about the world. The museums they built, smaller and perhaps less well known than their cousins in New York or Chicago, better reflected the ways in which knowledge was shifting and evolving in the late nineteenth century. Though it has not been thoroughly explored by historians who have worked from the present backwards, looking to explain how New York became New York, and how Chicago became Chicago, Philadelphians led the nation at the end of the nineteenth century in the application of science to solve problems in areas such as medical research, industrial engineering, and chemical processing. They likewise led the nation in trying to create public institutions that would shape the latest knowledge and put it on display.

In broadening my focus, I have done so selectively. This study does not pretend to be a comprehensive study of museums in America during these fifty years—such a study would be impossibly big. Rather, I have chosen to look at institutions that best represent the larger intellectual issues I want to explore. In this sense, I have, like the museums themselves selecting specimens, chosen the museums I feel best represent the intellectual currents flowing in American intellectual life between 1876 and 1926.

~

The task museum builders set themselves—to embody the world's knowledge in museum objects through an object-based epistemology—proved quixotic. That, however, should not diminish our appreciation for what they tried to do. The museums of the late nineteenth century should be seen as the last great encyclopedic project, undertaken at a moment when many believed that objects, systematically arranged, could make perfect sense of the world. Each of the museums Goode proposed in his six-part scheme represented a volume of that encyclopedia, and the objects contained within, the entries. A complex of museums including all six, presumably, would successfully complete the encyclopedia set.

Yet Goode's straightforward scheme masked myriad questions. What was the relationship between these different bodies of knowledge? What was the difference between anthropology and natural history? Where did art and history intersect? Just as the collections inside museums proved tricky to classify and arrange satisfactorily, so too the distinctions between different museums, and therefore between different objects and the different bodies of knowledge those objects stood for, turned out to be more complicated than Goode seemed to recognize.

By the first quarter of the twentieth century, objects could no longer hold the meaning with which they had been invested. In an intellectual world now dominated by theoretical and experimental knowledge produced at dynamic and expanding universities, objects, and the museums which housed them, remained static. When the curtain fell on an epistemology based in objects, museums left the center stage of American intellectual life.

TWO

⌒

"Naked Eye Science": Museums and Natural History

> Eventually I plucked up the courage to ask . . . How does one
> study fossils? How does one understand what they tell us
> about the history of life? The answer? "You look at them long
> enough, and they speak to you."
>
> IAN TATTERSALL

"Girl number twenty . . . Give me your definition of a horse."

An uncomfortable silence.

"Girl number twenty unable to define a horse! . . . Girl number twenty possessed of no facts, in reference to one of the commonest animals! Some boy's definition of a horse."

Responding to the challenge, young Bitzer recites, "Quadruped. Graminivorous. Forty teeth, namely twenty-four grinders, four eye-teeth and twelve incisive. Sheds coat in the spring; in marshy countries, sheds hoofs, too. Hoofs hard, but requiring to be shod with iron. Age known by marks in mouth."

Pleased with this recitation, the teacher concludes: "Now girl number twenty you know what a horse is."[1]

This famous classroom scene opens Charles Dickens's 1854 novel *Hard Times*. The speaker is retired businessman and schoolmaster Thomas Gradgrind, one of Dickens's most memorable caricatures. Described by the author, Gradgrind is "a man of realities. A man of facts and calculations." In the novel's first line Gradgrind announces his view of the world:

"In this life, we want nothing but Facts, Sir; nothing but Facts!" As surely as Ebenezer Scrooge is a man of money, Gradgrind is a man of facts. And just as money has shriveled Scrooge, the facts to which Gradgrind is so faithfully wed have desiccated his humanity.

Like Scrooge as well, Gradgrind is redeemed by the end of the novel. But it is not his redemption that interests us here. Instead, we begin with the observation that the reason Dickens could create the Gradgrind caricature is that his readers recognized the type. Gradgrind functions successfully as a literary device because he represented with wry accuracy someone familiar to readers in Victorian England. By creating Gradgrind, Dickens reminds us that mid-nineteenth-century Britons, and their American cousins, were surrounded by people who wanted nothing but the facts. Exaggerated to be sure, Gradgrind was a faithful enough rendering of character to have resonance.

In Gradgrind's eyes—and, as Dickens suggests, in the eyes of most nineteenth-century scientists, both professional and amateur—a horse is simply the sum of the observable facts: quadruped, hard hooves, etc. Even schoolgirls can be observed, quantified, and catalogued, as in Dickens's sardonic gesture, where Gradgrind reduces Sissy Jupe, the poor, picked upon girl in the classroom, to a classificatory number 20. Dickens's classroom scene wonderfully describes, albeit in a highly exaggerated way, a way of looking at the world shaped by natural science, a way that reached a kind of ascendancy in the West by the middle of the nineteenth century.

Relentlessly empirical, nineteenth-century natural history made a fetish of the observable fact. Careful observation followed by taxonomic classification drove the pursuit of scientists and provided a guide with which the natural world could be understood. Natural history, as it was practiced by mid-nineteenth-century researchers, seemed poised to figure out the essential organization of the natural world, and in so doing, to reveal the very secrets of nature, God's very design for the planet. Dickens may have been suspicious of this kind of thinking, but most of his contemporaries were not.

This approach to understanding the natural world matured and flowered in the natural history museums and collections that sprang up around the United States through the nineteenth century. Natural history museums served as the institutional nexus for this pursuit of science, linking the collection of specimens in the field with the study, preservation, and arrangement of specimens by natural historians. In a very

real and important way, museums stood on the frontier of scientific understanding through the century, and they presented that understanding to the public through their displays. Museums, and the kind of knowledge they embodied, also contributed significantly to the creation of
what we now recognize as the modern biological sciences, but by the
early twentieth century they ceded their centrality in the pursuit of natural science to university-based research laboratories. In this sense, the
museums formed the institutional span between an older conception of
theologically inspired natural philosophy and a newer notion of scientific research.

Science in a New Nation: New Museums, Old Ideas

Americans recognized Gradgrind too, and many shared his way of looking at the world. And perhaps more so than in Britain, in the United
States research in natural history had important connections to national
identity as well. Throughout the nineteenth century, natural history, the
museums that displayed it, and American national ambition were intimately linked. As a private citizen Thomas Jefferson famously studied
the natural world around him. As president, among the first things he
did with the Louisiana territory after completing its purchase was to
sponsor the Lewis and Clark expedition to explore the region. The Long
Expedition, another exploratory trip to the American West, followed
shortly afterwards. A generation later, in the wake of the Mexican-
American War, Smithsonian secretary Joseph Henry reported happily in
1849 that "our new possessions in Oregon, California, and Mexico" offered rich fields for research "particularly in the line of natural history."[2]
Looking back on the first fifty years of the Smithsonian, Frederick William
True observed that "the Museum is essentially a natural development
springing from the activities of the government, growing with their
growth, and expanding with their expansion."[3] The link between American expansion, museums, and the natural history which provided the
intellectual framework for both underscored that, while the vast expanse
of the American frontier was tamed physically, it needed intellectual conquering simultaneously.

Significantly, Jefferson presented the minerals collected by the Lewis
and Clarke expedition to Peale's Museum in Philadelphia, and through
that gesture he symbolically asserted the nation's control over the newly
acquired area.[4] By so doing Jefferson drew a correlation between the
nation's project of taming and ordering the wilderness and the way

Peale's Museum functioned to do the same metonymically and micro-cosmically. When Charles Willson Peale lifts the tasseled curtain in his life-sized self-portrait—surely one of the most theatrical gestures in the history of American art—to reveal his museum gallery, he invites us to view the hierarchical way in which he, naturalist, artist, and museum proprietor, has arranged the natural world. At their top, the gallery walls are lined with Peale's portraits of famous and prominent contemporary figures. Beneath the portraits dozens of stuffed and preserved birds and other animals stare impassively at the museum visitor from behind glass cases. Finally, at Peale's feet in the foreground of the painting, a turkey slumps over a case of embalming tools and three fossil bones from Peale's mastodon lie haphazardly waiting to join the rest of the skeleton, visible just behind the curtain.

Here Peale has twice ordered the world: once as he has arranged his museum, and again as he has painted and presented it to us. With representations of his contemporaries at the top of the hierarchy, with representative specimens of extant species in the middle, and with the fossil remains of mysterious and unknown species (along with specimens awaiting their final resting place on display) at the bottom, Peale's self-portrait in front of his museum presents a natural world which moves from highest to lowest, where each species has its place fixed in the natural order, and where human beings represent the supreme achievement of creation. Behind the curtain, the Great Chain of Being is on display.

Peale's Museum, the first museum of any importance in the United States, became more resolutely a natural history museum in 1786 when Peale took a somewhat disparate collection and shifted its focus toward what he called "natural curiosities." Fossils, preserved animal specimens, and geologic samples joined Peale's collection of portraits, and he augmented his museum objects by offering lectures on natural history. In the Introduction to those lectures Peale explained why natural history held such crucial importance for Americans: "The farmer ought to know that snakes feed on field mice and moles, which would otherwise destroy whole fields of corn. . . . To the merchant, the study of nature is scarcely less interesting, whose traffic lies altogether in material either raw from the stores of nature or *wrought* by the hand of ingenious art. . . . The mechanic ought to possess an accurate knowledge of many of the qualities of those materials with which his art is connected."[5] Peale offered a view of natural history that connected it to the growth of the new republic. By emphasizing the importance of natural history for the farmer,

4 Charles Willson Peale, *The Artist in His Museum* (1822). Late in his life, Charles Willson Peale shows us perhaps his greatest creation, the nation's first important museum of natural history. (Courtesy of The Pennsylvania Academy of the Fine Arts, Philadelphia, Gift of Mrs. Sarah Harrison, The Joseph Harrison, Jr. Collection)

the merchant, and the mechanic, he suggested that natural history and democracy went hand-in-hand. Natural history was not an arcane topic, reserved for the well educated or for the wealthy with time to dabble. Instead, natural history, if made available to the populace through vehicles like his museum, would make possible the prosperity of ordinary citizens. But if Peale articulated explicitly why the study of natural history was critical for ordinary Americans, he said implicitly with his museum that museums were the best way to present the results of its researches and that, therefore, museums should perform a vital educational function for a democratic citizenry.

Peale's Museum, while it arguably made the most compelling link between science and national identity in the republic's early years, did not survive beyond the first half of the nineteenth century. After the founder's death, the museum moved to Baltimore before it slowly evaporated. Back in Philadelphia, however, natural history took a more long-lasting institutional form when a group of gentlemen met to form the Academy of Natural Sciences in 1812.

The date marks, as George Daniels observes, the beginnings of nineteenth-century American science, a science closely associated with ideas of natural theology and dependent on the collection, examination, and classification of God's creations. As the Unitarian Orville Dewey put it in 1830, "It is not enough to say, in the general, that God is wise, good, and merciful. . . . We want statements, specifications, facts, details, that will illustrate the wonderful perfection of the infinite Creator."[6] At this moment, Philadelphia still held its prominent place as an American center of science. Benjamin Franklin, the quintessential figure of the American Enlightenment, and David Rittenhouse still cast long shadows across the city's intellectual landscape. The city ranked among the best in the English speaking world, for example, as a place to study medicine. Peale's Museum might have vanished from the city's scientific scene, but Philadelphia remained a lively center of scientific pursuit.

At its inception, the Academy of Natural Sciences was firmly rooted in Enlightenment ideas about the gentlemanly pursuit of knowledge. The original qualifications for membership in the Academy, according to W. S. W. Ruschenberger, president from 1869 to 1881, "were friendliness to science and good moral reputation and nothing more." In keeping with this founding principle, and also expressing the democratic impulses of the new nation, eminent scientists shared Academy membership with ordinary working men—and even some women.

The Academy's membership criteria reflect both a democratic impulse and a cultural reality. Unlike the academies of Europe, where social exclusivity governed membership, the Academy of Natural Sciences wanted to share the inclusive aspirations of the new nation. At the same time, the Academy's qualifications for membership underscored that in the early years of the nineteenth century there did not yet exist a community of what we would recognize as professional scientists distinct from amateurs. The men who came together in 1812 founded the Academy as a projection of what the nation hoped it would be, and as a reflection of what the scientific world was. Its founders hoped that the Academy would be a place where the two would intersect.

For nearly fifteen years after the Academy commenced its activities, it pursued its work without a museum. The purpose of its founding had been for scientific research, and a display of objects had not seemed central to that purpose. By 1826, however, the Academy had opened a display to the public. By opening the museum, those at the Academy built an institution designed to present the public with the object-based epistemology central to nineteenth-century Americans' understanding of the world. The museum's opening signaled a shift from the Academy's eighteenth-century roots. More so than Peale in his museum, Academy members worked hard to link the study of the natural world with the objects put on display in their museum. Peale had displayed objects arranged according to a conventional understanding of the natural world, but his institution did little to promote advances in natural science. With the opening of the Academy's museum serious research in natural science now included the collection and display of objects along with their description and classification. Eighteen twenty-six thus marks the beginning of museum-based natural history in this country.

As natural history developed in this country through the nineteenth century, it was deeply connected with museum work. The connection was a straightforward transitive one: the study of natural history depended on close, careful work with specimens. Museums existed to house and display specimens; therefore museums were the logical place to study natural history. Twenty years after the Academy opened its public museum, when Congress chartered the Smithsonian Institution in 1846, members felt that establishing a museum would best fulfill James Smithson's instruction that his money be used to increase and diffuse knowledge, though the bequest itself made no specific reference to a museum. Four years later, Smithsonian secretary Joseph Henry hired Spencer Baird to be assistant secretary in large part because of Baird's expe-

5 This retouched daguerreotype may be the oldest extant photograph of an American museum. Amidst the Academy of Natural Sciences' collections stand Joseph Leidy *(center)* and Edgar Allan Poe *(left)*. (Courtesy of the Ewell Sale Stewart Library, The Academy of Natural Sciences of Philadelphia)

rience classifying and recording zoological specimens.[7] Henry believed Baird had the talents necessary to develop a great museum collection.[8] Having collected, described, and classified the constituent parts of the natural world, what remained finally for natural scientists was to create orderly, systematic displays of representative specimens. As a final flourish to the work of natural history, museums dazzled the public with science's ability to control and order the world, to put it under glass, to put it literally on the end of a pin.

To put objects, and therefore the museums that exhibited them, at the center of an epistemology of natural science meant refining and recreating the concept of what a museum was. Henry, his assistant Baird, and their colleagues in Philadelphia had to distinguish their museums from mere collections of curiosities. In this redefinition, a true natural history museum became a place both of public learning and education and of scientific research. Peale, after all, had specifically referred to his museum as a collection of natural curiosities, but a generation later there would be no mistaking these new natural history museums with

the freak shows, circuses, and other disreputable displays of objects
that competed for the attention of the American public. As Joseph Henry
reported to the Smithsonian's Regents in 1856: "It is no part of the plan
of the Institution to form a museum merely to attract the attention and
gratify the curiosity of the casual visitor," but instead to create a place
"to facilitate the study and increase the knowledge of natural history."
These new institutions of natural history, quite apart from the Barnumesque dime museums and traveling sideshows, would be sober places of
learning and knowledge.[9]

As the nineteenth century wore on, these museums had to distinguish themselves not only from the freak shows that purported to exhibit
exotic natural specimens but also from other collections of objects. In the
second half of the century, Americans became increasingly surrounded
by objects of all kinds, especially consumer products. The 1876 Centennial Exposition in Philadelphia served to celebrate one-hundred years of
the American political experiment, and, after the bloodshed of the Civil
War, it became a place of national reconciliation. Just as importantly, it
also provided the first post-war opportunity for Americans to put a
world of objects on display. William Leach has observed that the Centennial was probably the most influential of America's fairs because "it un-
locked the floodgates to what became a steady flow of goods and fantasies about goods."[10]

Natural history museums had to display important and meaningful
objects, whose value lay not in the world of commerce but in the world
of science. Otherwise museums ran the risk of becoming simply another
part of the new world of vulgar, meaningless objects. Academy of Natural
Sciences president Ruschenberger drew the distinction sharply when he
responded to a plan that the Academy advertise itself more aggressively
to the public. Ruschenberger made sure to articulate the difference between a natural science museum and a department store like John Wanamaker's: "But the plan and policy—including a series of advertisements
as alluring as bits of fiction or romance—which have made Wanamaker's
great and unrivalled retail market for everything so wonderfully successful and admirable, are not adapted to promote the welfare of scientific
societies."[11]

One way to make sure people saw the difference between the two
was to concentrate on presenting museum objects in a way that enabled
them to be examined but not in a way that caused them to titillate, excite,
or otherwise amuse. Ruschenberger recognized that the museum of the
Academy served an important public function, translating scientific in-

formation to a general audience. Ruschenberger also understood that each specimen needed to be displayed properly if viewers were to learn all they could:

> The value of a specimen as an instructive or educational implement in a museum depends very much on the perfection of its display. A single specimen of any species of bird, for example, artistically mounted so as to present accurately an expression of the creature while alive, and distinctly labeled with its systematic and popular names, and the region of its nativity, and so placed that its individuality may be readily observed by the visitor, is of more immediate value to the general public than numerous unmounted specimens packed loosely in drawers or cases.[12]

Understanding natural history depended on the application of one's senses; it was not intended, however, to be in any way sensual. Ruschenberger insisted that the museum should be "a place of learned occupation or study," not "a place in which are collected chiefly animal monsters and effigies of strange and curious things . . . in a word, a wondermongerer's device to allure the curious and gaping many to amusement."[13] Ruschenberger and his Academy colleagues did not object to enjoyment. Indeed, according to Ruschenberger, "a grand museum is a source of pleasure." But the Academy would prove pleasurable because it provided a source of uplift: "It stirs no sensual emotions, provokes no admiration for what is false, but inclines the observer to perceive that the truth, nature itself, is more worthy of respect and admiration than any imitation or likeness of it."[14] The last barb doubtless made reference to art galleries, whose paintings represented "imitations" of nature, and which some members of the Academy saw as suspicious. Members of the Academy's Building Committee, for example, compared the effect of their new museum to the effect of fine art galleries: "The influence of pictures and statues upon beholders is entirely emotional and sentimental in character, sometimes kindling only sensual ideas which are not always as evanescent in effect as 'the lascivious pleasings of a lute.'"[15]

Ruschenberger was doubtless right that the embalmed specimens in glass cases never stirred any sensual emotions in anyone. But the control over the natural world that museum displays orchestrated represented more than an intellectual and physical conquest of nature for its own sake. Most natural scientists in the first half of the nineteenth century saw their work as an instrument of religious worship. In an equation of taxonomy with religious devotion, natural scientists collected the products of creation in order to understand the Creator better. Through this equation, natural history museums participated in what Lawrence Levine has described as a process of sacralization, where certain ostensibly secular activities became invested with religious significance.[16] They became temples of naturalism in which visitors could worship science's understanding of the creation. Mid-nineteenth-century natural scientists served then as moral teachers, and in their hands the carefully arranged objects that filled their museums thus became moral objects as well.

In his role as public spokesperson for natural science, Louis Agassiz, imported from Europe to teach at Harvard, enjoyed considerable celebrity. Agassiz drew the connection between his work as a naturalist and his religious beliefs as a Christian almost every time he had the chance. For Agassiz, this equation certainly extended to include museums. He believed that the "great object of our museums should be to exhibit the whole animal kingdom as a manifestation of the Supreme Intellect."[17] Agassiz, however, was only the most visible and famous of these devout naturalists. Joseph Leidy, for example, associated throughout his career with the Academy of Natural Sciences and one of America's preeminent scientists of the mid-century, was described as "a high-priest of Nature standing at the threshold of her mysteries."[18] When the natural scientists observed and categorized nature, arranging it all with taxonomic order, they held up a mirror not only to creation but to the Creator. In this sense, museums thus became places of research and education with the very highest moral purpose.

This, then, was the intellectual baggage that natural scientists carried with them across the threshold of the mid-nineteenth century: a belief that the world could be understood through the collection, observation, classification, and display of objects; and a certainty that this work served the higher purpose of illuminating God's plan for the world and humans' place in it. These beliefs not only contributed to considerable progress in the fields of natural science; they also permitted that progress to be profoundly reassuring. As Harvard president Charles Eliot Norton put it in 1878, "modern science has discovered and set forth the magnificent idea of the continuity of creation. It has proved that the development of the universe has been a progress from good to better, a progress not without reactions and catastrophes, but still a benign advance towards ever higher forms of life." In Norton's view, science had "laid a firm foundation for man's instinctive faith in his own future." Science had "exalted the idea of God," and in Norton's opinion, this was surely "the greatest service that can be rendered to humanity." [19] Norton made these remarks to the crowd gathered for the opening of the American Museum of Natural History in New York.

~

The Civil War is surely the watershed event of the American nineteenth century. While American museums of natural history had deep roots in the antebellum period, they blossomed after the Civil War. In Philadelphia, for example, by 1865 the Academy of Natural Sciences possessed over 200,000 specimens and needed a new building to accommodate growing numbers of visitors. In New England, Louis Agassiz finally got his life-long wish when ground was broken for the Museum of Comparative Zoology at Harvard in 1859; the building opened to the public late in the following year. Agassiz believed that the collections at the Academy of Natural Sciences were the only ones in the United States which rivaled those in Europe, but he was confident that his museum would ultimately surpass all others.[20] Philanthropic New Yorkers founded the American Museum of Natural History in 1868. To the South, the Smithsonian acquired the objects accumulated by the now defunct National Institute and, joined with the objects it already possessed, these objects formed the core of an expanded museum, housed in its own building. By the early 1870s Congress appropriated money for a museum separate from the rest of the Smithsonian's operations. The new museum was largely completed by 1881.

Each of these museums responded to different local pressures as they grew, and the details of their institutional histories are surely unique. Yet all four were built according to the same intellectual plan. Each museum presented visitors with a science which placed objects at the center of understanding the natural world. One historian has written about the founding of the American Museum: "The trustees preferred to support research that had spectacular physical objects and large concrete facts such as dinosaur skeletons . . . for its subject matter." [21] In addition, these museums invested moral authority in the objects they displayed. When the cornerstone of the Academy's new building was laid on October 30, 1872, Ruschenberger reminded those gathered that "in God's creation there is no conflict or contradiction of parts. When accurately interpreted the perfect harmony of their relations will be manifest, the book of nature is entirely free from error; it contains no misstatement of any kind. Surely such a book may be studied without perverting

the mind from truth or establishing a preference for what is not reality." [22] Ruschenberger and his colleagues remained convinced that the
natural history museum was the best approximation of the "book of nature," and the objects displayed inside those museums constituted the
pages.

If the Civil War marks the beginning of great institutional expansion
for natural history museums, then it also brought a coincidental intellectual revolution which undermined the very foundations upon which the
new museums were built. In 1860 Harvard botanist Asa Grey reviewed
Charles Darwin's recently published *The Origin of Species by Means of
Natural Selection.* His sympathetic notice of the book began the debate
in this country over the theory of natural selection and the role it played
in the evolutionary process. Philadelphia honored Darwin almost simultaneously when the Academy of Natural Sciences became the first scientific society in the United States, if not in the world, to offer Darwin
membership after the publication of *The Origin of Species.* In 1860, Darwin wrote to his friend Charles Lyell, telling him about election to the
Academy: "This morning I got a letter from the Academy of Natural Sciences of Philadelphia, announcing that I am elected a correspondent. . . .
It shows that some naturalists there do not think me such a scientific
profligate as many think me here." [23] Darwin's significance to natural history had been recognized by Joseph Leidy, one of America's most distinguished naturalists and a figure central to the Academy through the second half of the nineteenth century. Darwin wrote an appreciative letter
especially to Leidy: "Your note has pleased me more than you could
readily believe: for I have during a long time heard all good judges speak
of your paleontological labours in terms of the highest respect . . . appro-
bation from you has gratified me much." [24]

Although Darwin received these and other gestures of welcome to
the United States, the general reception of his ideas would prove more
complicated. [25] While Darwin was acknowledged by Grey and Leidy, the
natural history museums built after the Civil War maintained pre-
Darwinian principles of natural science even as those principles were
challenged fundamentally. Darwinian natural history might at first fit
comfortably into natural history museums. His theory of natural selection helped explain the Great Chain of Being these museums put on display. Ultimately, however, Darwinian theory shook the foundations of
these museums and the kind of natural history they fostered. The theory
drew natural history into new areas of research, away from morphology
and toward genetics, from whole organism biology into cellular biology,

from science that could be conducted with the naked eye toward science that needed a microscope. Just as importantly, though few people grasped it initially, natural selection eroded the confidence and optimism these museums projected. At its starkest, a Darwinian world was indifferent to Victorian notions of progress: it had no great design, and perhaps, therefore, no great designer. In brand new buildings, these museums presented the public with an understanding of the natural world which would eventually evaporate in the wake of Darwinian thinking. Darwin relied on the inherited techniques of an older natural science, but the theory he developed made possible the beginnings of a new one.

Dinosaurs and Darwinism

By the late 1860s, the old quarters of the Academy of Natural Sciences had been literally over-run by visitors. In 1869 nearly 100,000 people had trooped through the Academy's exhibits, even though the museum was only open two days a week. The annual report of that year worried that the fragile specimens in the collection might be in danger of destruction.[26] In fact, the crowds had become such a problem that in 1867 the Academy began to charge a ten cent admission fee in the hope of discouraging people from visiting.[27]

The huge popularity enjoyed by the Academy surely had one source: the hadrosaurus. The Academy possessed impressive collections of mollusk shells, and handsome specimens of stuffed birds, but without a doubt people came to the Academy to see the dinosaur.

The hadrosaurus fossils had been found in New Jersey in 1848, and when they made their debut at the Academy in 1867, they were the first dinosaur bones ever mounted in this country. In the new building, the hadrosaurus greeted visitors as they entered the main hall. J. S. Kingsley described the spectacle for readers of *Popular Science Monthly:* "On entering the hall, the visitor sees almost immediately in front of him, towering to a height of fifteen feet, a skeleton of Hadrosaurus, a kangaroo-like reptile from the greensand of New Jersey." [28] The obvious first moral of this story for natural history museums is, then as now: exhibit dinosaurs and they will come. Beyond its marquee value, however, the hadrosaurus represented the most dramatic example of mid-nineteenth-century paleontological research. The Academy's terrible lizard demonstrated to an eager public the fantastic extent of what Nature could dream up, and more importantly, what scientists could unearth.

In 1867 the hadrosaurus found itself not only as the star attraction

6   The first reconstructed dinosaur in the country *(Hadrosaurus foulkii)* made its debut in the galleries of the Academy of Natural Sciences. Here the beast towers over Benjamin Waterhouse Hawkins, the man brought from London to mount the fossil. (Courtesy of the Ewell Sale Stewart Library, The Academy of Natural Sciences of Philadelphia)

of Philadelphia's natural history museum. Like other creatures known only through fossils, the hadrosaurus played a crucial role in the debates over Darwin's recently published *The Origin of Species.* The study of fossils could address two important questions: first, did species evolve over time; and second, had some species become extinct as a result of purely natural processes, and not as the result of the biblical flood? These important connections between Darwin and paleontology also meant that natural history museums, at least those with good collections of fossils, found themselves at the heart of the Darwinian debate. Paleontology developed within the frameworks of the natural history museum. Paleontologists discovered and described extinct creatures, compared them with others, and through this work developed a taxonomy of a disappeared world. In this sense, paleontology represented the most spectacular achievement of the old natural history.

The exhibitionary spectacle of paleontology began in Philadelphia when Peale put his mastodon skeleton on display at the end of the eighteenth century. In the last half of the nineteenth century, however, as the "boneyards" of the American west opened up, American paleontology took off, and paleontologists raced to keep up with the finds coming out of the ground. Three men—Joseph Leidy, Edward Drinker Cope, and Othneil Marsh—bore primary responsibility for the growth of this discipline. The contributions these three made to the study of paleontology can most easily be measured numerically: before they entered the field, both metaphorically and literally, fossils of approximately one hundred North American genera and species had been discovered. To this number, Leidy himself added 375; Marsh discovered another 536; and Cope eclipsed them both by adding 1,282 genera and species to the total known through fossils.[29] With Leidy and Cope at the Academy during this period, Philadelphia was probably the most important center for the study of old bones.

Joseph Leidy ranks as perhaps the most prolific and successful naturalist of the mid-century, and he deserves to be recognized as the founder of paleontology in this country. He published his first paleontological paper in 1847: "On the Fossil Horse in America" (one wonders if Thomas Gradgrind had assigned it to his class). In part this paper gained attention by demonstrating that horses had existed and become extinct on the American continent thousands of years before the arrival of the Spanish. The following year, Leidy conducted the examination and classification of the hadrosaurus. Like the scientific expeditions to the American west, Leidy's pioneering work in a new field of natural history had nationalistic as well as scientific implications. Leidy helped put American science on a par with European science; his paleontological work "turned the eyes of the savants of the Old World to their younger brethren in the West," according to one eulogist.[30] Nathan Reingold has pointed out that in the nineteenth century, paleontology was one science where Americans could match or even outdo the Europeans.[31]

While Leidy was a gentleman and a scholar of the old school, Cope and Marsh, his two younger colleagues, carried on a famous, and often unseemly, rivalry. Stories of their competition and animus have become the stuff of scientific legend. Their antics often blurred the line between Victorian science and Victorian melodrama. Cope, for example, kept a secret notebook which he referred to as his "Marshiana." In it he documented all the scientific mistakes he believed Marsh had made. When he felt he had accumulated enough damaging material, he had the notebook published in the Sunday edition of the *New York Herald,* hoping that it would destroy Marsh's reputation. Unbeknownst to Cope, Marsh too had been keeping a journal and had his "Copeiana" published in the same paper the following Sunday. In their mutual hatred, Cope and Marsh may have spurred each other on to greater achievements in paleontology, but they also drove Leidy out of the field. Uninterested in the increasingly personal invectives, and unable to keep up financially with Cope and Marsh, who both financed their work by spending from family fortunes (Marsh was a relative of the Peabodys), Leidy essentially quit the world of paleontology by the 1870s.[32]

While the hadrosaurus and other such paleontological curiosities drew gawkers by the thousands, paleontology occupied center stage in the scientific debate over Darwin. Darwin himself understood the potential importance of paleontological discoveries to the discussion of his theory. He devoted two chapters in *The Origin of Species* to the topic. In one, he referred to "the imperfection of the geological record" to explain why his theoretical version of the history of life seemed to have so many gaps. In the other, he scanned the existing paleontological record for trends which would provide evidence for this theory.[33]

Paleontological discoveries revealed that extinction was a part of the natural cycle. That species could not only change but simply disappear altogether through natural processes, and not because of providential interference, unsettled an earlier understanding in which species remained fixed, unchanging, and timeless. When, for example, Peale's mastodon went on display, most people, Thomas Jefferson among them, assumed that the skeleton represented a species still living but as yet undiscovered in the American interior. Theorizing in the absence of modern genetics and other kinds of biological understanding, Darwin realized that extinct species brought to light by paleontologists seemed the most persuasive kind of evidence for his theory. The discovery of ancient beasts demonstrated that species did in fact evolve over time and did become extinct as part of the evolutionary process. In his letter of thanks to Joseph Leidy, Darwin recognized both the achievements of the great scientist specifically, and the importance of paleontology generally, to the development of his theory.

As Peter Bowler has observed, by 1860 paleontology had already begun to erode the foundations of early nineteenth-century understanding.[34] Fossils demonstrated that species did not remain fixed, and their disappearance from the planet might not have anything at all to do with biblical events. In that same year, Asa Grey's sympathetic review of *The Origin of Species* inaugurated the debate in this country over the theory of natural selection. That debate is usually told as the exchange between Grey and his Harvard colleague Louis Agassiz. If Grey lined up in Darwin's camp, then Agassiz, the more famous of the two, held a staunchly antagonistic view of Darwin. The struggle tends to be seen as one between those who understood Darwinism and saw its truth, and those who did not. This narrative, however, misses a third side of the debate: those who embraced and wrestled with Darwin and who took his ideas in other directions. In this group, no one made a more significant contribution than paleontologist Edward Drinker Cope.[35] To understand Cope's career is to understand the way in which paleontology, and the museums which provided its institutional home, tried to fashion a compromise between the old natural history and the new.

When *Popular Science Monthly* devoted an entire issue to examining Darwin's legacy in 1909, Herman Bumpus of New York's American Museum of Natural History contributed an essay entitled "Darwin and Zoology." In it, he claimed that Cope had been the central figure in initiating the Darwinian debate in America. Cope did so with the publication of a paper in the Academy of Natural Science's *Proceedings* playfully entitled "On the Origin of Genera." According to Bumpus, the essay represented "the first important direct contribution to the subject of evolution made by one not directly under the influence of the Boston academics." Tipping his cap to Philadelphia's Academy, New Yorker Bumpus continued: "I believe that I am perfectly safe in saying that no academy in America has ever published a paper that reflects more to its credit than this extraordinary essay of Cope."[36] In writing his own history of the Academy at the turn of the century, Edward Nolan went even further. Of Cope's essay, he wrote: "Indeed, it has been claimed that it was the most important contribution *to science* published in America up to that time."[37]

In the essay, Cope began by announcing his support of Darwin's ideas: "That a descent, with modifications, has progressed from the beginning of the creation, is exceedingly probable. The best enumeration of facts and arguments in its favor are those of Darwin, as given in his various important works." But rather than agree or disagree, Cope tried to push the issues Darwin raised further. Natural selection, in Cope's view, was the "second law" of evolution. This law might well explain differences between species, but according to Cope natural selection did not explain how different groups or genera appeared. From his reading of *The Origin of Species,* Cope concluded that "Darwin is aware of these facts to some degree, but . . . he does not dwell on them. Where he does, he does not attempt to account for them on the principle of natural selection."

Cope proposed two laws governing what he termed the "modes and means" of the evolution of life. The second was Darwin's natural selection. The first was what he termed "the law of acceleration and retardation." In his essay Cope argued that "while natural selection operates by 'preservation of the fittest,' retardation and acceleration act without reference to 'fitness' at all; that instead of being controlled by fitness it is the controller of fitness."[38] Natural selection, properly understood, introduced randomness into the process of evolution; Cope, in theorizing this mechanism of "retardation and acceleration" gave direction to that process. Without retreating from what he saw as Darwin's important insights, Cope tried to restore some sense of order to natural processes.

In addition to reaffirming the sense of order which the older natural history had given the world, Cope also wanted to preserve the role of religion in natural history. Sometime after 1885 he began a manuscript entitled "The Theology of Evolution." In it, he tried to relate theology to his paleontological work. "The object of the present essay," he began this unpublished manuscript, "is to point out briefly what science has done for theology up to this time." Quickly, Cope described how evolution explained the origins of the nonbiological as well as the biological. Paleontology provided critical evidence for this: "The great gift to mankind in the science of paleontology is the irrefragable evidence which it affords that life and consciousness (or mind) has in the order of time, preceded structure. The part played by consciousness in the history of animal life is that of a personal creator."[39] In this formulation, biological imperatives do not drive, but are driven by, the capacities of mind. Cope was not defining new questions here—philosophers wrestled with different versions of this same concern. There is something vaguely Lamarckian about this, and his ideas about "inner-directed" evolution, sometimes called "orthogenesis," were influenced by the botanist Karl Nageli.[40] But Cope, as one of the two preeminent American paleontologists, used his considerable scientific expertise to formulate a theory where the randomly operating mechanisms of Darwin could be harmonized with the more directed and personally controlled forces of mind. Put more simply, Cope used paleontology to synthesize the old natural history with the new.

Cope, according to Ronald Rainger, "was one of the first Americans to put forth a comprehensive evolutionary theory."[41] Like many Americans, however, he remained a Lamarckian as he envisioned an evolutionary process that preserved a role for volition, will, desire. Cope's evolution thus was not the random, aimless process that Darwin described. Cope's ideas, while more extensively developed perhaps, and with more paleontologic experience behind them, resonated with those of other Americans at the time. As Peter Bowler has observed, the combination of progress and Lamarckism—the theory that characteristics can be acquired during the life of an individual and then passed down to succeeding generations—appealed to many late Victorian thinkers.[42] Likewise Cynthia Russett has pointed out that Lamarck attracted Americans because his theory seemed to offer a scientific basis for the American faith in self-improvement.[43] Darwin's notion of evolution challenged not simply the idea of God's creation; for Americans he put into question the belief in individual effort and initiative. Some time ago, historian Charles Rosenberg suggested that rather than seeing a dichotomy between progressive supporters of Darwin and regressive defenders of theology, those who study the period would do well to "describe and understand the intricate yet ever-changing symbiosis which they maintained."[44] Cope's essay, neatly tying together theology, evolution, and progress, searched desperately for a synthesis.

～

In 1930, toward the end of his own life, Henry Fairfield Osborn, paleontologist and the man responsible for creating the paleontological collections at New York's American Museum of Natural History, published a biography of Cope. The thick volume served as a double tribute. At one level, it placed Cope among the first rank of nineteenth-century American scientists, calling him a "master naturalist" in the book's subtitle. Osborn viewed Cope as something of a mentor. While on the faculty at Princeton, Osborn had sided with Cope in his rancorous squabbles with Marsh. Osborn then left Princeton for the American Museum in New York and made an international reputation for himself by creating the Department of Vertebrate Paleontology. Through his efforts, New York supplanted Philadelphia as the premier place in the world for the study of vertebrate fossils. He began building the department by purchasing his mentor's collection of fossil mammals. A few years later, in 1899, Osborn added Cope's collection of fossil reptiles, and by the early twentieth century he had assembled the most extensive collection of vertebrate fossils in the United States.

Osborn made the department and the museum his private domain, and from this castle on Central Park West he became the leading force in paleontology in the first quarter of the twentieth century. Not content to make the American Museum the center of the paleontological world, Osborn also wanted to use his paleontological experience to formulate his own theory of evolution. Like most of his contemporaries, Osborn could not accept the naturalism and randomness of Darwin, and he worked to create a theory which would satisfy both scientific fact and late Victorian sensibility. Osborn tinkered with and refined the ideas of his mentor Cope. Convinced that only some guiding, and presumably divine, principle could explain the multiple examples of parallel evolution that his own collections of fossils illustrated, Osborn tried to preserve teleology within a theory of evolution. Like Cope a generation earlier, Osborn tried to unite God, morality, and science.

As the shaper of the major paleontological collection in the largest natural history museum in the United States, Osborn brought all of the frameworks that governed traditional natural science into the twentieth century. With its reliance on discovery, collection, morphological description, and classification, and finally through public displays, paleontology was the apotheosis of an older natural history. Produced within the frameworks of this older understanding, paleontology also retained natural science's commitments to Christian morality and to Victorian progress. Through their paleontological work and displays, the natural history museums of the late nineteenth century constructed a natural world where Darwin, Progress, and God resided comfortably together.

The growth of paleontology was bound up in the growth of natural history museums. Yet paleontology flourished in the late nineteenth century largely because more and better fossil specimens became available for study, not because there was an exciting intellectual ferment among the paleontologists. Reliable train service between the East Coast and the American West had as much to do with developing paleontology as did any new ideas.[45] But at the turn of the century, museums were the only institutions with the resources to mount the expensive bone-hunting expeditions. First and foremost, of course, was Osborn's work for the American Museum, but the Carnegie Museum in Pittsburgh, the Academy of Natural Sciences in Philadelphia, and even small places like the Natural History Museum in Denver all played the fossil-hunting game.

Beyond the money, the museums provided the intellectual architecture for paleontology. Museums served to display specimens, after all, and no specimens were more displayable than the apatosauruses, titanotheres, and megalonyx recovered and reconstructed by the paleontologists. In this sense, paleontology was the last, most significant contribution made by the museums to turn-of-the-century science. Paleontology was the apotheosis of the older natural history and its last stand.

Yet even as fossils came by the boxcar load to New York, Philadelphia, Pittsburgh, and Chicago, the frameworks which provided the logic of paleontology were under assault by experimental laboratory biology. Ronald Rainger has described it this way: "Conceptually and methodologically, the study of fossil vertebrates was peripheral to the most important work being done in the biological and geological sciences." Likewise, Peter Bowler describes an "almost complete breakdown of communication" between the new experimental biology and the older areas like paleontology. Consequently, the study of extinct animals, taking place almost entirely in museums, was stagnating intellectually, and, according to Rainger, it was increasingly "a marginal subject at institutions of American higher education."[46]

Darwinism arrived in America at roughly the same moment that the hadrosaurus went on display at the Academy, and in the context of scientific understanding of that time, the importance of dinosaurs and other extinct monsters to the study of evolution seemed unquestionable. By the end of the century, however, the commitment to paleontology meant, implicitly or explicitly, that the museums had made a choice. Dinosaurs still packed in the crowds at the museums, but they no longer drew the attention of scientists in the same way.

Creating Knowledge: Museums,
Universities, and "Original Research"

On July 11, 1883, W. S. W. Ruschenberger had an unpleasant run-in with Edward Cope in front of Philadelphia's St. George Hotel. The two had a brief but tense discussion which Ruschenberger reported later with some agitation. Cope, Ruschenberger wrote, wanted to elevate the Academy of Natural Science's professors to sit on the Academy's governing council. In addition, he proposed to restructure the Academy's professorships so that they would number thirteen, and therefore more closely resemble a university faculty.[47] Cope announced to Ruschenberger that he planned to pack the next council meeting with his supporters to push the measure through. Ruschenberger disagreed with the idea, then complained bitterly: "My conviction is that Mr. Cope is ambitious, selfish, unscrupulous and wholly unreliable and unfaithful."[48]

Cope may well have been all those things, and on the surface the encounter seems to have been a nasty bit of institutional infighting. At stake in Cope's challenge to Ruschenberger, however, was whether the Academy's professors would continue to serve the role they always had, or whether they would come to resemble their increasingly specialized and professionalized counterparts at universities. Cope recognized that the nature of scientific research was changing rapidly and fundamentally. He envisioned his proposal to turn the amateur professors at the Academy into professionals as a way for the Academy to keep up. By making this proposal, though, Cope implicitly suggested that the Academy abandon the principles upon which it and other museums of natural history had been founded.

~

When Congress solicited suggestions for how to best apply the Smithson bequest, members worked from the vague instructions left by James Smithson, who wanted the money to contribute to the increase and diffusion of knowledge. Beyond this, he left no stipulations. The idea of establishing a college or university with the money surfaced several times. John Quincy Adams finally scotched that idea when he reminded his colleagues that the purpose of a college was not to increase knowledge but to diffuse that which already existed.[49] When Congress finally chartered the Smithsonian in 1846, members thus decided to use the money to start a library, an art gallery, and a museum. Joseph Henry, recruited from Princeton to be the Institution's first secretary, was not enthusiastic about a museum. In his reports he complained that the expense of adequately maintaining a museum building and collection would drain the Smithson funds. He insisted that public museums were places of "great importance as a means of intellectual improvement,"[50] but he foresaw that a museum collection useful to researchers would not necessarily be attractive to the general public.[51] Congress, however, remained committed to a museum as the most effective way to "increase and diffuse knowledge."

At virtually the same moment, several hundred miles to the north, Louis Agassiz began complaining to Harvard president Everett that he needed a museum to pursue research in natural science. Writing in 1848, he asked for "some resolution" about the museum, reminding Everett that "without collections lectures will remain deficient." When, in the late 1850s, Agassiz finally got his wish (and the money to make it come true) to establish a broadly conceived natural history museum in Cambridge, he commanded enough prestige—and had enough influence with the major donor—to establish a museum independent of the emerging university. The museum would not be a part of any other school at the university, and it would have its own faculty. Far from turning his back on the university that gave him his American position, Agassiz believed that his independent Museum of Comparative Zoology would serve to elevate Harvard's sagging prestige. The episode reminds us that many in the mid-nineteenth century saw the order of intellectual prestige reversed from what it is today. A great museum, Agassiz believed, would make American universities competitive with European ones, and he was further convinced that a great museum collection would even draw students from Europe to study in the United States.[52]

Agassiz was not alone and was by no means unusual, except perhaps in the resources he could muster and the autonomy he could preserve. Many American colleges, big and small, established natural history museums, or at least collections, during the nineteenth century. From Yale in Connecticut, to the College of Charleston in South Carolina, from Cornell to Berkeley, American colleges believed that collections of natural history specimens were necessary to teach students about the natural world. Many colleges encouraged students both to participate in collecting specimens in the field and to study them in their classes. Agassiz, after all, had admonished his students: "study nature, not books."[53]

By the mid-nineteenth century, America's institutions of higher learning were sleepy at best, moribund at worst. Agassiz's project at Harvard seemed like a perfect opportunity to wake a university up through the activity of a museum. By the end of the century, however, that goal would seem a faded memory indeed. The leadership of university administrators such as Charles Eliot Norton at Harvard, William Pepper at Pennsylvania, and Daniel Coit Gilman at Johns Hopkins brought renewed intellectual life to America's campuses, without relying, by and large, on large-scale museums. In their new incarnations, America's universities directly challenged museums for intellectual leadership. The stakes in this intellectual tug-of-war centered around which kind of institution would function to produce new knowledge, and which would simply diffuse the old. As the last quarter of the nineteenth century began, the museums held the honor, but they found themselves aggressively challenged by upstart universities. As the nineteenth century moved into the twentieth, all the major museums of natural history would feel an intellectual competition from universities.

In 1874, nearly thirty years after the chartering of the Smithsonian and Agassiz's first correspondence about a museum, the Building Committee of the Academy of Natural Sciences reported that the architect of the Academy's new building, James Windrim, had chosen the "collegiate Gothic style of architecture" for the building. That style enjoyed a vogue in the 1870s; the University of Pennsylvania was simultaneously erecting its first building on its new West Philadelphia campus in the same style. Like "College Hall" at the University, Windrim faced the new Academy building with green serpentine stone, creating an unusual and striking facade. But Windrim's architectural choice represented more than fashion. By choosing the "collegiate" style, Windrim, unwittingly perhaps, expressed a complicated and increasingly tense relationship between natural history institutions like the Academy and newly expanding universities like Pennsylvania.

Through much of the nineteenth century, natural history museums took on the dual task of producing new knowledge and relating that knowledge to the public. Most American museums in the nineteenth century tried to work out versions of what historian Joel Orosz has called "the American Compromise."[54] Recognizing that their role in a democratic society should be different from that of European museums in hierarchical societies, American museums tried to forge a balance between serving the needs of scientists and appealing to a larger public. This struggle to define a space within American society should, however, be seen as an intellectual struggle at least as much as a social and political one. By insisting that museums and their collections of specimens could serve both a general audience and a specialized clientele equally well, those who ran the museums tried to preserve not only a social balance but a method of studying the natural world inherited from the late eighteenth and early nineteenth centuries. To deny the importance of museums in the creation of knowledge about natural history meant nothing less than abandoning one kind of epistemology and replacing it with something new. We have already seen that this older epistemology placed great emphasis on working directly with objects, and museums—filled with carefully arranged specimens—were therefore the logical institutional creation of this epistemology. Those in charge of the natural history museums after the Civil War used this method of understanding the world to shape their growing institutions.

In New York, for example, the founders of the American Museum of Natural History seem on the surface to have been less self-consciously aware of the relationship between knowledge and museum collections. Without defining their educational goals with any specificity, they simply assumed that careful examination of specimens would produce useful educational results. They were also less concerned than their counterparts in Philadelphia, Washington, and Cambridge that the museum should amass as complete and representative a collection as possible. In place of systematic collecting, those who paid the bills in New York preferred to buy rare specimens or famous collections that were also being sought by other institutions. Though it arrived on the museum scene later than either the Academy of Natural Sciences or the Smithsonian, because of the tremendous financial resources available to it, the American Museum quickly grew to rival any other natural history museum in the country. Driven not so much by scientific considerations but by trustees who enjoyed accumulating objects the way they enjoyed accumulating money, the American Museum stood more as a monument to what the trustees could buy than to what science might achieve.

Even so, these trustees were familiar enough with the way in which natural history was pursued to believe that through their acquisitions they were buying knowledge. They referred repeatedly to the museum as a "treasure house of facts," and as a "storehouse of knowledge." Having accumulated so many facts and so much knowledge in the form of objects, Morris Jesup, a driving force behind the American Museum as well as its president, began to wonder in the 1880s whether "the Museum should begin to aid original research in a more active manner." When Henry Fairfield Osborn came to build his empire on Central Park West in

1891, he abandoned a career at Princeton in part because he realized it would never have the museum facility he felt was necessary to study paleontology. That Osborn cast his lot in with the museums, not with the universities, suggests that even in New York, where civic pride and personal aggrandizement played at least as much of a role in building the American Museum as the pursuit of scientific knowledge, the American Museum could be viewed as a place where scientific research could go on.[55]

While all of these natural history museums felt the hot breath of the universities breathing down their institutional necks, none felt it more than the Academy of Natural Sciences. Its struggles with the University of Pennsylvania, which we will look at in some detail, epitomize the tensions between an older natural history conducted essentially by amateurs and a newer science pursued by professionals. When construction began on its new building in the 1870s, many at the Academy of Natural Sciences believed confidently that a public museum could serve both to create and to diffuse knowledge. Academy president Ruschenberger reminded readers in an 1871 essay that research, not entertainment, lay at the heart of the Academy's mission. The museum was integral to this purpose: "The popular notion that the purpose of forming this great museum of natural history is purely for exhibition is most erroneous. Its object is to facilitate the labors of students and the investigations of naturalists."[56] In describing the museum shortly before the opening of the new building, the Building Committee divided the Academy's constituency into three groups, and they seemed convinced that the Academy could accommodate all of them: "The museum, which is suitably furnished to answer the requirements of the original investigator, as well as the purposes of the systematic teacher and his pupils, is also well adapted to popular inspection."[57] In its new building, the Academy remained committed to the unity and wholeness of knowledge and to the essential unity of its audience. It might consist of three groups, but they could all be served by the same institution, and by the systematics which organized that institution.

Ruschenberger advocated as strenuously as anyone the position that museums remain at the center of what he termed "original research." In a report to Academy members in the Centennial year, he stated flatly: "Original research is a primary object of the Academy."[58] But Ruschenberger also believed that supporting "original research" meant precisely supporting a public museum. Writing on "The Value of

Original Scientific Research," Ruschenberger challenged Dickens's Thomas Gradgrind and his method of memorization and drill: "A knowledge of material things is easily acquired when submitted to examination of the senses; a horse, mule or ass, once seen are ever to be recognized." Ruschenberger saw the observation of material things as directly opposite to the rote and drill of learning from books. Horses, mules and asses might be easily distinguishable to those who had seen all three, "but a written description of those animals, committed to memory, would not enable one who had never seen them, to know and distinguish the horse, mule or ass, when he should meet them for the first time, though his information about them from written description, were entirely accurate."

Put more succinctly, Ruschenberger was convinced that "the boy or youth to whom book studies are repugnant—and there are many of this sort . . . is sometimes made to suspect his error while surveying the contents of a museum. He is fascinated with this or that object or class of objects."[59] By defining this kind of learning as the most effective, Ruschenberger implicitly made a statement about the authority of object-based knowledge over the memorization of stale fact associated with book learning. Knowledge derived from the direct inspection of objects was gained without mediation and therefore was more genuine. As if to underscore Ruschenberger's point, *The Museum,* a new magazine designed for young people and aimed at encouraging their pursuit of natural history, appeared in 1885.

If Ruschenberger remained committed to the method of natural science upon which the Academy's work had been built, then he also believed firmly in the socio-political goals the founders had in mind as well. By insisting on the importance of museums to the study of natural science, Ruschenberger and his colleagues saw themselves promoting a democratic kind of science. If the pursuit of science was predicated on the careful examination and study of objects, then anyone with access to the specimens could be trained to the task. Museums would provide democratic access to that knowledge and thus they would be places where new knowledge was created within the context of American democratic aspirations. The question of who should have access to the latest knowledge about the natural world was also at stake as the universities wrestled the museums for intellectual control. Universities were by their very nature exclusive and restricted places. American museums purported to be open and inclusive. What Peale had made available to the farmers, merchants, and mechanics of the late eighteenth century, the Academy would provide for their grandchildren.

Ruschenberger articulated his understanding of scientific research when he revised the rules governing the Academy's Jessup Fund scholars. The Jessup Fund was established in 1860 to provide scholarships for deserving students to study at the Academy. The scholarships were given to poor students, and through this scholarship fund the Academy tried to translate its egalitarian commitments into genuine practice. Between 1860 and 1893 fifty-seven men and one woman studied as Jessup scholars; seven of those went on to make careers in science.

In 1892, Ruschenberger formalized the guidelines of the scholarship. One action he took—reminding us again of the highly circumscribed nature of American democratic notions—was to eliminate women from consideration.[60] (This apparently angered one Jessup descendant. In 1893, Ruschenberger reported that he had received a $5,000 check from Mrs. Clara Jessup Moore to set up a study fund for young women.) In addition, candidates had to be American citizens. Reflecting an uneasiness, perhaps, with the influx of new immigrants to the city, and also remembering that the Academy was founded with distinctly nationalistic goals, he explained that "it seems both proper and expedient to regard and treat the Jessup fund as the bounteous gift of an American for the benefit of Americans." He admonished: "We should not forget that the Academy of Natural Sciences is an American institution and that its work should be American."

Having detailed who would be eligible for the scholarships, Ruschenberger went on to describe what they would study, and here he detailed his perception of how science should be pursued. Jessup students would learn "physics, chemistry in connection with mineralogy, and methods of collecting; French and German; a bit of Latin and Greek." These subjects would best prepare students for the kind of natural history that had been at the center of the Academy's work since the beginning. To make sure that selected students would be capable of this work, Ruschenberger stipulated that each applicant should be given a kind of physical: "Candidates will be examined in reference to their sense of sight, hearing, etc. and moral character."[61] In outlining these rules for the Jessup Fund scholars, Ruschenberger described the ideal natural historian: of sound moral character, with good sensory skills with which to carry out careful observation; versed in foreign languages and methods of collecting. Written at the end of the nineteenth century, it was a description more apt for an earlier generation.

While Ruschenberger remained committed to his notion of "original research," in the last quarter of the nineteenth century the definition of what constituted important scientific advance shifted. If Ruschenberger did not understand that, his colleague Edward Cope did. In March 1876, as the Academy made its move to new quarters, Cope wrote an assessment of the institution for *Penn Monthly* magazine. His primary concern in the article was that Philadelphia's preeminence in the sciences had begun to slip: "The danger is that our city will be shorn of her strength in this field before many years have elapsed." One solution that seemed to offer itself was a closer connection between the Academy and the University of Pennsylvania, which was then waking from a period of somnolence and transforming itself into a dynamic modern university. In Cope's vision, "The Academy of Natural Sciences should bear the relation to the University of Pennsylvania, that the Jardin des Plantes does to the medical and other schools of Paris." [62] For the rest of the century, the Academy would view the university with some degree of suspicion, more as a competitor than as a partner.

The relationship between the two institutions reflects the way in which the study and understanding of the natural sciences changed in the late nineteenth century, and it reflects the ways in which the Academy, with its museum-based way of studying the natural world, struggled to deal with those changes. By embracing the professionalizing world of experimental laboratory science, the Academy would turn its back on its tradition of democratic accessibility, thus severing the connection between science and the American democratic experiment that existed from the time of Peale's Museum. To remain committed to what now amounted to amateur science meant that more people might have access to the Academy's learning, but the Academy would no longer be at the forefront of scientific development.

From our vantage point, Cope proved an incomplete visionary. He may have proposed a closer relationship with the university in 1876 as a way to secure the Academy's future, but his understanding of the way natural history should be studied remained firmly rooted in the practices of the past. In his view, the study of natural history still relied on museum specimens, and he complained that a lethargic collecting policy had hampered research in several areas. "An institution of original research in the natural sciences," he explained drawing a peculiar gastronomic metaphor, "embraces three departments, viz: collections, publications and library. The first constitute the raw material of nature, the comprehension of which is the object of the investigator. . . . An institution without new collections, is a stomach without food." He went on to tell his readers: "As a matter of fact, the Academy has almost ceased to extend its museum excepting in one or two departments. Consequently original research based on its collections has very nearly come to an end." [63] That might soon change, as the Academy had built its new facility precisely to have the room to expand its collections, but the pressure the Academy felt from the university would not ease.

Less than ten years after Cope published his article, university provost William Pepper wrote to Joseph Leidy with a bold proposal. Pepper, more than any other person, began the transformation that turned Penn into a modern, research-oriented university. He wanted to talk with Leidy about how to shape the development of science in the city. "Sir," he began, "There is an unquestionable public demand that there shall be enlarged facilities for advanced Biological study in Philadelphia." With this said, Pepper insisted that he wanted to avoid competition in such study between the two institutions. "Realizing the immense amount to be done by each institution," Pepper went on, "it has been felt by many mutual friends that it would be very unfortunate that two separate Biological Laboratories for similar investigations should be simultaneously established by these two institutions." Ultimately, Pepper proposed a limited cooperation. He suggested sharing professors so that "the appointment of Professors . . . shall, as far as possible, include the gentlemen teaching corresponding branches in the Academy." [64] The plan does not seem to have produced much of the desired cooperation, but for those at the Academy, Pepper's letter served as an implicit gauntlet: the world of laboratory science based at modern universities was moving ahead rapidly; either the Academy would join the university in entering this field, or the university would pursue it on its own. [65]

Five years later, the University of Pennsylvania, again through the person of William Pepper, proposed an even more extensive partnership with the Academy than it had in 1884. This time Pepper suggested that the Academy move to join the university on its new campus in West Philadelphia. And again the Academy turned down Pepper's proposal. Rather than move in the 1890s, the Academy decided to build and renovate on its existing site. In rejecting Pepper's proposal, board members felt that the Academy's "immediate neighborhood is made up of dwellings of the better class," and that "the locality is readily accessible from all quarters by street rail ways." [66] The Academy's directors clearly had other concerns beyond neighborhoods and trolley lines. Ruschenberger worried that a move to join the university in West Philadelphia would erode the Academy's autonomy, and that "in the course of a few years the Academy would be absorbed by the Biological Department of the University."

Ruschenberger foresaw more than simple institutional competition. He, and others at the Academy, believed that their society and the university pursued two entirely different missions: "In brief, the purpose of the University is to teach what has been ascertained and is already known for compensation. The purpose of the Academy is to ascertain what has been hitherto unknown, and freely give whatever new truth it may acquire to any person or persons who may seek it."[67] In a final sardonic jab, he conceded, "But [the Academy] does not teach high-jumping, baseball or any form of athletics, now recognized to be essential to the highest grade of intellectual cultivation and polish."[68]

Toward the end of the century Ruschenberger simply re-gave the speech John Quincy Adams had given in the 1840s when Congress debated what to do with the Smithson money. But in drawing this distinction between institutions like the Academy and the university, Ruschenberger was not alone, nor was he hopelessly out of date. George Brown Goode of the Smithsonian, in a speech given in 1889, told his audience that there were two kinds of "intellectual work . . . the one tending toward the increase of knowledge, the other toward its diffusion." Sounding much like Ruschenberger in his critique of Penn, Goode spoke damningly of colleges in general: "The college which imparts only secondhand knowledge to its students belongs to a stage of civilization which is fast being left behind."[69]

Neither Ruschenberger nor Goode seemed to realize or acknowledge that American institutions of higher education were in fact changing and that the museums were in fact "fast being left behind." More than anything else, the new universities organized themselves around the intellectual principle of specialization. Societies like the Academy neither kept up with this fragmentation institutionally, nor would they accept it intellectually. Natural history museums presented the world as a unity, its parts related and finite, not as fragmented, and knowledge about it infinite. Ruschenberger had begun to complain about this trend in the early 1880s. Writing in the *Proceedings* for 1880, he compared the drive toward specialization with the Academy's original purpose. When the Academy was small, and "both museum and library were easily contained in one small room," Ruschenberger reminisced, the propriety of admitting to its membership those who possessed no other qualifications than friendliness to scientific pursuits and personal respectability was not questioned. But since the possessions of the Academy have grown to be extensive and of great value in every sense, there are individuals who lament that they are not greater. . . . Ignoring all that is recorded in the sixteen volumes of the first and second series of the Journal of the Academy and in the thirty-two volumes of its Proceedings, they imagine that it sadly lacks the afflatus of pure science and does nothing to promote research. . . . They seem to believe that the collections should be placed under the control of expert specialists . . . that the society should consist of proficients exclusively, or at least include a privileged class of experts.[70]

Sounding more upset the following year, Ruschenberger summarized his complaints: "To specialize is the order of the day. All the great meetings of men interested in the advancement of the different departments of knowledge are splitting into sections and special societies."[71] The Academy's Angelo Heilprin also understood the shift taking place when he penned a report for the Academy in 1889. In it, he worried about the diminishing attendance at the Academy's scientific meetings. The reason for this lay not with "any lack in the scientific workings of the institution" but rather with "a differentiation of the work into distinct and more or less independent departments." For Ruschenberger and Heilprin, the world of natural history, in a quite literal sense, was splitting apart.

In Heilprin's view, the dilemma was straightforward: if the Academy followed the rest of the scientific world toward increasing specialization, then it risked losing its primary constituency, those who were not "specialists" but who still took a "general interest" in science. Speaking before the Biological Society a year before Heilprin wrote his report, George Brown Goode summarized the change in natural science more succinctly. "It may be," he told the assembled biologists, "that the use of the word naturalist is to became an anachronism, and that we are all destined to become generically biologists, and, specifically, morphologists, histologists, embryologists, physiologists."[72] The choice facing the Academy—and it was a choice faced with greater or lesser urgency by other natural history museums—was whether to pursue science in the directions along which it now developed, or to stay faithful to the ideal and purpose of its founding. To choose the first option meant breaking with the Academy's past; to choose the second meant being left behind by the developments of twentieth-century science. In rejecting the offer from Penn to move west, the Academy recommitted itself to founding principles. But as it built a new facility, the Academy found carrying out its original mission increasingly difficult. Penn's offer to move symbolized the pressure the Academy felt from a professionalizing scientific world as it tried to stay its original course.

Whether they chose to admit it, by clinging so tenaciously to an older method of understanding the natural world, those at the Academy made themselves increasingly marginal to what came to be regarded as the vanguard of scientific research. The work of biological science was moving away from the classificatory and toward the theoretical, from the whole specimen to the level of the cellular, and from museum halls and into university labs. These tensions were felt at the Academy in its lecture hall.

In 1876, however, the Academy recommitted itself to making its knowledge more available to the general public. In that year, the Academy began offering public lectures in addition to its public museum. And as Ruschenberger reminded people regularly, these "public courses" did the universities one better because this teaching was offered for free. By 1887, however, the lectures became the source of a controversy that highlighted the difficulties the Academy had keeping up with the changes happening in science.

The Committee on Instruction, which oversaw the program of the public courses, began to question the content of some of the lectures. Committee members became concerned with "the possible danger which might arise to the Academy from the Popular course if at any of the lectures theories should be urged which might cause offence to a portion of the public, in which case it feared the blame would be visited upon the Academy." The committee insisted that such scientific disagreements could be discussed at the Academy, but it felt that such disputes "are hardly proper subjects for a lecture to an unscientific public." The record of this controversy does not indicate which theories offended, but the committee did go on to suggest that the lecturers confine themselves to "undisputed facts . . . without enunciating theories on which scientific men themselves are not agreed."

Moreover the committee worried that by lecturing on controversial theories the Academy would be seen as giving affront to the very public upon which it relied. "Mere theories," the committee offered, "should yield place to facts in science where the theories are known to be regarded with strong disfavor by a portion of the community to which the Academy must look for moral as well as financial support."[73] The committee passed a resolution asking its professors to refrain from controversial or offensive discussion. With that resolution, the Academy acknowledged that the changes taking place in the natural sciences would not be part of what the Academy presented to its public.

By insisting that lectures be confined to the "facts," the committee wanted lectures to reflect the older brand of natural history, rooted in observation and classification. Like Gradgrind, the committee wanted facts, nothing but facts. These kinds of facts were, for the most part, indisputable, and, like the frameworks of natural history themselves, they did not change. These facts did not change, of course, because they reflect God's plan for nature, as Ruschenberger often pointed out. The new science, however, was driven by contentious and abstract theory, not simply by observable facts. Theories needed facts to prove or disprove them, but those facts were ultimately less interesting than the theories themselves. But unlike the "facts" of the old natural history, these new theories were precisely disputable, and in the most troubling ways. Indeed, the whole endeavor of the new science was predicated on conflict and debate.

Now, the Committee on Instruction implicitly said, the hotly contested topics at the cutting edge of scientific understanding should be reserved for the sanctum of the Academy's learned meetings. Other topics, less controversial, but therefore less vital to the development of science, were the only ones suitable for presentation to the general public. In its popular lectures—next to the museum perhaps the most important forum through which the Academy communicated with the public—the Academy was no longer committed to giving general audiences a "thorough furnishing" in the natural sciences.

Though the professors at the Academy rejected the committee's proposal "contemptuously," the committee seems to have prevailed. During the academic year 1899–1900, for example, Benjamin Sharp offered five lectures on the topic "Comparative Anatomy and Physiology," Philip Calvert gave five lectures on "The Means of Defense of Animals," and Witmer Stone taught a five-lecture course on the "Structure and Morphology of Birds." [74] Interesting and informative lectures no doubt, but hardly the cutting edge of science. Like the museum displays themselves, lectures became viewed as a way to entertain and inform the general public, but not to make them aware of the most important developments and changes in natural science.

At the end of the nineteenth century, Ruschenberger saw the world of science headed away from the Academy in two directions. Down one road lay the emerging universities, which were shaping themselves to become the major institutional home of original scientific research, even as Ruschenberger complained that they only concerned themselves with teaching. Science as a source of amusement and entertainment—a vulgar popularizing—lay at the end of the other road. In the turf struggles with the university, Ruschenberger fought for a middle ground where genuine scientific research would be appreciated and made available to—indeed, even conducted by—ordinary citizens, and not simply specialized students. In short, Ruschenberger tried to find a place for the Academy in the late nineteenth century by holding onto the ideas with which it had been founded in the early nineteenth century. If Dorothy Ross is correct that the Gilded Age marked the "decisive period in which the balance shifted from theological toward naturalistic world views," then natural history museums helped make that transition.[75]

~

Just as the Academy of Natural Sciences was putting green serpentine stone on its new "collegiate gothic" facade, plans were under way in Baltimore for a new university. When the Johns Hopkins University opened in 1876, it had no museum. Most historians point to Hopkins as the exemplar of the new, experimental, European-inspired research institution in this country. No museum for Hopkins in 1876, but when its new biology and physiology labs were opened in 1883 they were regarded as the best in country. (Harvard followed suit at the same moment, building a new laboratory designed solely for biological research). Advanced students at Hopkins never laid their hands on museum specimens.[76] The transformation from natural history to biology carried with it a whole series of institutional implications concerning how such research would be funded; who would conduct it; and, perhaps most significantly, who would have access to the knowledge produced. George Brown Goode worried out loud that "professional men of science" were growing "strangely indifferent" to the question of how "the public at large is to be made familiar with the results of their labors." Natural history museums exist, after all, to put the fruits of scientific research on public display. University research labs are decidedly "off-limits" kinds of places. In the mid-nineteenth century Agassiz had encouraged his students to study nature; by 1900 botanist John Coulter could announce: "The legitimate off-spring of the laboratory is the seminar."[77]

The relocation of scientific research from natural history museums to university research labs mirrors a larger shift in the nature of scientific knowledge. The new academic biologists replaced a concern for description with an emphasis on experimentation, a search for design with the construction of theory, and focus on form with one on function. Ultimately they displaced a view of the natural world which stressed the connection between the past and the present with one which focused on the present and the future.

In 1910, several years after Ruschenberger's death, the original part of the Academy of Natural Sciences building, executed in Windrim's collegiate gothic style and faced with green serpentine, was covered over with "granite brick." Ostensibly this was done to stop the deterioration of the old building and to bring it into architectural harmony with a new one, but it also served as a marvelous symbol of the Academy's attempt to distinguish itself from the university.[78] In the space of thirty-five years, the two institutions had evolved in dramatically different ways. As the twentieth century began, the collegiate gothic was covered up and there would be no confusing the Academy and the university, architecturally or otherwise.

The Extinction of Natural History? /
The Natural History of Extinction

On February 16, 1909, the Academy of Natural Sciences of Philadelphia hosted a tribute to Charles Darwin to mark the hundredth anniversary of his birth. It seemed fitting that the Academy should sponsor such an event. As we discussed earlier, the Academy had been the first to extend an institutional hand to Darwin. Those who celebrated in February 1909 not only paid tribute to Darwin; they also applauded the foresight the Academy had demonstrated in 1860.

Charles Darwin was surely the nineteenth century's most significant naturalist. Indeed, speaking at the centenary celebration, Edwin Conklin called him "one of the last of the great naturalists."[79] At the same time, the Academy's own history, nearly contemporary with Darwin's, was impressive as well. Founded in 1812 by Philadelphians concerned with promoting scientific research in the new republic, the Academy enjoyed the distinction of being the first, and, through the nineteenth century, a major center of scientific learning in the United States. Many of the important nineteenth-century scientists in the Euro-American world had some connection with the Academy.

Through the years of the nineteenth century, the Academy would not stray from its original conception. When Ruschenberger described membership criteria in 1879, he added emphatically, "To this day candidates are not required to possess any other qualifications."[80] The Academy began in a world without distinctions between amateur and professional scientists, and in the years following the Civil War, it remained committed to this principle. "The Academy has never claimed to be a society composed exclusively of scientific persons," Ruschenberger reminded readers, and he continued, "Though the register of its members contains the names of very many true scientists, a large majority of the members of the society has been and is now composed of gentlemen who, to use an expression of the founders, are 'friendly to science' and its cultivation."[81]

The election of Darwin to the Academy, however, symbolized more than the recognition of a controversial and brilliant naturalist by a well-respected institution. Darwin's theories, as they would be pursued in the last quarter of the nineteenth century, represented the end of the natural history paradigm with which the Academy of Natural Sciences began. Benjamin Smith Lyman tacitly acknowledged this in 1912 when the Academy celebrated its own hundredth birthday. For its first fifty years, Lyman told the crowd, the Academy was occupied "with collecting, describing, naming and systematizing the natural forms that could be found in near and distant parts of the world." Since then, Lyman continued, Darwin's theory, "appreciated at once by our Academy, has immensely enlarged the scope and interest of the study."[82] Darwin's ideas, and the way they would be debated, irrevocably altered the conception of natural history. He had come to his theories using the techniques of the older natural history—observation, collection, and classification. The results of his work, however, led biological science into whole new areas. In so doing, Darwin helped initiate dramatic changes not only in the ways scientific knowledge would be pursued but also in the ways it would be institutionally organized. Just as Darwin represented the intellectual link between an older world of natural history and the pursuits of modern biological science, so too the Academy of Natural Sciences, more so than any other institution in the country, embodied the difficulties such museums had in fitting new ideas into older frameworks.

In the years following the publication of *The Origin of Species,* the Academy of Natural Sciences wrestled to define its purpose in the midst of a revolution in the study of science. It tried to balance its original mission to be a place for amateur, and therefore democratic, scientific

study against the demands of an increasingly specialized and professional scientific world. And it tried as well to find ways to present the
post-Darwinian world of natural science to the public within older pre-
Darwinian frameworks. The older notion of the world promised fixity,
while the newer seemed troublingly fluid.

In many respects neither the Academy nor its companion museums
successfully struck that balance. By the 1920s academic science had replaced museum science as the vanguard of new knowledge. The Swedish
Academy began awarding Nobel Prizes in 1901 to recognize the most
important contributions to science. The categories honored by the prize
are instructive: physics, chemistry, and physiology/medicine. No prizes
for the fields related to the older natural history, and there would be no
Nobel Prizes for scientists working in museums. In New York, by the
1920s, those directing the American Museum traded in their old displays
of specimens and bet the museum's future on the development of "habitat halls." By 1929 five such halls had already opened to the public or
were planned. The habitat halls presented animal specimens in attractively arranged displays to make them appear more "natural."[83] Gone
now were the systematic displays of taxonomy which had been the heart
of the museum and of natural science in the nineteenth century. These
new habitat halls, or dioramas as they were often called, placed a pre-
mium on visual appeal—they were less concerned with conveying scientific understanding to the visiting public.[84] In a further irony, while the
endless glass cases containing countless specimens monotonously displayed might have seemed hopelessly static in a world increasingly bom-
barded with new visual imagery, the new habitat halls proved even more
so. The dioramas might be flashier than the exhibits they replaced, but
they were much harder to change. Having invested a great deal of money
to create the dioramas, the American Museum was stuck with them—
some for over a generation.

Much the same story can be told in Philadelphia. When the Academy
of Natural Sciences celebrated its centennial in 1912, its exhibits continued to illustrate the systematics of nineteenth-century natural science.
Speaking at the Academy's celebration, Samuel Dixon told those gathered: "While we have thus built up world-renowned study collections it
has been impossible to develop the popular exhibits that sister institutions . . . have been enabled to install. We have, however, kept our collections systematically arranged."[85] When Dixon made his speech, older
members of the Academy still believed that the systematically arranged

cases of specimens served as the best way to teach the public about the natural world.

By the end of the 1920s, however, that had changed. In the midst of corresponding with Academy member Clarence Moore about his collection of Native American artifacts, collector George Heye made a trenchant observation about the direction of the Academy under the leadership of new director Charles Cadwalader. Heye confided to Moore about Cadwalader: "He seems a rather energetic young man, but does not know, or does not claim to know anything about science. He wishes to run the Academy from a business point of view."[86] What Heye meant, presumably, was that the Academy, under Cadwalader's leadership, would now see its museum as primarily a place of public education and entertainment.

Cadwalader's task was precisely to develop "popular exhibits," and his appointment signaled that the Academy, having resisted the professionalizing force in the sciences by trying to adhere to the mission of its founders, had conceded a kind of defeat. The Academy acknowledged in the 1920s that the old way of displaying natural history was neither vital to science nor able to attract the public in the way it once had. The Academy's new exhibits, particularly the lifelike dioramas, and the old favorites, like the hadrosaurus remounted, did draw big crowds, just as Cadwalader and those who hired him had hoped they would. But the Academy could no longer claim that what those crowds saw represented the important breakthroughs of scientific research. The natural history museums which had given an institutional home to a nascent American science would, one hundred years after the first museum opened, no longer be major contributors to the growth of scientific knowledge.

$\sim$

In 1976, as part of Philadelphia's Bicentennial festivities, the Academy of Natural Sciences held a symposium to consider: Changing Scenes in Natural Sciences, 1776–1976. An ambitious enough historical task, but the papers published from the conference reveal less a concern with the past than with the present. The papers presented at the Academy were grouped into the following categories: Evolution and Systematics; Population Genetics; Terrestrial Ecology; Aquatic Ecology; Behavior and Sociobiology.[87]

At the end of the twentieth century, perhaps we have come full circle.

Those categories represent, more or less, the way in which nineteenth century natural history has survived into the twentieth. And they represent, more or less, the areas of research pursued in many natural history museums.

Universities did indeed eclipse the natural history museums as the places where knowledge about the natural world would be produced. And while it would be an exaggeration to say that the pendulum has now swung back—natural history museums simply cannot compete with universities for resources and prestige—it would also be inaccurate to say that natural history museums have ceased altogether to be places of scientific research.

Having made the choice to pursue an older form of natural science, having ceded laboratory and experimental science to the universities, places like the Academy of Natural Sciences now find themselves, ironically, newly relevant. With our society's increasing concern for environmental problems, ecology came to public attention in the 1960s. Ecology, the term and the concept, dates back to the late nineteenth century. Ernst Haeckel is generally credited with defining both. Though Haeckel's nineteenth-century concerns did not include problems like soil erosion or groundwater contamination, he did conceive of the earth as a balanced, unified whole.[88] At a basic level, then, ecological research is an updated version of nineteenth-century natural history, with its focus on whole organisms, whole populations, and even whole ecosystems, with its focus on unity and interconnectedness. The papers given at the Academy in 1976 make that clear. Scientists have certainly not forsaken the techniques and technology developed over the last hundred years, but some are beginning to apply them to environmental research. Biological inventories, habitat assessments—counting, classifying, and collecting. This is one kind of research the Academy and other such institutions are positioned to do.

Environmental science—whether it be population studies of plants in Amazonia, or watershed analysis in central Ohio—is driven at some level by a sense of urgency. Since the environment became a potent political issue in the 1960s, we have all lived with the gnawing dread that the planet will not survive the strain we have put on it. In fulfilling their public educational mission, many natural history museums now include exhibits dealing with environmental degradation, endangered species, and the like. And this has given their specimens an ironic relevance. Many of the birds, butterflies, mammals, and reptiles collected in the nineteenth century to be metonymic now increasingly stand as unique, rare, and lonely. They are no longer representative of the natural world as it is, but as it was. In many cases these specimens illustrate not the seamless continuum of a great chain of being, but the severing of the natural present from the natural past. In the galleries of natural history museums, whether wandering in the galleries of fossils or in front of dioramas filled with stuffed animals, visitors confront all that remains of extinction.

7 *Neither science nor art.* As American museums accumulated large collections of anthropological objects, they struggled to create a category for them in between science and art. Here, at Chicago's Field Museum, sculptures from Central America and the Pacific Northwest share the same gallery space. (Courtesy of The Field Museum, Neg. #1187, Chicago)

THREE

~

Between Science and Art: Museums and
the Development of Anthropology

The museum is no less essential to the study of anthropology
than to that of natural history.

GEORGE BROWN GOODE

In 1918, Lewis Mumford, twenty-three and buoyantly enthusiastic, proposed a marriage. In an essay written for *Scientific Monthly,* the young
critic suggested a wedding between science and art by joining together
the American Museum of Natural History and the Metropolitan Museum
of Art. The two had more in common than they realized, Mumford wrote,
and spinning a not altogether successful metaphor he went on: "Both
science and art are means of opening that oyster, which is the world;
and if the one seeks chiefly to dissect the bivalve while the other loses
itself in contemplation of the pearl, this should not obscure the fact that
they must open the same oyster, and that they may well, for the attainment of this mutual end, take hold of the same instrument and use their
forces jointly." Mumford mused about the intersection between these
two institutions and the bodies of knowledge contained within each. By
1918, in Mumford's assessment, the presentation of nature had grown
more artistic, and the presentation of art more scientific, and so much
the better for both.[1]

Whether he realized it or not, Mumford proposed this union precisely thirty years after George Brown Goode, assistant secretary of the
Smithsonian, had also suggested that the time had come for the two to
produce an offspring. In a speech delivered in 1888 in front of the American Historical Association, Goode focused on the distinctions between

these two kinds of institutions. "As a matter of convenience," he told the assembled historians, "museums are commonly classed in two groups—those of science and those of art. . . . On the one side stand the natural history collections, undoubtedly best to be administered by the geologist, botanist, and zoologist. On the other side are the fine-art collections, best to be arranged, from an aesthetic standpoint, by artists."[2] And by the late nineteenth century, art galleries and museums of natural history could be found in many American cities.

As Goode spoke, however, this division of the world between science and art no longer sufficed. The intellectual geography of the era had become more complex. Goode defined this new terrain for the historians, and suggested a new kind of museum to occupy it: "Between is a territory which no English word can adequately describe—which the Germans call Kulturgeschichte—the natural history of civilization, of man and his ideas and achievements." Further, Goode told his audience, no institution had yet attempted to exhibit "the natural history of civilization." "The museums of science and art," he concluded, "have not yet learned how to partition this territory."[3] In this speech, Goode presaged the way in which anthropology would emerge from the intellectual frameworks of natural history and from the institutional matrix of natural history museums, and would try to situate itself between science and art.

The Natural History of Humankind

Whether he meant to or not, Goode insulted those in his audience who had come from Cambridge, Massachusetts. Twenty years earlier, Louis Agassiz had directed the establishment of the Peabody Museum of American Archaeology and Ethnology at Harvard. Harvard's Trustees turned over the operation of the museum in 1875 to Agassiz's student Frederic Ward Putnam, who, though trained as an ichthyologist, took to the task with enthusiasm. Though it grew under Putnam's leadership, the Peabody had apparently not succeeded in occupying the territory Goode described very satisfactorily because in 1888 the museum apparently did not serve as a model for Goode or for the historians to whom he lectured. Putnam too must have sensed that his ambitions to create a museum of "Kulturgeschichte" in Cambridge had not been altogether successful. Technically, Putnam continued his association with the Peabody for the rest of his life, but when the opportunity to oversee the anthropological section of the World's Columbian Exposition presented itself, Putnam jumped at the chance and left for Chicago.

That the 1893 World's Fair served as a watershed event in the development of American anthropology is now a standard refrain in the narrative of the discipline's history. By the time the gates of the Exposition opened, the field had already begun to develop its own professional identity. Among its milestones: 1880, when Lewis Henry Morgan became the first person associated with anthropology to be elected president of the American Association for the Advancement of Science; 1886, when the University of Pennsylvania appointed Daniel Brinton to be the first professor of anthropology at any American university; 1888, when the journal *American Anthropologist* began publication. The fair, thus, became for anthropologists a chance both to consolidate their emerging field and to present the fruits of their work to an eager public. Putnam certainly did his part by bringing together the leading lights, such as they were, in the field, and by assembling a dazzling array of objects from around the world to represent the world's cultures. The millions who came to Chicago saw, really for the first time, a new science on display.

Without assessing the immense impact the fair had on the development of anthropology, we pause long enough to make two observations: first, the connection between the fair and the growth of anthropology serves as a reminder that anthropology as a discipline began as an object-based field. At the Congress of Anthropology held at the fair, an entire afternoon was spent discussing and examining "the extensive collections of anthropologic materials brought together by the exposition."[4] Second, Putnam's goal in organizing the anthropological section was to use it as the basis upon which to found a great museum. In Putnam's vision, the discipline of anthropology in the United States would grow from museum roots.

Putnam began agitating for this museum at least a year and a half before the fair opened. In a speech given to Chicago's Commercial Club late in 1891, Putnam warned his listeners that the Exposition would bring to Chicago the material necessary to start a new museum, and he sought to convince the club's members that Chicago needed such a museum. "Surely this opportunity," he intoned, "must not be lost." The newly arrived Putnam made sure to appeal to the civic pride which drove the fair in the first place. A grand new museum was necessary for the city's "culture and fame. . . . For the city to longer remain without such a museum seems impossible." This appeal to Chicago's sense of itself helped push the museum plan ahead. Putnam joined other Chicagoans who agreed that the city could create a new museum from the objects brought to the city for the Exposition. When retail giant Marshall Field wrote a check for one million dollars, the Field Museum was born. Amidst much ceremony, the museum opened to a throng of expectant visitors on June 2, 1894.

The Field Museum broke no new ground when it opened in 1894, either literally or intellectually. Instead, it did much to enshrine the past. Physically, the museum occupied the Fine Arts Building of the World's Columbian Exposition. That building had been intended as the only permanent structure built at the fair—the rest of the White City had been torn down immediately and transformed into Jackson Park. The Field Museum thus gave Chicagoans a connection with the proudest moment in their young city's history. When the museum opened, "it was all like a memory of the fair," according to the *Chicago Times*. With "memories of the Grand Exposition revived by the event," the crowds listened to speeches and cheered the beneficence of Marshall Field before being allowed through the gates to see what was described as "a permanent memorial of the glories of the summer of '93."⁵ (In fact, the museum's collections had to compete for space with historical memorabilia from the fair. The central spaces in the building were filled with Columbus statuary and other such material).⁶ In June 1894, Chicagoans returned to the only remaining physical presence of the fair, and when they went inside they saw some of the very objects they had seen in "the summer of '93."

Intellectually, the new Field Museum also preserved an older way of conceptualizing the scientific study of human beings. Though the anthropological collections assembled under Putnam's guidance proved among the most significant exhibits of the Exposition, Putnam wanted to build a natural history museum with the material from the fair. Putnam, and the wealthy Chicagoans he enlisted to support the plan, never seem to have envisioned a museum strictly for anthropology. The anthropological collections would certainly be the highlight of the new museum, but Putnam and others saw the museum as a broadly conceived museum of natural history, encompassing zoology, botany, and geology as well as anthropology. Putnam described exactly such an institution to the members of the Commercial Club. The 1893 World's Columbian Exposition may have signaled the beginning of anthropology as its own field of endeavor, but when anthropology was given a permanent museum home in Chicago it rented rooms from natural history.

George Stocking and others have observed that American anthropology first took institutional root in museums. In Stocking's phrase, museums lay at the "center of the political economy of anthropological research" in the second half of the nineteenth century.[7] Museums, in fact, may have literally created "anthropology" by helping to consolidate the mid-nineteenth-century endeavors of linguistics, ethnology, and archaeology under the same terminological umbrella and under the same institutional roof. After the turn of the century, those other studies would now largely be seen as subsidiaries of the larger anthropological project.[8]

What has received less notice, however, is the relationship, both intellectual and physical, between natural history museums and anthropological collections. Throughout most of the nineteenth century, the study and presentation of other cultures occupied one branch of natural history. At Philadelphia's Centennial Exposition in 1876, for example, the Smithsonian's "Indian Department" exhibit promised that "curious people can learn more about them in this section than he [*sic*] could in any other way, except by living with them."[9] Two large totem poles from the Northwest attracted the most visitor attention and were spectacular enough to merit a full-page illustration in *Frank Leslie's Illustrated Historical Register of the Centennial Exhibition.* The exhibit, however, remained firmly rooted within the context of natural history displays. Ethnographic objects were juxtaposed with the stuffed birds and mineral samples from the Department of Natural History.

If anthropology resided as an adjunct to the larger field of natural history, then anthropological objects were expected to function in precisely the same metonymic way that natural history objects did. With objects at the center of anthropological understanding, anthropology, as it grew up in museums, tried to develop its own visual language, through which the objects would speak. To facilitate the comprehension of this language, anthropological objects displayed in museums demanded the same careful presentation, and the same systematic arrangement, as shells, geological samples, and plants. Just as natural scientists had done for some years with the specimens with which they dealt, the new anthropologists used objects to stand for whole cultures and replaced original contexts with classificatory schema.[10]

By including anthropology as a part of a natural history museum, the creators of the Field Museum simply stretched the conventional paradigm of natural history. The English journal *Annals of Natural History,* for example, began publication in the 1830s and included botany, zoology, and geology as the constituent parts of natural history. At the Field Museum, anthropology became a fourth part of natural history. Museum director Frederick Skiff described how anthropology inhabited the new museum with the rest of natural history: "The space in the Field Museum is divided by an imaginary line drawn north and south through the central court, man and his works occupying the east half of the building and the works of nature the west." [11]

Anthropology may have been conceived of intellectually as twenty-five percent of natural history, but Skiff's description of the building makes it clear that in terms of square footage, anthropology occupied a far larger place in the museum. Because it began with the large collection of anthropological objects from the fair, the museum's anthropological department "sprang into existence as an accomplished fact, and from its very beginning could claim a place among the leading anthropological museums of the world." [12] Much like the city itself, Chicago's Field Museum seemed to emerge fully formed and already self-conscious of its place.

But, as some would say about Chicago as a whole, although the Field Museum's anthropological collection might have been large, it lacked a certain refinement. Frederic Putnam persuaded museum organizers to hire his assistant at the Exposition to take charge of the anthropological department. Franz Boas, who left a job at Clark University to work under Putnam, oversaw the installation of the anthropological displays. Boas was less impressed with the quality of the museum's collections than were others. Writing to Skiff about the collections from Western Asia, for example, Boas reported dryly: "There are a few large specimens which are not particularly good and which do not convey any important information to the public." [13] In an object-based epistemology, Boas reminds us, not all objects functioned equally well to transmit metonymic knowledge.

The problem with the Field's collections, as Boas saw it, lay with their provincialism. As he wrote to Skiff, the central idea behind the anthropological section at the Exposition had been to display material from the Americas. "The effect of this fact," Boas continued, "is that in the Anthropological collections of the Columbian Museum, Indian material predominates to an undesirable degree. It may safely be said that about four-fifths of the Anthropological collections of the museum refer to America, while the remaining fifth refers to all other continents." And in what surely must have been a slap to the hubris of Chicago's museum builders, Boas informed Skiff: "For this reason the Museum takes at present a high rank among other Museums devoted to the Anthropology of

America while it is decidedly inferior to even small Museums regarding matters pertaining to other continents."

Whether he understood it or not, Boas put his finger on one of the major tensions pulling at American anthropology. The field in the United States had its origins in various and loosely connected studies of Native Americans. Not surprisingly perhaps, incipient American anthropologists through the first three-quarters of the nineteenth century studied the languages, physical characteristics, and archaeology of the indigenous peoples of this country, who were at that very moment being conquered.[14] By the end of the century, however, American anthropologists eyed the whole world as a potential field of study, and they wanted to shake the regional provincialism they felt held their discipline back.

Boas finished his complaint to Skiff by sketching an ambitious plan to create just such a globally focused museum of anthropology. "The Department of Anthropology," he insisted, "ought to be made to cover the Anthropology of the whole World as equally as possible." He went on to outline how the cultures of the world could be divided up at the museum:

A. Physical Anthropology
   1. Comparative anatomy of races
   2. Comparative physiology of races
B. Psychological Anthropology
      I. Primitive people
   1. America
   2. Asia and Europe
   3. Australia and Isles of the Pacific Ocean
   4. Africa
      II. Civilizations of Asia, Europe and Africa
   1. China and countries influenced by China
   2. India and countries influenced by China
   3. Semitic civilization
   4. Egypt
   5. The rise of civilization of Greece & Italy
      III. Special comparative exhibits [15]

Having conceived of this ambitious plan for the Field Museum, Boas never had the chance to carry it out. Like his sponsor Frederic Putnam, Boas quickly had a falling out with those who paid the bills. By the end of 1894, both had left the Windy City in disgust with it and with the arrivistes who ran the museum. Chicago, which seemed uniquely poised to do so, did not become an important center for anthropology at the end of the nineteenth century. The permanent museum which grew from the 1893 World's Fair had not quite answered George Brown Goode's challenge successfully.

Kulturgeschichte in Philadelphia

While Chicago prepared for the World's Columbian Exposition, and while Putnam and Boas assembled the anthropological collections for it, several prominent Philadelphians, most associated with the University of Pennsylvania, also began to formulate plans for a museum of "Kulturgeschichte." The museum of the University of Pennsylvania was among the first institutions in this country—and probably the most ambitious—to create a separate space, both physically and intellectually, for the display of human artifacts apart from collections of natural history specimens. Proposed by the University provost as early as 1889, the University Museum, when it moved from temporary quarters to its new home in 1899, tried to do what the Peabody and the Field museums had not yet done—occupy the space between science and art.

Philadelphia had already assumed some prominence in the study of humankind. The American Philosophical Society maintained a small collection of anthropological artifacts, as did the Academy of Natural Sciences. More significantly, the academy served as the final resting place for Dr. Samuel Morton's collection of skulls and skeletons, from which he made his famous study of racial types. And, as mentioned earlier, the University of Pennsylvania had taken a lead in developing the academic discipline of anthropology when it appointed Daniel Brinton to be the first university professor of anthropology in the country in 1886.

Trained originally as a physician, Brinton became the one of the most important anthropologists of the last quarter of the nineteenth century. Franz Boas, looking back to that time, felt Brinton to be one of the three founders of modern American anthropology.[16] Brinton lectured in anthropology at the Academy of Natural Sciences in the 1880s and 1890s and wrote the "Current Notes" on anthropology in *Science* magazine between 1893 and 1896. In addition, he served as president of the American Association for the Advancement of Science. Brinton's primary contribution came in the area of linguistic studies, but the doctor was also interested in the issue of racial differences. In 1891 he published his most important book, *American Races*. The book had its origins in the lectures Brinton delivered at the Academy of Natural Sciences.

Though Philadelphia had this history, the new museum was something else altogether. Enormous in scale as originally envisioned, the University of Pennsylvania's museum would provide a proper home for anthropology, one which could both accommodate the discipline's growth and help to shape it. The very design of the new institution signaled its novelty and innovation. According to the comments of the day, the building borrowed loosely from the architectural vocabulary of Northern Italian Romanesque. Architect Ralph Adams Cram, an influential though by no means typical architectural critic, fell over himself praising the new museum in an *Architectural Record* review: "How shall we speak of the Archaeological Museum, the building which should be era-making and which is the result of the fusion of the brains of Messrs. Eyre, Cope, Stewardson and Day? . . . I am a little afraid to speak of this structure at length for it makes so instant and overwhelming an appeal to me that I doubt my judgment. Personally, I feel increasingly that it is at the very least one of the most significant works of art yet produced in America."[17] The impression the new building gave, as Cram suggested, was at once of novelty and of familiarity. This was not a palatial temple of art, such as could be found in Boston or New York. Nor was the building simply another example of Romanesque revival. In fact, like the exhibits inside the building, Wilson Eyre's design had no easy precedents. The design was clearly and richly historical. Though the historical references were distant, both in time and place, they served nonetheless to draw an architectural connection between European history, which provided the source of the building's design, and the rest of the world, which provided the source of the objects inside. In this sense, the building captured the ingenuity of this new kind of museum collection. The trajectory of the University Museum's development, more so than that of the Peabody or the Field, mirrored the changing frameworks within which anthropological knowledge was produced. That change was embodied in the building's very architecture. Neither science nor art, the University Museum, like the field of anthropology, proposed to be simultaneously both—and something entirely different.

As we have already discussed, the study of anthropology grew from, and at other museums remained rooted to, an older conception of natural history. When Pennsylvania provost William Pepper—a truly remarkable institution-builder called by many in Philadelphia a latter-day Benjamin Franklin—embarked on his museum scheme, he, too, originally hoped to link his new museum with the existing collections at the Academy of Natural Sciences, a union that would create "a grand center of scientific and educational activity."

Pepper was certainly not the only university administrator who coveted a close relationship with an existing museum. Pepper's colleague at the University of Chicago, William Rainey Harper, proposed a similar union between his institution and the Field Museum. As they helped define modern research universities, both Pepper and Harper believed that museum collections were still vital to the production of knowledge. Universities may have needed museums at the turn of the century, but museums apparently did not need universities. The Academy of Natural Sciences' trustees rejected Pepper's plan in 1889, and the Field Museum's trustees scorned Harper similarly in 1904. Both museums regarded these proposed mergers as something less than equal partnerships. Harlow Higinbotham of the Field Museum wrote with some suspicion that "evidently President Harper would like very much to make some arrangement that would enable the University to reap a larger benefit from the Museum." Instead, Higinbotham urged, the museum "should hold itself aloof."[18] Unlike Harper, however, when Pepper found his offer rejected, he went ahead with plans to build a major museum of the university's own.

These short-lived attempts to create a cooperation between major institutions of learning represent an episode in institutional growth and competition. But the exchange between the University of Pennsylvania and the Academy of Natural Sciences also represents the institutional manifestation of the intellectual tension described by George Brown Goode to the AHA in 1888. The course of museum development that Goode predicted in his address had been followed, at least in part, by Philadelphia institutions. While Pepper and others at the university already planned to develop an archaeological and anthropological collection, he initially tried to cooperate with the city's premier natural history museum. Unable to do this, the university went ahead to build its own institution, located intellectually between science and art.

Initially, the University Museum's efforts were directed by a university Department of Archaeology and Paleontology and by a private organization known as the University Archaeological Association. That "archaeology" and "paleontology" should be joined in a single department made sense at several levels. Paleontologists peeled away strata to unearth the remains of ancient species, and, similarly, archaeologists dug through human deposits to reveal the relics of past cultures and civilizations. In addition, as Peter Bowler has noted, the archaeological evidence dug up during the late nineteenth century seemed to demonstrate a social progression from "primitive" to "civilized" that was akin to the biological progress of species.[19] Both paleontology and archaeology rooted themselves in the systematics which lay at the core of natural history: discovery, description, and classification remained primary concerns. The discoveries made by paleontologists filled in pieces of the great evolutionary puzzle; archaeologists used their discoveries to fill in the evolutionary tree of human society. Because of the spectacular finds made by both groups of scientists in the last half of the nineteenth century—from gigantic dinosaurs to extinct civilizations—each enjoyed a tremendous public prestige. Nineteenth-century paleontologists and archaeologists literally resurrected natural and human worlds which had ceased to exist, and by putting their discoveries on display in museums, made those worlds real for the public.

But while the two fields shared a methodology and background derived from natural history, and while both captivated the public imagination, by the end of the nineteenth century the link between the study of fossils and the study of human artifacts had become increasingly strained. By the turn of the century, the study of human beings was outgrowing the frameworks of natural history. As a result, although it had been one of the original sections of museum interest and was included in the title of the department, paleontology never assumed an important place in the University Museum's collection. Though the museum accumulated artifacts at a furious rate during the 1890s, by 1900 paleontology had been officially dropped as an area of museum concern. This minor administrative decision taken in the late 1890s actually reflected a huge intellectual shift in the organization of knowledge. It reflected nothing less than the emancipation of the social sciences from the natural sciences.[20]

By moving away from the natural sciences in the last decade of the nineteenth century, the University Museum led the way in a larger shift away from studying human beings in the context of natural history and toward developing a new "natural history of civilization." W. J. McGee described this transformation for readers of the *Atlantic* in 1898. "At first," McGee observed, "man was studied simply as an animal and men were classed in races defined by characteristics shared with brutes." This had given way, according to McGee, to a more sophisticated approach: "a notable advance was forecast when students perceived that man occupies a distinct plane, in that his essential attributes are collective rather than individual." The result of this realization was "a new ethnology, in which men are classified by mind rather than by body, by culture rather than by color."[21] John Wesley Powell, in charge of the Federal Government's Bureau of Ethnology, put the matter more succinctly: "Man is an animal," he wrote, "and may be studied as such; and this branch of science belongs to biology. But man is more than an animal. Though an animal in biotic function, he is a man in his anthropic activities."[22]

This kind of distinction between the anthropic and the biotic had not been honed sharply at the Field Museum. It amounted to an imaginary line in the floor. When he described the grand sweep of the Field's exhibits, Frederic Ward Putnam said: "The installation begins with the formation of the earth, and concludes with the age of invention."[23] Though it is not entirely clear what Putnam meant by the phrase "the age of invention," it is clear that he saw humanity in two distinct categories: those groups whose development placed them before that age, and placed them therefore in the natural world, and those who came after. A natural history museum was not, apparently, the appropriate place to study the latter.

In giving institutional form to this newly emerging sense of "anthropic" activities, Philadelphians found themselves ahead of their counterparts in New York and in Washington as well. In the Capitol, John Wesley Powell did an able job of making the Bureau of Ethnology an important center of research on the indigenous people of North America, and part of that work included "a massive effort to collect Indian artifacts." This meant that the collections in Washington suffered from the kind of provincialism that Boas had complained about in Chicago. More personally, Powell remained more interested in linguistic and cultural studies, and consequently did not believe in the efficacy of an anthropological museum. Museums, Powell believed, could not accurately represent cultures through objects: "an anthropological museum, therefore, is an impossibility."[24] Further, the National Museum, under the leadership of Spencer Baird, remained a museum primarily of natural history and secondarily of technology. An 1888 plan of the National Museum reveals that "Ethnology" occupied two exhibit halls out of a total of sixteen, and in one of them, ethnological objects shared space with "Transportation and Engineering." American antiquities were displayed in two of the other smaller halls, but these objects were not given as much space as the display of stuffed mammals.[25] Baird remained deeply committed to an older kind of natural history during his tenure at the Smithsonian, and as a result anthropology remained a stepchild in the Washington museum throughout the second half of the nineteenth century.

Similarly, the newly independent study of anthropology did not find New York any more hospitable. The American Museum of Natural History grew quickly to be one of the world's important museums of natural history in the late nineteenth century. Frederic Ward Putnam, eager to make a fresh start after Chicago, hoped to build both an anthropological department and a collection of the first rank at the American Museum. Briefly, in the 1890s, he succeeded in assembling a staff of talented young researchers. But just as quickly, in 1903, Putnam left the museum and in 1904 removed to California, where Phoebe Hearst lured him to build both an academic department and a museum at Berkeley.

Putnam surely left New York in part because he was unable to convince the New Yorkers to develop museum-based anthropology in the way he envisioned. Many at the American Museum simply did not see that anthropology merited their attention or resources. Putnam's 1896 budget request left museum president Morris Jesup (1881–1908) "startled," and the museum board "saw no other course than to review and reduce it to reasonable proportions."[26] Further, some at the American Museum were unconvinced that anthropology was worth studying in the first place. As museum president Osborn (1908–1933) put it in a letter to W. B. Scott, "Between ourselves much anthropology is merely opinion, or the gossip of the natives. It is many years away from being a science." As Osborn's tenure at the American Museum progressed, he became less and less willing to commit museum resources to anthropological research or display.[27]

As anthropology emerged as a professional discipline in the last years of the nineteenth century, Philadelphians, through their University Museum, were the first ones in the United States to take George Brown Goode up on his challenge. In this way, the University Museum made the most dramatic gesture to literally split "culture" as a subject for scientific analysis away from natural history.

Upstairs, Downstairs: Culture or History?

When the University Museum opened the doors to its permanent quarters late in 1899, it gave architectural shape to the scientific study of humankind. Walking through the fountain courtyard of the museum and up a broad flight of steps, a visitor in 1899 faced two great wooden entrance doors. Above those doors two figures carved in stone held—and

8, 9 *Upstairs and downstairs.* Above, the Graeco-Roman installation in Pepper Hall of the museum at the University of Pennsylvania early in the twentieth century. Below, a school visits the American section of the museum c. 1912. A hierarchy of the world's cultures was built into the very fabric of the museum's building. (Courtesy of the University of Pennsylvania Museum, #S4–142533 & S4–141709)

still hold—a medallion. The medallion is inscribed: "Free Museum of Science and Art." The "free" part of the name was easy. Philadelphia mayor Edwin Stuart traded city-owned land to the university for the promise of a museum open to the public without charge. "Science," and "Art," which presumably defined what the visitor would find behind those grand wooden doors, proved more complicated.

Passing through the entrance doors of the new building in 1899, the visitor found him or herself immediately on a landing. From the landing, the visitor could either ascend to the second floor or descend to the first floor. On the second floor, according the museum *Bulletin,* visitors would find artifacts from the ancient Mediterranean world and objects secured by the museum's famous expeditions to the Near East.

Should a visitor choose instead to go downstairs from the landing, he or she would discover something of a hodge-podge: a collection of objects connected with Buddhism; "ethnological objects of asiatic origin; material from central and South America"; and "collections illustrative of the life of the Colorado cliff dwellers, and other American aborigines and collections . . . recently brought from Borneo and adjacent islands." [28]

The symbolism in the design of the museum was not subtle: from the entrance landing, one *rose* to find the civilizations of the Near East and the Mediterranean; conversely, the visitor went *downstairs* to find Native Americans from all parts of the New World, Buddhism, and the objects from the primitives of Borneo. The University Museum may have helped pioneer the study of human culture as distinct from natural history. The institutional emancipation of anthropology from natural history represented by the opening of Penn's museum did not, however, accompany a complete intellectual break. Those associated with the University Museum brought to their understanding of human culture models refashioned from the natural sciences, demonstrating how influential, pervasive, and enduring the museum models provided by natural history proved to be.

Chief among these was a progressive model of human social development which, according to many at the turn of the century, applied to all human groups. Elaborating the evolutionary metaphor from biology, many who studied human culture felt that all cultures, like the development of organisms from lowest to highest, went through a progression from savagery, through barbarism, to civilization. (American ethnographer Lewis Henry Morgan, for one, elaborated this to include three phases of barbarism.) This concept was neither new nor uniquely American. General Pitt-Rivers had used this approximately Darwinian framework to arrange his museum in England.[29] As David Jenkins has suggested, this sense of evolutionary hierarchy could be further reinforced by arranging objects from simplest to most complex. Otis Mason, of the National Museum, for example, felt it was "crucial to arrange artifacts . . . from the most primitive to the most advanced, in order to facilitate the study of their evolution."[30]

Philadelphia's Daniel Brinton played a significant role in developing and refining this conception of humanity. Brinton placed a universal psychic unity at the center of his ethnological theory. His study of particular ethnographic material served simply to underscore his belief in "the sameness underlying the range of culture among diverse groups."[31] In an 1895 address to the American Association for the Advancement of Science, Brinton described his progressive view of human society: "We know beyond cavil or question that the earliest was also the lowest man, the most ignorant, the most brutish, naked, homeless, half-speechless. But the gloom surrounding this distant background of the race is relieved by rays of glory, for with knowledge not less positive are we assured that through all hither time, through seeming retrogressions and darkened epochs, the advance of the race in the main toward a condition better by every standard has been certain and steady."[32]

Clearly, this evolutionary view of culture placed Western civilization at the apex of cultural achievement, and it served to relegate other cultures below it in the hierarchy. But this ladder of cultural development also helped simultaneously to explain the differences people observed between cultures, and to link all human groups in a progressive chain. To explain cultural differences in a way that created a sense of human unity under the umbrella of Western superiority had become an increasingly urgent task as nineteenth-century imperial and commercial adventures brought people from the West into contact with human cultural groups in all their dazzling variety. Almost reassuringly, William Pepper told the crowd assembled for the opening of the museum's first major exhibition in 1892 that the objects on display served to underscore the essential "unity of the race, and the undying force of the aspirations and affections which are guiding it painfully upwards and onwards through the stages of its evolution."[33]

The institution's collections were assembled to facilitate comparisons between different groups in order to plot the location of each on this universal scale of social development. The point of comparing cultures, of course, was to observe how far each one had traveled along the social evolutionary path. Moreover, just as human beings represented the triumph of biological evolution, a comparison of the world's cultures would unambiguously demonstrate that Western civilization marked the highest achievement of social evolution.[34] George Byron Gordon, trained as an ethnologist at Harvard before he took over as Curator of General Ethnology at the museum, made this point in a letter to university provost and museum board president Charles Harrison: "At the present time certain peoples are relatively backward, such as the Indians of North and South America, the African negroes, the inhabitants of the South Pacific Islands, the tribes inhabiting the plains of Siberia and the mountains of Central Asia." But he assured the board president that while "the distance between these more backward peoples and those that are at the head of the procession to-day is very considerable," the evidence clearly indicated that "all peoples were from the beginning capable of making progress . . . proved by the fact that even the most primitive folk have arts and industries."[35]

By using an evolutionary model to explain human cultural development, the Philadelphians who founded the University Museum tried to conceive of an anthropology that linked the savage and the civilized in the same intellectual construct. By creating a new museum to display the "natural history of civilization," those at the university anticipated institutionally a reorientation taking place in the organization of knowledge about the human species. They built a museum that would house under the same roof the artifacts of human cultures both before and after "the age of invention." To build this bridge, and with this universal model of human cultural development at the center of the museum's intellectual architecture, those who built the University Museum solidified distinctions between two kinds of culture. One, an Arnoldian version of Culture extended backward in time, was linked to history, art, and permanence. The other, a newer, anthropological conception of culture, became almost synonymous with primitivism, science, and transience. These were the distinctions given architectural form when the museum opened its doors to the public in 1899, and they served to define how anthropology emerged as a discipline in the late nineteenth century and how it would develop in the twentieth.

Having distinguished the study of human culture from the study of the natural world, there were tensions at the museum, and in the field as

a whole, over which cultures should receive greater institutional attention. Boas's complaints about the geographic imbalance in the Field Museum's collections were a version of the conflict that took place throughout the early years of the University Museum's growth between those
who wanted to focus on the issues of American and other "primitive"
cultures and those who wanted the museum to be a leader in the archaeological discovery of the ancient, Old World civilizations. At stake,
therefore, in the squabbles between Old World and New World interests,
was how museums would negotiate between the presentation of human
cultures as a part of human history and the understanding of human culture in the social scientific frameworks of anthropology.

Old World archaeology developed, and indeed continues to be seen,
as a branch of historical study. Working without the kinds of written
documents available to their Old World colleagues, however, archaeologists interested in the recovery of the indigenous American past culti-
vated stronger ties with anthropology. Through this approach to the
past, history and culture became virtually synonymous. In reconstruct-
ing the past of "primitives," cultural change and historical change were
the same.

When dealing with the history of so-called primitive peoples, anthropologists saw few distinctions between past and present. According to
one newspaper reporter writing in 1894, "ethnology in America is nothing less than a succession of stories of living, human histories."[36] In a
letter written to Smithsonian secretary Spencer Baird in 1880, John Wesley Powell broke the study of Native Americans into eight categories. The
first seven, including "Philology, Mythology, Habits and Customs," had
no historical specificity. The eighth, "History of Indian Affairs," focused
on changes experienced by native peoples after their contact with Euro-
Americans: "treaties, cession of lands; removals; progress in industrial
arts."[37]

In a speech given at the University Museum, Frank Hamilton Cushing, employed by the Federal Government's Bureau of Ethnology and regarded by some as America's first professional ethnologist, complained
that "American ethnology has been comparatively neglected."[38] Museum curator Charles Abbott agreed and felt that the museum's primary
area of concern ought to be with American archaeology and ethnology.
A circular Abbott sent to Philadelphia doctors in May 1890 solicited contributions to a museum of "American archaeology," and he titled himself
curator of the Museum of American Archaeology in his first annual report. At the same time, the University Archaeological Association and

the Department of Archaeology sponsored excavations in the Near East and subscribed to Flinders Petrie's Egyptian Exploration Fund.[39] Certainly the museum's most important and most visible project took place in Nippur, where the museum sponsored the excavations formative in Sumerian studies.[40]

At its most prosaic, differing opinions over the issue of geographic focus created administrative problems. Stewart Culin, an ethnologist, had the largest hand in the museum's day-to-day operations. He also designed most of the early exhibits. Sara Stevenson, who along with university provost William Pepper was the driving force behind the planning and growth of the museum, had a particular interest in Egyptian archaeology. She expressed a clear administrative divide to Edward Clark in a letter in 1895: "Mr. Culin, although he has the title of Director, is for practical purposes only in charge of half the museum."[41] Culin may indeed have been in charge of half the museum, but it was not an equal half. The Report of the Board of Managers for 1893, for example, records that the Egyptian, Mediterranean, and Babylonian sections received nearly $8,000 while the American and Prehistoric section—and notice the link between the two—received $331.20.[42]

That the museum should devote more of its resources to the Old World projects simply reflected, on one level, the desires of the wealthy Philadelphians who funded the institution. Discoveries made in the Near East, Egypt, and in the Mediterranean generated far more excitement than broken arrowheads or crude pots ever could. Consequently, Old World archaeological projects attracted greater sums of money, both in this country and in Europe. To a certain extent, the museum's activities followed the wishes of its funders.

The institutional friction between these two camps at the museum paralleled larger intellectual tensions in the late nineteenth century. Old World archaeologists, whose discoveries at places like Troy, Assyria, and Egypt's Valley of the Kings captivated the public imagination, worked within frameworks of biblical and classical texts. Their finds played large roles in the debates over the legitimacy of those texts. American archaeologists, concerned primarily with questions of human antiquity in the New World, and the new ethnologists, interested in describing and cataloguing the world's primitive and exotic peoples, tied their interests to the emerging discipline of anthropology.

While these two camps at the museum fought over financial resources and administrative turf, the larger question with which they wrestled was how the notion of history would be defined and how it would be recovered. Old World archaeologists made discoveries that filled gaps in the history of Western civilizations. Their excavations provided tangible proof for the existence of and established the chronological framework for these vanished societies. In this sense they helped tell the story which ultimately ended with the contemporary West: from the Near East, through the civilizations of the Mediterranean, to Europe, and finally to the United States.

Ancient civilizations had specific histories and chronologies. They had, thanks to the recovery work done by the archaeologists, identifiable events, traceable dynasties, even decipherable languages. Primitive groups, be they Native Americans or people from Borneo, had instead a life course. Each group might be expected to follow a predictable and progressive path of development, but that development from savagery to civilization had no temporal specificity. It happened apart from the chronological markings that are the essence of historical understanding. The ancient civilizations of the Old World changed historically, just as the West did. Primitive groups, however, evolved ahistorically from one stage of development to the next. The difference between upstairs and downstairs at the University Museum then, became one of chronometers. The history of those civilizations upstairs could be measured and understood with calendars, clocks, and chronology. Human groups on display downstairs, however, existed not in the time of human civilization but rather in a "natural" time, like animal species or geologic formations.[43]

This difference between understanding some human groups historically and others culturally became increasingly the difference between art and science as well. The University Museum, in trying to define a space to encompass the two, did so architecturally. Art came on the second floor, associated with the ancient civilizations and thus with history. Sara Stevenson wrote to Charles Harrison in July 1893 about the possibility of sponsoring excavations in Cyprus. In advocating this excavation she wrote: "Moreover classical art is archaeology and more widely interesting to the general public than any other."[44] In expressing this view she echoed the ideas of many archaeologists, including the famous German excavator Adolf Michaelis. Michaelis reflected on his own forty-year career in 1908 and informed his readers: "By the term archaeology is meant the archaeology of art; the products of civilization in so far as they express no artistic character will only be mentioned incidentally."[45]

For Old World archaeologists, a chief goal was to recover art objects, architectural remains, or artifacts of obvious and recognizable historical import, such as the cuneiform tablets brought back to Philadelphia from Nippur. Science, therefore, would be represented on the first floor with the primitive cultures from around the world, reflecting again the connection between anthropology and natural history. The functional and religious items collected from existing primitive groups had no value as art, but they could be studied instead as scientific specimens. By the turn of the century, therefore, the categories of art and history helped define the difference between civilization and primitivism when Western eyes gazed on ancient societies or contemporary primitive groups.

Permanent Histories, Vanishing Cultures, and the Value of the Primitive

On October 6, 1876, Henry Gillman, an amateur scientist based in Detroit, wrote to Frederic Ward Putnam. Gillman was collecting material from the Ojibwa people for Putnam, and he reported on his progress. Sadly, he informed Putnam, "I have been disappointed in not getting more. But the Indians are fast moving away or dying out."[46] Gillman's letter summarized an increasingly urgent refrain among those engaged in anthropological collection during the last quarter of the nineteenth century. In an article describing the Field Museum's new quarters, the *Christian Science Monitor* noted that "special attention has been paid to securing complete exhibits of the rapidly changing tribes of North America."[47] The cultures, and often quite literally the people, from whom anthropological collections were taken disappeared before anthropologists' very eyes.

That disappearance, and the sense of loss it engendered among some in the field, underscored another distinction between history and culture. This distinction, too, was given architectural form at Penn's museum. If the first and second floors of the University Museum described the differences between science and art, between culture and history, then the final distinction between upstairs and downstairs was between permanence and transience.

Old World archaeologists saw themselves recovering the remains of the past as they excavated intrepidly through the buried accumulations of human history. Their discoveries waited for them. The ethnologists/anthropologists, on the other hand, saw themselves rescuing the artifacts and information of cultures that seemed to be vanishing. George Byron Gordon melodramatically summarized the sense of urgency many ethnologists felt when he wrote to the museum board president: "The records of the American Indian are a burning house; they are fast disappearing, when lost, they are lost forever." [48]

The race against perceived cultural extinction—what George Stocking has nicely dubbed "salvage ethnography"—gave the anthropologists and ethnologists yet something else in common with natural historians. The loss of species, like the perceived loss of cultures, prompted, at least in part, the voracious collecting of natural history museums. The American Museum of Natural History, for example, decided to create exhibits featuring the fauna of California "owing to the fact that the larger California mammals are fast approaching extinction." [49]

The destruction against which ethnologists like Gordon raced had a specific source. Writing to Sara Stevenson, Howard Furness, another Penn ethnologist, talked less politely about the difficulties facing his own work in the Carolines: "They are glorious fields and must be reaped quickly before trades' unfeeling train usurps the lands' entirely and the d——ned (excuse me!) missionaries destroy the pure minds of the natives and cram down their throats the fruit of that forbidden tree, whose mortal taste has played hob with us for so many thousand years." [50]

Furness and his brethren in the field raced against the march of civilization, which would inevitably reach even remote places like the Carolines. Gordon agreed. In a memo to Charles Harrison, Gordon reminded the board president about the need to rescue the artifacts of what he termed "backward peoples" quickly: "The more progressive part of the human race has now launched itself upon the whole world, with the result that the more backward peoples, even those with a relatively high civilization, are receiving, whether they wish it or not, the uniform stamp of modern culture. The immediate effect of this impact is the obliteration of many ancient landmarks preserved in the customs of savage folk and of peoples who, like the Chinese, are exchanging their native culture for foreign customs." [51] For these scientists, the notion of progressive social development was thus a two-edged sword. All human groups might eventually attain civilization and therefore history. In so doing, however, they would lose their culture and thus be lost to science.

Furness's evocation of Milton is revealing. In trying to get to the Carolines ahead of the missionaries, Furness believed with other ethnologists that so-called primitive peoples existed in a state of timelessness and purity. Furness felt that the inhabitants of the Carolines remained "pure" until commerce, Christianity, and knowledge corrupted them. What Furness reveals is that when he and his fellow ethnologists made their explorations of the exotic cultures of the world, they believed or imagined that they were making contact with cultures that had not changed. In the view of ethnologists, it was only the influence of the West that brought change to these otherwise changeless people. In the anthropological hinterlands the two chronometers of human culture collided, and in the collision the relentless progress of the West disrupted the flow of "natural" time. When these cultural explorers arrived in some remote place, they experienced the fantasy of every historian: they came into direct contact with the past, just as that past was slipping away.

Fretting over the disappearance of the world's "primitives" might have been prompted by a humanitarian impulse on the part of anthropologists who had grown to respect and admire these other cultures. But it may have also reflected a more selfish sense that Western society had lost touch with its "wild" side. Merwin Henry Childs mused on the problem of "Being Civilized Too Much" for readers of the *Atlantic*. According to Childs, humans were "a compound of feeling and intellect." Savages might be over-influenced by the former, but Westerners, Childs argued, were ruled too much by the latter. In a late-nineteenth-century version of Rousseau, Childs concluded: "The true problem is, not to eradicate the savage in man, but so to train and control him that his strength of feeling, his spontaneousness and promptitude shall be at the service of man's higher powers." [52] Childs' choice of the word "eradicate" seems particularly pointed in this context. The possible sources from which Americans might learn "spontaneousness and promptitude" were quite literally being eradicated as Childs wrote his article. But Childs and the anthropologists who worried about cultural disappearance revealed a central problem for anthropological museums. On the one hand, they displayed a cultural hierarchy with civilization at its apex. On the other hand, in Childs' words, perhaps the West had become too civilized. What then, were visitors to glean from anthropological exhibits—Western superiority, or, with Rousseau, that the savages really had noble qualities, or some confused combination of the two?

As early as 1893, when he worked on anthropological displays at the World's Columbian Exposition, Franz Boas had begun to grow suspicious of the "public" anthropology of the kind conducted at museums and world's fairs. According to Curtis Hinsley, the fair provided Boas with "the first of a series of shocks" to his faith in public anthropology. The second came with the Spanish-American War, and "by 1900 he had begun to retreat from American museum anthropology as a tool of education or reform." [53]

Boas probably cringed when he heard about a new exhibit of Native American culture—and I use that term loosely here—that opened at the Field Museum in 1908. Under a big headline which screamed "Chicago's Growing Tribe of Savage Redskins—They're in the Field Columbian Museum all done in plaster and they perpetrate horrible tortures and follow their warlike rites in glass cases," the *Chicago Record-Herald* went on in tabloid tones to describe the exhibit:

> Not only is Chicago's permanent population of aborigines growing rapidly and living realistically, in tepee and wigwam; . . . but rites and ceremonies, all of them ancient and many of them bloody and barbarous, are presented without interference from the authorities of city, state, or nation. Young girls are sacrificed in propitiation of Tedawa, god of the Pawnees, the only plains tribe which includes a human sacrifice in its ceremonials. . . . Salish and Hopi tribes are represented in their weird and ghastly rites as well as their home life and industrial activities; the savage Haida of the Northwest coast, whose emblem is the eye; their neighbors the cannibal Kewauks . . . Rickarees, the warlike Sioux, and the basket and blanket weaving Navajos, all are represented, and strangely enough, those who anciently were bitter enemies live harmoniously on the same reservation.[54]

Historians have long noted the connection between turn-of-the-century anthropology and Western expansion, and the connections are quite naked in the *Record-Herald* newspaper report. The headline shocks because, after all, any Native Americans who might once have lived in Chicago had been chased away years ago. The "Savage Redskins," not living, of course, but represented in plaster, are described in almost hysterical language as grotesques, but they are ultimately safe savages because they have been contained in glass cases. Most remarkable of all, the Field Museum—a "reservation" in this account—succeeded in taming these formerly lawless savages. Now, thanks to the museum and to anthropology, these groups live "harmoniously."

The Euro-American efforts to master cultural knowledge about natives has, from the early seventeenth century, been inextricably bound to the destruction of those cultures. Whether it was mastery of native languages in order to subdue native peoples through missionary work, or the understanding of Plains Indians' reliance on bison, which then drove the wholesale slaughter of those animals, knowledge has always preceded conquest. (And what was true for Americans on this continent, of course, was true as well for other Europeans as they created empires around the world.) In what sounds today more like a threat than a news report, the *Record-Herald* informed its readers about the Field Museum's plan to study people around the world: "If any of the inhabitants of the globe have any customs, characteristics or language they want to hide from Chicagoans they had better be getting them under a bushel at once, for the Field Museum of Natural History is hard on their trail. A visit to nearly every kindred, every tribe, no matter how remote or wild, is contemplated by the museum management." [55] The staff at Chicago's Field Museum may have been no worse than any other, but in 1912 former Indian Service employee Angus McColl called the work in the Southwest of Charles Owens, Chicago's Assistant Curator of Ethnology, a "jackal operation." [56]

Penn's anthropologists also expressed a rapaciousness common to the anthropological endeavor. Writing about his plans to conduct research in Alaska, George Byron Gordon confided to a colleague: "I look forward with great confidence to the results of my work during the summer. I expect to clean out the last unexploited region in North American of its ethnological material." [57] Anthropologists may often have approached their research like bargain hunters at a fire sale. At the same time, however, it must be acknowledged that, at least at the University Museum, the motives behind the work of the anthropologists were more complicated. Collecting and displaying objects from cultures around the world was seen by many as contributing to a broader sense of human understanding. A 1924 writer quoted an editorial in *The Museum News* which made the claim that "the interest of the museums of America in the American Indian had helped create a more sympathetic attitude toward the Indians" and asked, "why shouldn't we . . . create an attitude of world understanding through our museum culture material." [58]

Without question, that understanding came on terms dictated by those who ran the museums. Nonetheless, in an era that saw increasing racial animosity manifest itself in Jim Crow laws in this country and which witnessed atrocities against indigenous people in European colonies, the University Museum tried to present a more humane and sympathetic view of the world's cultures. Indeed, Laurence Coleman, president of the American Association of Museums, saw the University Museum as leading the way. Crediting it in a 1939 book, Coleman wrote that the University Museum "long ago set an advanced example" by displaying New World [i.e. "primitive"] cultures "on equal terms" with Old World civilizations. [59]

To teach the public to appreciate "primitive" cultures became then the public role of the museum's displays. For the scientists at the University Museum, the collections housed there provided a comparative yardstick by which to measure cultural progress. For the public, these collections were intended to provide something more than mere tourism through time and space. According to museum director Gordon: "Bringing people into direct contact with the visible past [would have] a civilizing and humanizing influence upon our manners and habits of thought."[60] Ethnographic objects on the first floor of the museum brought turn-of-the-century visitors face to face with a different kind of history. The past to which Gordon referred was not a specific historical moment—that sort of encounter could be had on the second floor. Rather, visitors to the museum's first floor could view a generic human past when staring at the ethnographic displays.

All human civilizations, even that of modern America, therefore, could be traced back to the savage state in which these primitive groups still existed. The "civilizing influence" Gordon hoped for came because the museum introduced its audience to the evidence of their own roots, not specific historical roots, but their distant, anthropological origins. As a result, Gordon believed, collecting this "harvest of cultures" to place within the walls of the museum would ensure that "the museum becomes a center for the spread of a higher culture in the present and in the future for all time."[61]

～

Having ambitiously attempted to unite the study of history and culture, art and science, under the same museum roof, those at the University Museum discovered that this task proved more complicated than they had realized. In 1913, museum director Gordon outlined a three-part plan for the museum that he hoped would bring a greater cohesion to the museum's efforts. Gordon described his plan to Charles Harrison:

> The first, because the most urgent, is to assemble the best available examples of the handiwork of the various peoples known to history and geography, and left behind, as it were, in the march of events. The second method is to assemble, either by excavation or by purchase, collections of the relics which precede the records of the earliest civilization and which carry the history of man backwards a hundred thousand years and more to the beginning of his life on the planet. The third method consists in assembling examples to illustrate the

great civilizations of antiquity to which our own civilization is more directly indebted, namely, Egypt, Babylonia, Greece and Rome.[62]

The result of this plan, according the Gordon, would enable the University Museum "to reconstruct, in visible shape, the life history of the human race, exhibiting at once its progressive development and the rich variety and excellence of its attainments."

Much here is familiar: the distinction between history and geography, the difference between civilization and those groups "left behind." Familiar, too, is Gordon's assertion that all groups make gradual progress toward civilization and his alarm that these primitive groups have already begun rapid change through contact with the West. Many anthropologists saw cultural change as an almost natural process, like the evolution of species, that had a birth, development, and then a death or extinction. With this as their understanding, anthropologists like Gordon objected to what they saw as the artificial change brought on by Western contact. If these primitive groups could not be permitted to continue their natural development in the cultural vacuum imagined by anthropologists, then the University Museum could preserve cultural artifacts as evidence of the process interrupted.

When anthropologists like Gordon, Furness, and their colleagues both in this country and in Europe collected artifacts and recorded observations, they thought they were discovering the distant past, and they did so to exert a beneficial influence on the domestic present. At the same time, these researchers realized that progress and destruction were intimately linked. As Gordon suggested when talking about Native Alaskans, anthropologists borrowed a final concept from the natural sciences: the idea of extinction. Ethnic groups themselves might and probably would disappear as the progress of the West marched on. "Race extermination," as Gordon put it using "race" as a synonym for culture, for indigenous people seemed inevitable, but the anthropologists could at least preserve the artifacts associated with the culture of these people as a reminder to the contemporary West of its distant roots. Old World archaeologists rescued the past from historical oblivion, but the anthropologists and ethnologists had the far more elusive task of rescuing the timeless past of peoples who had no future from the inexorable processes of the present. If the groups represented by displays in the museum's downstairs had no history, unlike those upstairs, then at least by preserving their artifacts museums could give them a permanence through its exhibits.

Winners and Losers: Museum
Anthropology vs. University Anthropology

After leaving Chicago, Franz Boas returned to the East Coast to take a post at the American Museum of Natural History. Shortly thereafter, he began to split his time between the museum and Columbia University, where he had been given a professorship in 1899.[63] In 1905 Boas left his post at the American Museum to work exclusively at Columbia. When Boas headed uptown, he took the future of anthropology in America with him.

So goes the conventional narrative of the history of anthropology. Boas, perhaps more than any other practitioner, shaped anthropology into an academic discipline. Not an institution builder, Boas used Columbia as a power base from which to construct the professional network that shaped the direction of the field in the early twentieth century. Boas consolidated his influence over the field, the narrative continues, by producing most of the next generation of academic anthropologists. As his students spread to universities across the country, Boas's triumph became complete.

Boas certainly deserves much credit both for asking the intellectual questions that anthropologists tried to answer in the first half of this century and for creating the professional environment in which those questions would be addressed. I gloss over this essentially positivist view of academic anthropology not to argue with it—there is a rich literature that examines Boas's role in shaping the discipline—but to note that where there are winners, there must also be losers.[64] Boas's victory meant, among other things, that universities would now be the primary sites for the production of anthropological knowledge.[65] Museums, therefore, lost that role. It is this contest between museums and universities for possession of anthropology, not its final outcome, that interests us here. The outcome of the struggle profoundly affected the nature of the anthropological knowledge that would be presented to a public audience.

$\sim$

During the 1890s, the Peabody Museum at Harvard began to feel a squeeze. Exhibition space in the museum "was increasingly given over to classroom purposes," according to Curtis Hinsley.[66] Space, of course, is perhaps the most accurate barometer of prestige on university campuses, and the Peabody's loss of space was just such an indicator. Unlike the studies of natural history, which developed at a moment when American colleges languished in stagnation, anthropology grew alongside the transformation of the American university system. In Cambridge, the spectacular growth of Harvard University literally choked the Peabody Museum. At Harvard, as at other dynamic institutions, anthropology would finally belong to academic departments, not to museums.

The complicated relationship between the museum of anthropology and university departments played out nowhere more dramatically than at Penn. The tension had been present at Penn from the beginning. The university had appointed Daniel Brinton as the first professor of anthropology in the country before it had a museum, but according to Regna Darnell, when Brinton was at the university, he seems to have had little to do with shaping the emerging museum.[67] When Brinton gave the presidential address to the American Association for the Advancement of Science, he complained about the weak relationship between museums and universities: "We erect stately museums, we purchase costly specimens, we send out constantly expeditions, but where are the universities, the institutions of higher education, who train young men how to observe, how to collect and explore in this branch?"[68] Brinton's complaint suggests that universities were not keeping pace with museums as the places where anthropological knowledge would be produced.

Though Brinton articulated this problem, as the nation's first university anthropologist he did little to address it. His influence at Penn seems to have been slight. It is not clear that he taught very much, and more importantly for the future of the discipline, he trained no students to succeed him as academic anthropologists. Unlike Harvard, which produced under Putnam the largest number of Ph.D.s in anthropology, the new coin of the academic realm, Penn invested its resources in building the museum. Brinton's sole protégé was Stewart Culin. Culin would acknowledge Brinton's influence until the end of his own career, a career spent, significantly, entirely in the museum world and not in the academic. Though provost Charles Harrison proposed a memorial chair be established honoring Brinton's memory, after his death in 1899 Brinton was not replaced.

More than anyone else in its first ten years, William Pepper and Sara Stevenson gave Penn's museum leadership and direction. We have met Pepper already. Stevenson, Pepper's partner in building the museum, was herself possessed of considerable gifts. She was a respected, if amateur, Egyptologist, who lectured and published on the topic. In 1894, she became the first woman ever awarded an honorary degree by the

University of Pennsylvania. Through the 1890s, Stevenson served as president of the Philadelphia Civic Club, a women's reform organization, and from 1894 to 1901, she was the only female trustee of the Philadelphia Commercial Museum. At the end of her life, she was made a Chevalier de la Legion d'Honneur of France.

For her part, Stevenson was aware of the difficulties a woman like herself faced when working in the world of professional men. When the project of creating the museum was just beginning, she wrote to Daniel Brinton asking for his help: "As a woman, an enthusiast, I need such endorsement from the authorities of the University and from those who, like yourself, are identified with the archaeological work in this city, & indeed in this country."[69] Though she also served as the first president of the Equal Franchise Society of Pennsylvania in 1909, a eulogist made sure to note her domestic accomplishments as well: "Feminine accomplishments were not unknown to her. In spite of public duties and business engagements she found time to be a most admirable housekeeper. . . . She was also a fine needlewoman."[70]

Stevenson and Pepper clearly had a more than professional relationship. Pepper wrote often to Stevenson, sometimes twice a day. After his death, Stevenson transcribed and annotated Pepper's letters to her in a memorial gesture. That correspondence reveals two people who relied on one another to a great extent for professional and personal support. In Chicago together in 1893 for the world's fair, they shared a ride on the world's first Ferris Wheel, and Pepper complained about the time they had to spend apart. The correspondence is a remarkable window into the relationship of two married people, both in their middle years, as they shared personal and professional aspirations. After an evening spent at a university fund-raising event, Pepper wrote to Stevenson in a way with which many university administrators can surely empathize: "An evening absolutely wasted: gabble, gorge, and guzzle. Nothing useful, nothing interesting, no business—and I could have spent it in yr company in instructive and amusing talk." Stevenson and Pepper shared an intense love, whether or not their relationship had a physical dimension. Pepper described the difficulties created by Victorian propriety: "Perhaps there were never two creatures as capable of enjoyment as you & I—so penned in & restrained." Their relationship did attract enough attention to cause a scandal late in 1894. In her annotations to Pepper's letters, Stevenson insisted that there had been nothing improper between herself and Pepper.

In many ways, the museum was the child produced by these two extraordinary but perhaps thwarted people. He deprecatingly wrote to her in 1893: "Never will you give up your quest for a museum; and never shall I give up helping you according to my feeble powers." More arrogantly, Pepper believed that his partnership with Stevenson created an irresistible force. Writing in March 1894, he said: "It is so easy to assert one's power: for you & I always find I suspect that no one in the Company in which we are can stand against us."[71]

William Pepper had managed to keep a peace between the museum and the university, as the former grew and the latter transformed. His death in 1898, however, initiated a period of turmoil among those running the museum, and Stevenson lost her most powerful ally in keeping it as autonomous as possible from the growing centralized power of the university. In 1903, for a variety of reasons, Stewart Culin, the man most responsible for shaping the museum's displays and for bringing the museum's work to a national and international audience through exhibits at world's fairs, resigned to assume a position at the Brooklyn Museum. In 1904 the board polarized, in part because of a controversy concerning Hermann Hilprecht, the museum's chief Assyriologist. A pro-Stevenson faction vied with an anti-Stevenson/pro-university faction for control of the museum, and by 1905, Stevenson's group had lost out. Stevenson herself then resigned from the board on February 24, 1905, taking others with her. Though the administrative particulars of this upheaval do not interest us here, the root of the problem was a struggle over what the museum's relationship to the university should be.[72]

Charles Custis Harrison had replaced Pepper as provost in 1895. After graduating from Penn in the 1860s, Harrison made a considerable fortune as head of the Franklin Sugar Refinery. In 1876, Harrison was elected to be one of the university's trustees, beginning an administrative career with the university that lasted well into the twentieth century, and he brought to his work his considerable business and financial talents. Harrison created more departments and erected more buildings than any other administrator before him or since. By the time he left the provost's office in 1910, the size of the faculty had nearly doubled, the size of the student body more than doubled, and the value of the university's assets increased by a factor of four. By assuming the post of vice-president of the museum when he resigned as provost, Harrison acknowledged the prestige and importance of the museum. Six years later, now an old man, Harrison became president of the board.

As provost, Harrison did not have the educational vision of his predecessor. Nonetheless, that limited vision of the university did not leave room for an autonomous museum. As board president, he committed himself to bringing the museum's operations within the orbit of the centralized university. When Culin resigned in 1903, many saw an opportunity to bring the university and the museum closer together. His resignation enabled those remaining at the museum to contemplate a reorganization. Franz Boas certainly recognized the importance of this moment when he wrote to Stevenson: "I do hope that you will be able, in re-organizing the museum in Philadelphia, to bring about a close co-operation between the Museum and the University, and that you will find some one who will be able to use the great advantage of a museum position for the purpose of training a new generation of anthropologists." [73] That someone turned out to be George Byron Gordon, a Harvard-trained anthropologist who took Culin's job as Curator of Ethnology at the University Museum. Through a combination of tireless work and auspicious timing, Gordon became director of the museum in 1910, the same year that Harrison took charge of the board.

From the outset of his tenure at the museum, Gordon attempted to strengthen the ties between the museum and the academic program in anthropology. [74] Gordon was determined to revive academic anthropology at Penn, but to do so in a way which kept it connected to the museum. Echoing Boas's sentiments in a letter to the board in 1907, Gordon told them: "I believe that it will be of great advantage for the Museum to become more and more identified with the regular activities of the University, and experience at Harvard and Columbia as well as here has shown that interest in Anthropology within the student body is very considerable." [75] Gordon himself taught undergraduate courses in anthropology and supervised graduate students. He proudly reported to the Board of Managers on February 17, 1911 that anthropologists trained at Penn were receiving "important positions" in the United States and Canada. [76] In an act of powerful symbolism, on December 20, 1912 the board signaled the new relationship between the university and the museum by changing the latter's name from the "Department of Archaeology" to the "University Museum." Both Gordon's appointment and the name-change signaled a new attempt on the part of the museum's managers to strengthen the connections between the university and the museum. [77]

Gordon wanted to build a university program in anthropology that preserved a central role for a large museum. At the same moment that

Boas took anthropology out of the museum, Gordon tried to keep it there and tried to create at Pennsylvania a serious academic department of anthropology tied to a university anthropological museum. At one level, the different paths pursued by these two men represent the difference between anthropology's institutional future and its past. More than that though, the struggle between museum anthropology and university anthropology was a struggle over the meaning of anthropological objects and over how anthropological knowledge would be produced. As we have already seen happen in the natural sciences, by the first quarter of the twentieth century an object-based epistemology for anthropology had begun to evaporate.

Despite—or perhaps precisely because of—the fact that Boas had left the American Museum in 1905, he wrote in 1907 an essay for *Science* detailing "Some Principles of Museum Administration." In what might be perceived as a swipe at his two former employers, the Field Museum and the American Museum, Boas insisted in the essay on the separation of anthropology museums from natural history museums, just as George Brown Goode had done nearly thirty years previously. The two kinds of collections, he wrote, were "entirely distinct." There was no reason, he felt, "for the visitor to come into contact with the natural-history exhibits while passing through the anthropological halls."

Boas also affirmed the important role museums played in the production of knowledge. "I do not hesitate to say," he wrote, "that the essential justification for the maintenance of large museums lies wholly in their importance as necessary means for the advancement of science"— and this even at the expense of broader public education, which he felt could be better accomplished by small institutions. Boas then articulated what he felt to be the primary function of a museum: "It is the essential function of the museum as a scientific institution to preserve for all future time, in the best possible way, the valuable material that has been collected, and not to allow it to be scattered and to deteriorate." Boas here echoed the widespread belief that many of the world's cultures were on the verge of extinction and thus that museums can best serve the future of science by preserving relics of the past.

Having stated the case in favor of large museums, Boas spent much of the essay implicitly indicting the whole museum enterprise, especially as it concerned anthropology. As we have already discussed, the museums of the late nineteenth century strove for an encyclopedic completeness and for a perfected system of classification. Boas challenged both notions. Presenting knowledge in museum exhibits as complete would only point up "the uselessness of further effort. . . . Such a museum will fail to bring home the complexity of nature and an appreciation of the efforts required for mastery of its secrets." If that was not damning enough, Boas suggested that such a museum would stifle interest in further scientific research. He went on to attack the museum premise even further: "It is my opinion that the attempt at a thorough systematization of a large museum must be given up."

Boas went on from this to critique the way in which museum practice had hindered the growth of anthropology more specifically. From his office at Columbia, Boas turned and bit the institutional hand that had fed him and his field for two generations. "The strong tendency to accumulate specimens has often been a disadvantage to the development of anthropology," he told *Science,* "because there are many aspects of this science in which the material objects are insignificant as compared with the actual scientific questions involved. . . . Anthropology requires a broader point of view for its fieldwork than that offered by the strict requirements of the acquisitions of museum specimens." Objects could not serve to represent culture in the same way a clamshell might represent a species, Boas argued: "Any array of objects is always only an exceedingly fragmentary presentation of the true life of a people. . . . For this reason any attempt to present ethnological data by systematic classification of specimens will not only be artificial, but will be entirely misleading." Finally, Boas informed his readers, "anthropological inquiry" concerned itself with "complex mental processes" of which objects are primarily "incidental expressions." [78]

Incidental expressions.

There it was then. Boas in a few pages had deftly undercut everything upon which the museums of the late nineteenth century had been built: completeness, order, system, and the synecdochic value of objects themselves. Boas did not simply propose a shift in subject matter, though he did do that, from the incidental expressions to the mental processes behind them. More, Boas suggested that objects no longer served as the generators of anthropological knowledge. Whether he intended it or not, the "Principles of Museum Administration" stood as Boas's— and as anthropology's—declaration of independence from museums and from an object-based epistemology. [79]

Gordon, on the other hand, tried to fashion a future for anthropology based on the past. His own anthropological thinking and his ideas about the role of museums in anthropology remained stuck in the nineteenth century. Simply put, Gordon remained committed to an evolutionist conception of human groups—a progressive development from lowest to highest, from savagery to civilization. Further, Gordon believed that museums still functioned as the best place in which the details of this evolution could be studied and compared and the evidence for that evolution put on display for the public. Gordon was by no means the only anthropologist who held on to older ideas, even as those ideas were challenged by the Boasians. Boas had left the American Museum in some measure because of fights he had with museum president Morris Jesup. The latter wanted a series of exhibits displaying an evolutionary progression of human culture. Boas balked. In Chicago, as Curtis Hinsley has pointed out, Frederick Starr, the University of Chicago's first and only anthropologist from 1892 until 1923, held roughly the same set of ideas. "In my teaching," Starr wrote in 1922, "*evolution* is fundamental. . . . It would be evolution of man, of human types, of ideas, customs, arts and industries." [80] Demonstrating an even fiercer devotion to the past, when it opened its new building in 1921 the Field Museum preserved exactly the same division of natural history around which it had been founded nearly thirty years earlier—anthropology alongside geology, botany, and zoology.

At the end of 1912, Gordon wrote a lengthy piece for the museum's *Journal* in which he described plans for the museum's expansion. He took the opportunity to place his museum in a historical context. Somewhat more generously than Boas, Gordon acknowledged the debt anthropology owed to the systematics of natural history. The association, he wrote, "has helped the development of historical and anthropological collections along systematic lines because biological methods have exerted a favorable influence on the study of History and Anthropology." Agreeing with Boas, and with George Brown Goode as well, Gordon articulated the need for separate museums of anthropology. Sounding suspiciously like Goode, Gordon wrote: "In this final division of labor there will be on one hand the Natural History museum containing collections illustrating the mineral, plant and animal kingdoms including man in his purely physical aspects. On the other hand will be the museum of Fine Arts that will aim to present examples of the best either in classical art and the art of the renaissance or else the best in modern painting and sculpture and the related arts. Between the two will be the museum of Human History." [81] Gordon had a self-serving as well as a didactic purpose in tracing the trajectory of American museum development. He proceeded through this analysis of museums to assert that his own institution found itself on the cutting edge and was poised to succeed where the Field Museum and American Museum had failed. He concluded his historical look at museums by saying: "The University Museum has grown up along these lines and has in a measure been anticipating the general movement for museums to illustrate the life history of the human race." [82]

Having situated this new museum snugly between the two established kinds of institutions, Gordon described the museum of "Human History" as being "as much concerned with the earlier and cruder stages of development as with the more advanced." In fact, because the former occupied a greater period of human history, "a relatively large proportion of the collections in such a museum will be those pertaining to savage peoples, or to the prehistoric peoples of Europe, Asia, and North Africa." Gordon did believe that the civilizations of antiquity "such as the Egyptian, Babylonian, Mycenaean, Minoan, the Greek and the Roman and all the others that contributed so powerfully to modern culture should be represented." Finally, Gordon completed the division of human history by insisting on the inclusion of non-Western cultures in this new museum: "With equal interest must be included those nations whose culture was related more remotely or not at all to our own. Among these are the nations of India, Central Asia, China, Japan, Mexico, Peru and many nameless peoples of antiquity." Almost twenty-five years later, Gordon tried to define Goode's "Kulturgeschichte."

Gordon did not let go of his progressive and evolutionary notions of human cultural development, despite the obvious shifts taking place within the anthropological discipline. In 1913 he wrote to Charles Harrison with optimism and confidence that the University Museum remained "exceptional in centering its efforts on the systematic development of collections which will illustrate and reproduce the life history of man." [83] Saying much the same thing two years later, Gordon reiterated to the museum board that the "scope of the Museum has been defined as one which undertakes to illustrate the History of Human Culture," and that the museum's collection should present the "idea of progressive development in human history." This idea, he told the Board members "unites all the collections in one consistent whole." [84]

Yet it was exactly against this kind of schema, with its evolutionist basis and presumed cultural hierarchies, that the Boasians rebelled.

Boas's work fundamentally undermined the "evolutionary" assumptions about human culture upon which anthropology museums had been founded. Boas complained that the West did not fully value "lines of thought that have led to cultures different from our own" and called for "a just appreciation of the achievements of various races." According to historian Richard Handler, Boas "argued that the classificatory schemes of evolutionary theory—dividing the world into 'savage,' 'barbarian,' and 'civilized' peoples—were artificial." [85] The University Museum, however, had built this artificiality into the very fabric of its building, and fifteen years later Gordon stuck to this construction of anthropological knowledge.

With Boas leading the way, anthropologists lost faith both in the power of objects to convey meaning about different cultures and in the frameworks into which those objects had been placed. The belief shared by Stewart Culin, Frank Hamilton Cushing, and their colleagues in the last quarter of the nineteenth century that the ordinary objects of other cultures, collected and arranged systematically, could tell stories transparently had evaporated for many anthropologists by the time of the First World War.

Try as he might to strengthen the intellectual ties between the museum and the study of anthropology, Gordon swam against the currents of the emerging discipline. Under the influence of Boas, anthropology moved further and further from museum concerns.[86] By the First World War, according to Hinsley, the concerns of museums and academic departments had drifted far enough apart to make interactions between them "rare." By 1920 roughly half of the professional anthropologists in the United States made their institutional home in college and university departments, and that was the direction the traffic would continue to flow; after World War II, anthropology would become "the most highly academicized" of any of the social sciences.[87] When Gordon clashed with Frank Speck, the university's most visible Boasian, the conflict foreshadowed the split that would occur in the rest of the profession after Boas's censure by the American Anthropological Association. Even though Gordon's training and research interests were ethnological and not archaeological, his directorship of the museum positioned him as an enemy of the Boas group. "At the cost of the association with a major museum," Darnell observes, "the academic department at Penn went with Boas." [88] The partnership between the university and the museum which was implied when Penn's museum become officially the "University Museum" turned out instead to be more of an uneasy truce.

Both the museum and the university's department of anthropology would continue to prosper under the terms of the settlement, but largely on their own terms. The department would grow to be one of the major centers of academic anthropology, and the museum, in the 1920s, began to cultivate a broader public audience. That audience included business-people and designers—by cultivating closer relations with the former, Gordon hoped to increase the museum's holdings; the latter, Gordon hoped, would find the objects in the museum useful for study—and that audience increasingly included school children. In language reminiscent of Frank Hamilton Cushing, Gordon claimed that giving students the chance to handle objects "enables children more easily to realize the meaning of an object." The academic anthropologists might no longer believe in the power of objects, but Gordon could try to pass on a pint-sized version of an object-based epistemology to elementary school students.[89]

Penn's museum was not alone. As early as 1909 "public education" had assumed a larger place in the plans of the American Museum of Natural History. As a way to spur similar efforts at the Field Museum, the *Chicago Daily News* reported that "a large part of the work of the American Museum of Natural History . . . is planned directly for educational purposes." Quoting the American Museum's director, the *Daily News* continued: "The exhibition methods of the museum are frankly and chiefly for public and higher education."[90] Perhaps the prodding worked. In 1911 Chicago banker Norman Harris donated a quarter-million dollars to the Field Museum to develop a more extensive relationship with the schools. Likewise, in a stark measure of how current scientific information had been split from a broad public audience at the Field Museum, the guide book to its new museum ran to all of nineteen pages. The guide book which visitors used in 1894 was nearly 250 pages long.

These museums had always hoped to play an educational function, but by the first quarter of the twentieth century there had clearly been a shift in emphasis. The confident claims that museums would advance science had quieted. Consequently, these museums played a significant role in popularizing what were seen by professional anthropologists to be outdated ideas. What became regarded as the serious work of studying human culture was now taking place in university departments and was no longer available to ordinary people.

∼

10   The opening day crowds lining up to see the new Field Museum on May 2, 1921 did not seem to care that the anthropological collections were still housed in a museum of natural history. (Courtesy of The Field Museum, Neg. #44681, Chicago)

Science and art.

In 1933, Chicago's Field Museum made what were termed "radical changes" in its anthropological exhibits. Chief among these was the installation of nearly one hundred life-sized bronze busts depicting the world's different racial types. Executed by Malvina Hoffman, they captured much attention when they were unveiled in the museum's Hall of Races, and they remain on display today.[91] Unable to join together science and art, the Field Museum chose instead to replace science with art. The museum's new busts gave sculptural permanence and authority in 1933 to scientific ideas that had little currency in the scientific world. The space between science and art remained elusive ground for museums to fill.

11   The Philadelphia Commercial Museum was the largest—and indeed the only—
museum of its kind in the nation. It aimed to foster international commerce by putting
it on display. Here is an artist's conception, c. 1895, of how the building would look.
(Courtesy of the City Archives of Philadelphia)

FOUR

~

The Philadelphia Commercial Museum:
A Museum to Conquer the World

> The very name 'Commercial Museum' is a demand for recon-
> ciliation between two diametrically opposed ideas. What can
> a musty collection of specimens have to do with commerce?
>
> PAUL CHERINGTON

On May 3, 1897, Morris Jastrow, librarian of the University of Pennsylvania, wrote a breathless letter to the university's former provost, William Pepper. "I paid a visit to the Philadelphia Museum on Saturday," he reported, and continued: "It was my first . . . & I cannot resist the impulse to tell you what a revelation it all was to me. I had not the faintest conception of the gigantic scale on which this noble enterprise has been planned. I wandered through those rooms as in a dream." [1] The "Philadelphia Museum" that so entranced Jastrow would become better known as the Philadelphia Commercial Museum. Founded in 1893, the museum moved into its own building in 1897, and it received its official dedication in 1899. Although it was only four years old in 1897, it had already emerged as one of the fastest growing and most ambitious museums in the country. Eventually, the museum's complex would include several buildings, its own printing press, and countless exhibits. It proposed to facilitate American economic expansion overseas through spectacular exhibits and extensive publication of information. As the only such institution in the United States, the Commercial Museum gave Americans the opportunity to see the possibilities of a commercial empire given material form.

Yet while its exhibits dazzled visitors, the Commercial Museum served primarily two didactic purposes. From its inception, the Philadelphia Commercial Museum catered to the needs of American businesses as they tried to conquer foreign markets. Most especially through the international conferences sponsored by the museum, and through the publications produced by its Bureau of Information, the Commercial Museum provided American businessmen with advice and expertise as they expanded their enterprises around the globe. Its founder William P. Wilson described the museum's goal succinctly, if prosaically, in 1899: "The Philadelphia Commercial Museum is endeavoring to increase foreign trade of the United States . . . with every nation of the world."[2] The museum's exhibits, and its education extension work, tried to persuade Americans that such a commercial conquest was something devoutly to be wished.

Just as importantly, through the strategies of representation employed in the museum's exhibits, and additionally through the data produced by the Bureau of Information, the Commercial Museum tried to reassure Americans that commercial expansion could bring the benefits of imperialism without any of its attendant perils. Attempting, though not always successfully, to remain aloof from the rhetoric and political debate which swirled about American imperial designs, the Commercial Museum offered the practical and useful information which made commercial expansion possible. In this way, the founders of the Commercial Museum tried to design an intellectual framework for international commerce, one which would help give it systematic order and therefore scientific and social legitimacy.

The history of Philadelphia's Commercial Museum stands as an important, if largely forgotten, piece of a bigger narrative about American imperialism in the late nineteenth and early twentieth centuries. As Edward Crapol observed several years ago, the study of American imperialism and empire building during these years has languished in the last generation, the victim of increasingly sterile debates and "over-stated dichotomies." While some historians have demonstrated how analytical categories like gender can be usefully brought to bear on the question of American imperialism, Crapol's survey of the field led him to conclude that most practitioners remain suspicious of approaches that shift our attention away from the exercise of state power. Crapol ends his reconnaissance by endorsing the call of Warren Cohen, Phillip Darby, Michael Doyle, and others to pursue an "imperial history" that shifts our focus away from older topics and toward examining instead "the process of empire."[3]

To make such a shift means acknowledging that American imperialism in the years surrounding the turn of the twentieth century was not exclusively, or even most importantly, an episode in American foreign relations, presidential policy, or military history. Rather, "the process of empire" took place on a multiplicity of terrains—domestic and foreign, public and private. American imperialism has had, to borrow Amy Kaplan and Donald Pease's phrase, a variety of "cultures."[4]

Certainly part of the process of empire included the creation and control of knowledge about the rest of the world. Historians and theorists, most notably perhaps Michel Foucault, have explored the deep connections between discourses of knowledge and discourses of power. Recognizing these connections, it does not overstate the case to claim that the American empire, and the knowledge needed to develop that empire, were inextricably bound. C. A. Green understood as much, writing in 1897 that "one of the greatest obstacles in the development of trade with South American, African, Australian, and Eastern markets has been the lack of knowledge on the part of our manufacturers."[5] The significance of the Commercial Museum, then, lies in its attempt to design the intellectual architecture for an American commercial empire. By creating an epistemology of imperialism, the Commercial Museum stands as the most significant institutional manifestation of the cultural and intellectual apparatus that made American imperialism possible at the turn of the twentieth century.

To create an epistemology of imperialism the Commercial Museum relied first and foremost on objects. To do this, those who shaped the museum had to engage in two transpositions. The first insisted that the meaning inherent in objects of commerce, collected, arranged, and displayed by the museum, could substitute—indeed, even obviate the need—for the knowledge gained through experience. This transposition would level the playing field for Americans as they competed against European traders who could rely on the extensive colonial apparatus of their respective nations to provide them with on-site advantages Americans did not have. Once again, museum objects functioned metonymically—this time for the world's business, rather than its cultures or species. In fact, the Commercial Museum argued, because objects could substitute for experience, Americans could benefit from knowledge without being burdened by colonial responsibilities.

The second transposition involved the value of the objects themselves. The objects they put on display—raw materials, agricultural products, manufactured items, etc.—already had a real, utilitarian, economic value. The price of cotton or cocoa, after all, had real meaning in the world of commodities and markets. But by taking examples of these commodities out of economic circulation and putting them behind museum glass, the Commercial Museum stripped them of this value and reinvested them with a new value. Now these commodities, turned into museum objects, had an intellectual and educational value. No longer to be priced and traded, these objects were now to be examined and studied. The intended result of these dual transpositions for visitors to the Commercial Museum was an understanding of the world which placed commerce at the center of progressive civilization.

The dynamic growth of the Commercial Museum between 1893 and the First World War measures the successful institution building of the museum's founders and reminds us of Emily Rosenberg's observation that during these years, save for the "flurry of annexationist activity after the Spanish-American War, the most energetic expansionism [came] from private citizens." [6] That private activity took museum form spectacularly with the Commercial Museum. More metaphorically, however, the museum grew large enough to house the complex and often contradictory attitudes Americans had about overseas expansion. Alternately, often simultaneously wary and enthusiastic, bellicose and irenic, racist and humanitarian, the various positions in the debate over America's role in the world were embodied in the Commercial Museum and its ancillary activities. By investing commercial objects with the burden of these debates, however, the Commercial Museum tested the limits of an object-based epistemology. Ultimately the objects that carried this meaning could not bear the weight.

From World's Fair to Permanent Museum

The Philadelphia Commercial Museum had sprung from the mind of University of Pennsylvania botanist William Powell Wilson in 1893, who envisioned the institution during a visit to Chicago's Columbian Exposition. Wilson was unlike most visitors, who were simply dazzled or overwhelmed by Chicago's White City. Looking perhaps to put his scientific training to more practical use, Wilson saw at the fair a tremendous opportunity to create a permanent museum from the material collected for the temporary exhibition. [7] After negotiations with fair officials and with the governments of over forty countries, twenty-five railroad box-car loads of material arrived in Philadelphia to form the basis of the new institution.

Wilson, born in 1844 in Oxford, Michigan, was nearly fifty when he traveled to Chicago and had already achieved some success in the new world of academic science. From his boyhood home on the frontier, Wilson went East to attend Harvard College, graduating in 1878. After studying in Germany, where he received his doctorate in 1882, he became a member of the School of Biology at the University of Pennsylvania as professor of the anatomy and physiology of plants.[8] Academia, apparently, did not satisfy entirely. Wilson wanted to turn his academic talents to more current matters. A eulogist remarked: "Trained as a botanist, he was not satisfied with the botany of the period—the herbarium and the paraphernalia of species naming."[9] This mid-life career switch reminds us as well that even in the mid-1890s museums still held an intellectual legitimacy for those in the emerging academic world. Wilson's journey from the University of Pennsylvania to the Commercial Museum mirrors in its opposite the path taken by Franz Boas from the American Museum to Columbia University. Both careers underscore the competition for intellectual leadership going on at the time between universities and museums.

Wilson may have had personal motivations in creating the museum, but he was doubtless aware as well of current economic conditions in the United States. It is an irony of history that America's two most famous nineteenth-century celebrations of industrial progress—Philadelphia's 1876 Centennial, and Chicago's 1893 Columbian Exposition—took place during two of the nation's most desperate economic downturns. The prolonged depression which began in 1893 heightened the interest of Americans in foreign markets. According to an emerging consensus, foreign markets could provide the outlet for manufactured goods that were not consumed domestically.[10] Selling abroad, many Americans thought, would alleviate the economic problems brought on by overproduction. The drive to expand overseas manifested itself militarily when the United States fought a war with Spain at the end of the decade, but before any shots had been fired, Wilson's Commercial Museum had begun to lay the intellectual groundwork necessary for American commercial expansion.

Wilson also sensed intuitively the relationship between the world's fairs and American commercial expansion that historians like Rosenberg and Robert Rydell have subsequently demonstrated. According to

Rosenberg, Americans saw in Chicago "the cheap mass products, the dazzling technology, and the alluring mass culture" that they would endeavor to export around the world. Almost from its founding, the museum became the quasi-official repository of material from the many world's fairs which remain hallmarks of the age. As Robert Rydell has observed, the Commercial Museum became a "permanent world's fair," adding constantly to its collection from fairs in this country and abroad.[11] When the museum had its official inauguration in 1897, William Pepper told the assembled crowd: "Our Commercial Museum possesses the most extensive collections of natural products in existence in any country, and we have good grounds for expecting that these collections will be continually replenished and enlarged."[12] He was right.

Material from the fair in Liberia arrived in 1894; four-hundred tons of material came from the Central American Exposition in Guatemala in 1897, while Paris provided 500 tons for the museum in 1900. By 1900, the museum housed over 200,000 samples of foreign manufactured goods alone.[13] Such was the scale and scope of Wilson's undertaking that an English traveler, echoing Morris Jastrow's amazement, wrote less than ten years after its founding that the Commercial Museum "impressed me as much as anything I saw on the American Continent, not excepting the Falls of Niagara or the Congress Library."[14] By the turn of the century, Wilson had made the Philadelphia Commercial Museum the most significant institution in the country devoted to American imperial aspirations.

To create a "permanent world's fair" devoted to American commercial expansion seemed a contradiction to some. World's fairs by their very nature offered snapshots of the world at a particular moment. They opened with great fanfare, lasted perhaps a few months, and then closed.[15] To turn these snapshots into something permanent, to give them institutional form as a museum, presented a challenge for Wilson and his collaborators. What, after all, was a "commercial" museum?

To some, the concept of this museum seemed to defy the very notion of what a museum should be. Paul Cherington asked his readers: "The very name 'Commercial Museum' is a demand for reconciliation between two diametrically opposed ideas. What can a musty collection of specimens have to do with commerce?" What indeed? Oliver Farrington voiced deeper suspicions. Museums, he felt, should stay away entirely from "commercial and advertising features" as well as from objects having "great money value."[16] Cherington and Farrington clearly had not read the writings of George Brown Goode, who included commercial museums in his plan to create a museum complex comprehensive of the world's knowledge. But the two also missed a deeper, more popular connection between world's fairs and the world of things. These hugely popular events bound together commerce and the display of objects. As William Leach has observed, the most lasting influence of Philadelphia's Centennial Exposition was to unlock "the floodgates to what became a steady flow of goods and fantasies about goods." [17]

When the Commercial Museum built its own facility after several years in temporary quarters, Wilson began to answer some of these questions architecturally. He did so by returning to Chicago. Chicago's White City gave the Commercial Museum its architectural style. The Commercial Museum's main building came straight from the neo-classicism of the Columbian Exposition. Wilson undoubtedly chose this neo-classical style for the Commercial Museum to give added legitimacy to his museum enterprise. The facade of the museum presented orderliness and rationality while the interior displayed the products of commerce, a world increasingly frenetic and disorderly. Further, the design of the White City linked current notions of Western expansion, Anglo-Saxon supremacy, and a vaguely Roman, imperial past.[18] The architectural message sent to visitors was that Americans in the 1890s had inherited the glory that was Rome. By returning to Chicago for his architectural inspiration, Wilson tried to link commerce, empire, education, and display, an equation, after all, central to the 1893 World's Fair.

Challenging his doubters, Wilson believed that the objects on display in his institution could function like the objects in any museum. The Commercial Museum relied, as all late-nineteenth-century museums did, on an object-based epistemology which posited that objects, systematically arranged, could be studied by visitors to yield information. Wilson wrote to Edward Ayer of Chicago's Field Museum in 1894 summarizing this epistemology. "Museum material is worth nothing," Wilson told Ayer, "unless it is properly classified and scientifically described." He continued: "All Museum material should speak for itself upon sight. It should be an open book which tells a better story than any description will do. This it will do if properly arranged and classified." [19]

Further, Wilson explained to readers of *The Forum* how the Commercial Museum's collection could be used as the source of commercially useful knowledge: "By studying the character of these samples the manufacturer may also learn how the styles must be modified to suit the tastes of different peoples." [20] Wilson insisted that the museum could effectively encourage American commercial expansion overseas because the museum gave this endeavor a degree of intellectual order through the systematic presentation of the exhibits. Underneath this lay the assumption that commerce, like natural history or anthropology, could be understood through systematics and through objects that stood for those systems. The very objects of commerce thus stood not only as the products of commercial empire but as a source of knowledge used to construct that empire.

If Wilson insisted in his article that the Commercial Museum could function for overseas commerce in the same way that natural history museums functioned for science, then he also understood that the visual appeal of his exhibits was paramount. Wilson made it clear in *The Forum* that the museum would be of use to "the manufacturer" thanks to the elaborate and attractive exhibits he had created. By insisting, as he did repeatedly, on aesthetically pleasing exhibits, Wilson achieved two goals. First, the exhibits were designed to recapture the excitement of the world's fairs. Wilson wanted visitors to be awed when walking through the museum, and if the account of the English traveler quoted earlier gives any indication, he succeeded. Second, though, the elaborate displays announced that foreign trade constituted a serious, scientific body of knowledge. In a sense, Wilson's exhibits tried to persuade visitors, including perhaps businessmen themselves, that commerce was truly a noble enterprise, worthy of the kind of museum treatment that Wilson gave it.

The exhibit that greeted visitors as they entered the Commercial Museum taught a lesson. Walking through the Corinthian portico, a visitor to the Commercial Museum first saw an exhibit intended to "illustrate the history and development of commerce from the earliest beginnings to the present time." The core of this exhibit consisted of a collection of commercial products arranged "in the order of their entry into the world's demand." Along with these cases, the exhibit made the connection between commerce and civilization by including maps showing "the development and changes in trade routes and the concomitant rise and fall of the nations." Large photographs surrounded the cases of products and the maps. These photographs traced the evolution of transportation "from the most primitive type of human burden to the modern railway train, steamship, automobile, and airship." The exhibit was completed with a series of historical model boats. Because they were all constructed to scale, "the visitor can compare at a glance the relative size and capacity of the shipping of the Pharaohs, that of the Caesars and the Empires of the East, with the modern liners."[21] The les-

son here was not obscure or difficult to understand: civilization depended on commerce—the former could not exist without the latter.
Furthermore, the exhibit demonstrated that modern civilizations not
only succeeded but surpassed the achievements of the ancients.

A taxonomy of commerce, and ultimately of civilization, emerged
from the exhibits at the museum, developing systematically as Wilson
brought his training as a natural scientist to bear on these exhibits. From
lowest to highest, Wilson's specimens demonstrated that each development in commerce grew out of the one previous, and, as with natural
processes, each led in an orderly way to the next. Civilization, with
commerce as its engine, evolved ever forward. The frameworks around
which the Commercial Museum were organized put commerce at the
center of "progress." At the turn of the century all Americans, save for a
handful of intellectuals and cranks, believed in "progress."

Wilson's history lesson perfectly embodied Emily Rosenberg's observation that American internationalists—presuming without question
that the rest of the world was destined to follow the American model—
saw "no fundamental conflict between national advancement and global
progress."[22] At one level, late-nineteenth-century American museums all
exhibited progress—the evolutionary progress of species, the develop-
mental progress of cultures. The progress on display at these museums
culminated, one way or another, in Western humanity. But Wilson's museum made an even more persuasive case. It was quite specific that the
undeniable and quite tangible achievements of commerce lay at the root
of progress and of Western triumph.

To the untutored visitor, the world of commerce might be rough and
raw, but, the exhibit taught, it had a pedigree and lay at the center of all
things refined. Past, present, and future had been connected for visitors
as soon as they stepped inside the museum. Turn-of-the-century Americans might view overseas trade as a new endeavor, but Wilson's exhibit
demonstrated that it was as old as civilization itself.

Displaying the World's Commerce

History occupied center stage for visitors when they entered the museum, but the rest of the exhibits sought to order the rough and tumble
world of contemporary commerce and trade. The exhibits of objects
from around the world argued that all the world was a market, and all
the men and women merely traders. The museum took justifiable pride

in the extent of these collections. By 1909, Wilson could say confidently that "no such collection of African materials exists in any other museum in the world." From Asia, to South America, to Africa, in a few years, it seemed as if the museum had recreated the whole of the commercial world within its walls.

Looking at the exhibits from around the world, however, visitors to the museum saw them arranged in two ways. One part of this plan followed an approximately anthropological model, exhibiting the products of a particular region or produced by a particular people. The second part, following roughly a natural history model, grouped together products of similar type regardless of their origin. The first system followed geography, while the second put commercial products into something like a biological taxonomy.

Dr. Gustavo Niederlein, Wilson's assistant at the museum and a fellow botanist, explained this dual plan to the crowd gathered for the museum's official opening: "First, geographic displays, which show all the resources of each country by itself, and second, monographic displays which present for comparative study products of the same kind from nearly every country of the world."[23] Visitors would all have access to both collections, but we might presume that the general public would be entertained and informed primarily by the attractively arranged geographic exhibits, while businessmen would be interested more in the "monographic" exhibits. All visitors, though, were intended to learn that a commercial empire had two interrelated parts: such an empire could be located in specific places, or it could be achieved through specific products. In this way the dual classification and presentation of exhibits moved toward a scientific system for understanding international commerce. The geographic exhibits answered questions of "where" business could be conducted, while the monographic exhibits answered questions about "what" could be traded.

Paul Cherington challenged the Commercial Museum to reconcile the dynamism of commerce with the stasis of a museum. Wilson responded to that challenge by insisting that the objects be simultaneously as accessible and useful to people as possible and that the exhibits be visually exciting and engaging. Wilson understood that an object-based epistemology is an essentially visual, rather than a verbal, epistemology. He realized that his exhibits needed to have visual appeal in order to be educational, and he made it clear that the attractive presentation of the objects was a primary concern. "The installation and arrangement of the exhibits," he wrote in 1909, "have been done with an eye single to the best results from the standpoint of the observer. Many of the groups can find their counterparts nowhere else."[24] In expressing this concern, Wilson was no different from any other museum curator who fretted over proper systematic arrangement of objects. In trying to understand the world through objects, all museums recognized the crucial importance of presenting those objects to maximum effect. Wilson may have felt this more urgently because he put objects on display that might not have the same intrinsic appeal as dinosaur bones or Egyptian mummies. His concern, therefore, over how best to display his objects was nothing less than a concern over whether the Commercial Museum would prove successful. Like the world's fairs from which they sprang, the Commercial Museum's exhibits tried to turn the didactic into something exciting.

Wilson's promise to foster trade with every corner of the globe, however, reveals an apparent tension inherent in the museum's understanding of the world. Commerce and civilization were inextricably linked; the historical exhibit at the entrance made that clear. Yet how would the museum display objects from countries that lacked extensive commercial activity—societies that were by Wilson's very definition therefore "semi-civilized"? These people, after all, lay at the center of most European and American colonial ambitions. Wilson, for his part, saw no such contradiction, and he seemed particularly proud of the displays he created representing the "semi-civilized peoples": "No small degree of artistic taste has entered into the scheme of display. The daily life of the people, their peculiar habits, their dress, cooking, agricultural and manufacturing implements, are arranged in classified array and are most attractive to the visitor apart from what he can learn touching economics."[25] This description, and the attention it reveals to the presentation of this material, suggests how Wilson resolved the tension inherent in the museum's understanding of the world. He recognized that his museum needed to broaden its scope beyond commercial products to include more general information about the "primitive" groups with which Americans hoped to do business. In addition to "large collections of products of every kind," Wilson noted that the museum also displayed "much in ethnology." Taken together, these two kinds of exhibits illustrated "the habits, customs and life of the people and what they produce."[26] While other museums struggled to define anthropology, the Commercial Museum invented its own version of anthropology in which objects were not important because they yielded their ethnological secrets to the careful observer but rather because they might reveal information about commercial possibilities.

Presumably, American businessmen were not familiar with some of the "remote" parts of the world, and Wilson sensed that some people would need to be convinced that trade could be conducted with these "semi-civilized" peoples. He did this through the design of his exhibits, which titillated on one level by emphasizing the different and the exotic, but which reassured on another level by stressing the familiar—cooking and farming, for example. Wilson represented other cultures as different, yet ultimately accessible. These people might not be "civilized," but for the purposes of American businessmen they too could be regarded as producers and consumers.

Unlike the exhibits of non-Western people in anthropology museums, which stressed cultural attributes like religion within the framework of cultural development, these exhibits specifically highlighted the kinds of goods that might be bought from or sold to these people. A textile manufacturer or an agricultural broker could study these exhibits to get ideas about trading possibilities. By combining economic information with "much in ethnology," the Commercial Museum acted as the experienced field guide to intrepid American businessmen as they ventured into exotic and unknown corners of the world.[27]

The material from faraway lands represented for visitors less an intrinsic view of those exotic cultures than it did the dynamic between Western business and those cultures. The unequaled African collection did include products manufactured by Africans, including a "remarkable exhibit of textile art from savage hands,"[28] but it seems to have been primarily a collection of European products then being sold to Africans.[29] This exhibit did not promote an understanding of African culture for its own sake, or in an anthropological sense. Rather it promoted a strategy of understanding of African culture which would permit Americans to undersell it.

Wilson singled out the Madagascar display to describe in a 1909 booklet. Like the exhibit from the African continent, the collection from this island demonstrated what Americans might hope to sell to the natives. Wilson wrote: "The Madagascar exhibit is of exceptional quality. The textiles of this collection are of native make, and in many instances impossible to duplicate, since they have been gradually disappearing for a number of years and their place has been taken by the cheaper fabrics of foreign make."[30] Wilson put textiles of indigenous make next to those made in Europe and sold in Madagascar. In making this comparison, Wilson confidently communicated to his readers that "American manufacturers should have no difficulty in competing with Europe by supplying the Malagasy with textiles, provided the proper effort be made to give them just what they want." Wilson reminded his readers that the "Europeans are particularly successful in conforming their own ideas to the tastes of semi-civilized people and even the barbaric races." [31] Americans, by implication, would enjoy similar success if they, too, learned what it was Malagasy customers wanted.

Whether he understood it or not, Wilson had created something quite dynamic indeed with his Madagascar exhibit. His description of it reveals how the cultural process underlying imperial expansion could be put on display. When they saw fabrics originally made by Madagascans next to the European imitations that had replaced them, the objects bore witness, whether visitors understood it or not, to how cultures in foreign lands were disrupted by the arrival of European commerce. There was no indication in the exhibit, of course, of what happened to the native textile production; a complex process of cultural contact and interaction has been reduced to the shifting of market forces represented by the artifacts left over. Like all good salesmen, European merchants have simply given the island residents what they wanted. On the stage of Wilson's global commerce, all the world became a market, and all its peoples merely buyers and sellers.

~

Within ten years of its founding, the Commercial Museum, and its system of understanding and displaying the world of commerce, had catapulted to international prominence. In 1901, Richard Foley reported that Germany's Minister of Commerce, when considering "the best method of securing a knowledge of foreign conditions, said that the ideal plan would be the establishment of a national commercial museum." The minister, according to Foley, "pointed to the Philadelphia institution as a model." [32] By 1914, Wilson could write confidently that, in addition to being the only museum of its kind in the United States, "several foreign countries have made a very careful examination of the Commercial Museum in all its activities and have established commercial museums on a somewhat similar plan, notably Japan, Mexico, Brazil and others." [33] In creating a permanent world's fair whose useful lessons would not evaporate, Wilson had constructed an epistemology of commercial expansion and put it on display.

12   Central to the Commercial Museum's mission was the production of information through the Bureau of Information. Here the staff of the Translation Bureau help American businessmen negotiate language barriers with their overseas partners. (Courtesy of the City Archives of Philadelphia)

Collecting and Producing: The Bureau of Information

The Commercial Museum made order and sense out of a chaotic world by creating the intellectual frameworks through which to conceptualize commercial expansion, and it thus served as a bridge between that world and American commercial ambition. For visitors, this vital information came through the two-part arrangement of the museum's exhibits. But Wilson understood the inherent limitations of conveying information through objects: for those unable to make the trip to Philadelphia, the museum would be of little use. For them commercial knowledge would come in the form of quantitative and written data, not through object lessons. From the outset, therefore, Wilson intended his museum to produce two different kinds of knowledge.

Central to the museum's function, and to its mission as a whole, was its Bureau of Information. By including the Bureau of Information in his plans for the museum, Wilson believed that two kinds of knowledge—one based on objects, the other on more abstract data—could complement each other. He designed his institution to provide both. Pursuing an aggressive collecting policy, and combining it with an equally aggressive bureau to collect and produce information, the Commercial Museum could provide businessmen and the general public with the most thorough commercial education. It would be no musty institution.

The bureau's work had a tri-partite division: a publication service, an information service, and a translation service. The latter provided American businessmen with translations both to and from foreign languages, while the information service responded to individual requests of all kinds from subscribing members. The bureau's publications, however, became the vehicle through which commercial information was most widely disseminated. To promote the bureau's services, the museum published a pamphlet entitled *How a Commercial Museum Report May Aid an Exporting Manufacturer,* which listed several specific examples of how member businesses had saved time and money, and achieved commercial success, because they utilized bureau reports.

The bureau tried to function encyclopedically, collecting information with the same thoroughness that the museum collected and displayed specimens. It assembled "all Consular Reports, Statistical publications, publications on Commerce, Navigation and Surveys, with maps and official journals from all the different Governments, which show the possibilities of increased commercial relations."[34] Indexed, and collated with information culled from the "five hundred current journals on Trade, Commerce and Finance from all the countries of the world, which are regularly received and are open to consultation in the Reading Room," and from "the information secured from private agents in Australia, South Africa, South and Central America and Mexico, together with the replies to our Information Blanks which the State Department distributes for us," these data were sent monthly to subscribing businessmen. The museum charged no fee for this service, but asked that manufacturers pay for the expense of copying, compiling, and postage.

Just as the museum's objects functioned as metonyms for colonial possessions the Europeans had but Americans did not, so too the bureau's publications would help American businesses close the gap in the race for global commercial expansion. Without the elaborate, government-sponsored colonial apparatus which made entrée for European businesses easier, American businesses would have to rely on knowledge instead. Knowledge, assembled and produced by the Bureau of Information, would make up for the first-hand experience in foreign countries that Americans did not have. Touting his bureau, Wilson wrote: "It has served to give the business men of America an unusual opportunity to acquire, in a very short time, a great deal of information concerning the markets of the world; placing them in a position to compete successfully with those who, in the matter of experiences, have had an enormous advantage."[35] Because it substituted for the on-site but often costly and difficult colonial experience of the Europeans, Wilson believed that information compiled and ordered by his bureau had the advantage of being easier and faster to manage: knowledge could more quickly and effectively achieve for Americans what colonial possessions had, at greater expense, for the Europeans.

Wilson joined the Bureau of Information and the systematic, methodical way in which it collected information with the museum's visual displays to develop a natural science of commercial expansion. In Wilson's conception, the Commercial Museum would collect both artifacts and data; for Wilson, one kind of knowledge supplemented the other. In this way the museum could provide "object" lessons to people able to visit in person. Those unable to do so, or those who required different information, could get what they needed from the Bureau of Information. This new "discipline" drew from anthropology, which helped shape the way Americans saw foreign cultures, and from economics, which was becoming increasingly reliant on quantitative analysis to turn the messy world of business into neat charts and graphs. Information, scientifically collected and widely distributed, could provide for Americans what years of colonial involvement provided for the Europeans. In this way, American businesses could compete in a world colonized by Europeans, without becoming colonialists themselves.

The bureau's pamphlets often focused on a particular country and provided information, statistical and anecdotal, to help Americans increase trade with that nation. The museum published guides to trade with Siam, India, and Australia, for example.[36] Each was written by someone who had lived or done business in that country. "The best way to introduce American goods successfully into the Indian market," an 1898 bureau publication asserted, "would, of course, be by means of traveling salesman thoroughly versed in their work," while Colonel Bell, author of the commercial field guide to Australia, told those interested in trading with Australia that "it is better do business through well established commission houses." Though they might differ in specifics, all these publications asserted the need to collect information about the countries American businessmen hoped to conquer commercially, and they consistently emphasized that boundless opportunities existed in foreign markets for American businessmen, provided they armed themselves with the right kind of knowledge.

In addition, the information these reports provided often stressed cultural considerations, the "tricks" of a particular place, as Colonel Bell put it. Like the new generation of anthropologists who gathered information about kinship systems and religious rituals, the Commercial Museum wanted to teach Americans a different kind of ethnological knowledge, offering data on exotic forms of banking and credit. No less than the anthropologists then, Wilson ground an intellectual lens through which Americans could view the world. Visitors to the museum learned that other cultures could be understood, both in their similarities and differences, through their commerce.

The information on display in the museum galleries and that provided by the bureau's publications differed in a final aspect. The museum displays captured the excitement of the world's fairs that were at the root of the institution, but they concentrated on information that did not change quickly or regularly. The natural products of a particular region, and the habits of the people living there, were seen in museum exhibits to exist in a kind of stasis. Like the specimens at a natural history museum, these exhibits displayed objects as timeless, and the relationships between them as more or less fixed. The information produced by the bureau, however, was more ephemeral. As a result the bureau worked hard to make sure its charts were always current, and that its tables and pamphlets were updated as often as possible. The two kinds of knowledge were organized for the museum's public in different ways, but they complemented each other.

Yet what Wilson saw as the complementary nature of these two kinds of knowledge would ultimately prove conflicting. Wilson might have believed that commercial knowledge could reside in objects, like knowledge about the natural world, but his own Bureau of Information would demonstrate the difficulties of an object-based epistemology for commerce. Knowledge of the kind produced by the Bureau of Information would supersede knowledge produced by objects, and finally render the "museum" function of the Commercial Museum obsolete.

Finding the Road to Empire: The Commercial Museum's International Conferences

In 1899, William P. Wilson published a booklet entitled *The World's Commerce and the United States' Share of It.* In it, Wilson looked back to the Centennial Exposition, suggesting that that event "gave an impetus to our foreign trade by bringing to the notice of foreign visitors the character of our products." Since the Centennial, Wilson complained, the effort of American businesses overseas had been passive and anemic, merely following what he called "the line of least resistance." [37] That choice of phrasing seems curious. Wilson began his pamphlet with an historical allusion to 1876, but he chose not to refer to a more recent and momentous event. The publication date of *The World's Commerce* has obvious significance, even if it went unacknowledged by Wilson. A year earlier the United States had begun to take its share of the world's colonies, along with its share of the world's commerce, grabbing, as it were, with both hands.

Though Teddy Roosevelt's Rough Riders would take offense that their charge up San Juan Hill constituted the "line of least resistance," Wilson's use of the phrase, and indeed the tone of the whole pamphlet implicitly suggested that foreign commerce should be pursued with even more aggressiveness. But Wilson's decision not to make mention of the Spanish-American War admitted the contradictory—indeed, often hypocritical—attitudes Wilson and others manifested concerning American expansion. In a sense Wilson avoided the major question confronting Americans in 1899: could commercial expansion occur without military campaigns? could a commercial empire grow without a colonial empire?

By the turn of the century, as Lester Langley has pointed out, Americans had developed an exceptional definition of empire to "distinguish what the United States was doing . . . from what Europeans had implanted in their empires." [38] Economic exploitation, not territorial colonization, set the United States apart from the other Western powers, and this vision was shaped in part at the Commercial Museum. Wrestling with questions of domestic politics and drawing comparisons with European empires, those associated with the museum tried to navigate and to shape the evolving debate on American imperialism. The vision of American expansion sketched at the museum continued to cast commercial expansion and prosperity in the role of world civilizer and peacemaker despite events in Cuba and the Philippines. Unlike the European empires, which relied on military coercion, the Commercial Museum still insisted on an American empire where conquest came through peaceful commerce.

At virtually the same moment that the American troops went abroad to fight the Spanish, representatives from governments around the world came to Philadelphia. The Commercial Museum sponsored two international trade conferences which became forums to discuss how America could best define a road to commercial empire while avoiding the pitfalls of European-style colonialism. Once in 1897, and again in 1899, the Commercial Museum played host to governmental and extra-governmental representatives from around the world who met to discuss international commerce. The museum's essential ideas about how the United States should conduct its affairs overseas can be measured by examining these two conferences. Bracketing the Spanish-American War, the two conferences had similar agendas and came to similar conclusions. The inescapable alteration of the geopolitical situation seems to have had little impact on the discussions at the 1899 congress. That the events of imperialist war and annexation did not significantly alter the tenor and tone of the 1899 conference reminds us that the war itself may not have changed the "process of empire" as much historians have claimed. Before any shots had been fired in Cuba or Manila, Wilson's Commercial Museum had begun to lay the intellectual groundwork necessary for American commercial expansion. The war did not significantly shake those foundations.

In June 1897, President William McKinley traveled from Washington to Philadelphia to preside over the first four-day meeting of the Commercial Museum's International Advisory Board. His presence in Philadelphia underscored the significance both of the event and of the institution that sponsored it. The conference served as the museum's official inaugural, and on June 2, McKinley addressed the assembled delegates. In his speech he echoed the theme of progress so central to the museum's conception. Further, he reiterated the idea that the application of scientific methods could rationalize and systematize business: "The Museum is inaugurated on broad and progressive lines; its authors and promoters mean that the conditions for international commerce shall be directly promoted by systematic study, and demonstrated by scientific methods." [39] Speaking while the country still suffered the effects of its most recent economic depression, McKinley hoped that economic cycles could be scientifically tamed.

In his speech, William Pepper the medical scientist, who also spoke on the opening day of the conference, helped McKinley construct a rhetorical distinction between science and politics. The Commercial Museum was a scientific institution, Pepper pronounced, and as such "whatever may be the appropriations made by governments . . . it is essential to the scientific efficiency of the institution that it be wholly free from political influences."[40] McKinley and Pepper, speaking at a moment when political debate over American foreign policy swirled, perhaps protested too much. They might have believed that the science of commerce practiced at the Commercial Museum would resolve rancorous political debates, but they were quite confident what that resolution would be. Science would certainly determine the most efficient way to bring home America's share of the world's commerce.

Applaud though they might, delegates to the conference begged to differ with McKinley and Pepper and quickly began to raise issues of politics and policy. Indeed, several foreign representatives saw the application of science to commerce as precisely a way to achieve political ends. Both Cordeiro da Graca, representing the Society of Engineers of Rio de Janeiro, and Everardo Hegewisch, from the Mexican Chamber of Commerce, compared the American commercial expansion with European colonial domination and agreed that the American approach would be more successful. Da Graca told the delegates: "What I came here to admire to-day . . . is the very great conquest which you have made on this occasion. While Europe is armed to the teeth spending millions, sending soldiers to Africa, and all this only to acquire new colonies, this great country, in a way which makes civilization creditable, makes the same conquest by promoting peace, receiving us here as guests, rendering the interchange of commerce of real and practical value by means of friendship."[41] Da Graca, much like his host Wilson, linked commerce, civilization, and conquest in the same breath. But, as a representative from a foreign country, he also suggested a qualitative difference between European military aggression and American commercial expansion. Underscoring a familiar theme, da Graca connected trade and civilization, and set these in opposition to conquering armies. In da Graca's view, commerce led to conquest, but of a different sort.

Everardo Hegewisch concurred with da Graca that American commercial conquest would lead to peace and prosperity, while European military adventurism would not. "It is really gratifying," he told delegates, "to consider that, while in the Old Continent the greater part of the intellectual and material efforts of the official circles, as well as of those of private character, are wasted on war-studies and the discovery of machines to destroy human life, a group of men of all the American nations meets here to deliberate on the best methods of increasing the wealth of their respective countries by means of commercial relations." [42] Hegewisch drew a hemispheric distinction between the Old and New Worlds. The Old seemed bent on destroying itself, while the New looked toward a cooperative future. But unlike either American isolationists or American imperialists, Hegewisch, da Graca, and other delegates at the Commercial Museum's 1897 meeting envisioned a way for America to be involved actively in world affairs without becoming a military or colonial power. American commercial conquest of the world would lead to world peace.

The museum had its official dedication in 1897, but the 1899 groundbreaking for its new facilities in West Philadelphia provided another excuse for the Commercial Museum to hold an international event. The first International Commercial Congress convened in October and ran during the National Export Exposition, which was also being held in West Philadelphia through that fall. The Exposition proved as eventful as a world's fair. During the nearly three months it was open, from September 14 until December 2, the exposition attracted over 1,250,000 visitors.

The congress, held in conjunction with the exposition, was an equally impressive event. Over thirty foreign governments, including China, Japan, Romania and Russia, sent official representatives. In addition, dozens of trade organizations also sent delegates, including the Chamber of Commerce at Aden (Arabia) and the Business Interests of Teheran. The hundreds of official delegates were greeted by a crowd of 3,000 audience members when the Congress opened on October 12. Over the course of the next seventeen days, participants heard one hundred fifty papers ranging from assessments of the parcel post system to calls for universal standards in trade statistics reporting. It would prove to be, as the *New York Times* reported in anticipation, "the most notable gathering ever held for the discussion of trade and commerce." [43]

While the congress functioned to bring businessmen together from around the world to discuss trade issues, it also served notice that the United States had now emerged as an international commercial power. Wilson wrote in the publicity brochure: "It is particularly fitting that this, the first international commercial conference in the world's history, is to be held in the United States of America, which, having won for itself a dominant position in the world's industry, is beginning to claim a similar position in the world's commerce." [44] It was equally fitting that this congress took place at the Commercial Museum. As the most significant institution in the country dedicated to developing foreign markets and international trade, the Commercial Museum had brought objects, information, and now, on two occasions, representatives from countries around the world to the United States.

Between the two conferences, circumstances in the world had changed dramatically. The United States, under President McKinley's leadership, had taken its first steps toward precisely the same kind of empire the Europeans had built. This inescapable alteration of the geopolitical situation, however, seems to have had little impact on the tone and tenor of the discussions at the 1899 congress. Commerce and civilization, economic prosperity and world peace, still went hand-in-hand at the International Commercial Congress, despite, or perhaps because of, the Spanish-American War. Certainly the Philippines came up for discussion numerous times, both formally and informally, and sometimes controversially. Delegates, including some of the Chinese participants, debated whether the Chinese Exclusion Act ought now to be applied to the Philippines. (The consensus seems to have been no, because to do so would disrupt existing businesses too much.) But the absence of any real discussion of, much less debate about, Cuba or the Philippines simply demonstrates that the scientific frameworks for commerce that the Commercial Museum hoped to develop could bend and expand to include colonial acquisition. Moreover, the proceedings of the congress demonstrated how "scientific" discussions of commerce easily masked political agendas. The message of both conferences remained clear: scientifically organized commerce would create an American expansionism different from European colonialism. A year after the United States Navy steamed into Manila harbor, commerce, in the eyes of participants both American and foreign, remained the bearer of peace, thousands of dead Filipinos notwithstanding.

Those associated with the Commercial Museum may have seen a sharp distinction between their own global ambitions and those of the Europeans, but the collecting plan of the museum underscored what Amy Kaplan has called "the unacknowledged interdependence" between the United States and European colonialism.[45] This complex and complicated relationship between American and European colonialism meant that while Americans might eschew European-style colonialism, they certainly would take advantage of the groundwork laid by the European powers.

During 1894 and 1895, Wilson's assistant Gustavo Niederlein traveled throughout Europe to make contacts and to collect. His reports back to the museum's board indicate that Neiderlien paid particular attention to establishing connections between the Commercial Museum and European colonies. He reported to the board: "On my way to Europe I landed in Southampton and went immediately to London and directly to the South Kensington Museums and the Imperial Institute, the new museum of the English Colonies." In November 1894 he visited the French Colonial Museum in Paris and arranged with its director M. Bilbaut to get "specimens from the complete collections from all the French dependencies." He made a similar deal with a Dutch importing house for "products of the Congo Free States."[46] When Niederlein made his collecting trip to Europe, the United States did not yet have any colonial possessions of its own. But Neiderlien's work ensured that the museum would be filled with objects from European colonies. Through the work of the museum, American businessmen would enjoy the economic advantages of colonialism without worrying about the complications of colonial governing.

The Commercial Museum, through its exhibits and the international conferences it sponsored, remained unwaveringly committed to the fundamental assumption that commerce would lead to peace and civilization, even if on terms dictated, if need be, by military power. Wilson articulated this assumption perhaps most emphatically in a speech he delivered at the Pan American Exposition in Buffalo in 1901. The speech, entitled "Commerce as a Conservator of Peace," began with a predictable refrain: "While it will be found that the present tendency of commerce is undoubtedly toward the maintenance of friendly relations among the nations of the world, this result has only been reached by a process of evolution, in which the progress of civilization has brought with it conditions very different from those which obtained centuries ago."[47] Wilson then proceeded with a history lesson, reminding his audience of the historic connection between civilization and commerce: "A curious circumstance in connection with the fall of Rome was the fact that the tribes which were eventually her undoing were those with which she had developed practically no commerce. With all the rest of the world, her trade relations were intimate, and with all the rest of the world, peace prevailed." The fall of Rome, resulting from her poor commercial policies, led to the European dark ages. Wilson summarized these years by saying: "For nearly five centuries commerce lay dormant, and warfare was the chief occupation of man." Wilson's equation of commerce and peace also permitted him to explain the American Revolution to his audience: "Whatever political questions may have been the immediate cause of the War for Independence, the primary reasons were commercial. . . . The right to make the most of the resources with which nature had provided them, to sell in such markets as they pleased, and to buy in their own way, was the underlying reason for their rebellion." Ultimately, in Wilson's view, history taught that wars resulted from political conflict and that "the influence of commerce on the whole, has been steadily in the direction of peace and prosperity, until to-day it has become the one great factor in the prevention of war." Speaking to an audience doubtless aware of the "balance of power" between nations, Wilson said that his Commercial Museum created a comprehensive classification of resources and "an accurate estimate of the lines along which particular nations may best promote their commercial and industrial activity." As a result, Wilson concluded, "a trade balance has been struck, so to speak."[48] By promoting commercial conquest rather than military conquest, the Commercial Museum hoped to steer the United States on a road between isolationism on one side and European-style colonialism on the other. Following the path Wilson tried to lay out with his museum, Americans could enjoy all the material prosperity associated with colonialism and bring about world harmony at the same time.

The equation made over and over by Wilson at the museum was quite straightforward. Commerce formed the foundation of civilization. Civilization, with commerce as its driving force, linked peoples and nations together in a tight web of mutual dependence. With the modern Western world leading the way, civilization was evolving beyond the need for warfare. Commerce, therefore, was the essential requisite for world peace. This vision enabled Americans to pursue business activities without military adventurism, because military expansion would ultimately prove less fruitful. The Commercial Museum's energy was dedicated to the proposition that America could peacefully conquer the world by conquering the world's markets. Contradictory, perhaps incoherent, even hypocritical though it might have been, this was the path to commercial empire traced by the Commercial Museum.

Education and Empire: The Philippines

Although the museum was a popular Philadelphia destination both for locals and for tourists, it undoubtedly reached its largest public audience, fittingly enough, through its participation in world's fairs. The museum had drawn its inspiration, and much of its initial collection, from Chicago's White City. Its collections had been enriched from several sub-

13   The living fruits of empire. William Wilson was responsible for overseeing the Philippine exhibits at the 1904 Louisiana Purchase Exposition in St. Louis, including the "reservation" of Filipinos shown performing here. (Courtesy of the City Archives of Philadelphia)

sequent fairs.[49] Designed to be a permanent world's fair, the museum also reciprocated and contributed to these fairs as well. The most important of these opportunities came in 1904 in St. Louis, when Americans celebrated the centennial of the Louisiana Purchase.[50]

St. Louis played host to the most significant fair since Chicago's Columbian Exposition of 1893. Indeed, the 1904 Louisiana Purchase Exposition, itself a centennial celebration of American expansion, was designed to outdo Chicago's 1893 fair. The White City commemorated America's "discovery" by Europeans, but by 1904 empire, rather than discovery, was much on the mind of many Americans. The commemorative book published by Pennsylvania's Commission to the fair, to cite one example, was entitled *Pennsylvania: The Building of an Empire.*[51]

The Louisiana Purchase Exposition marked the anniversary of America's expansion into the trans-Mississippi West. Set against the background of the recently concluded war with Spain, the St. Louis event therefore became doubly a celebration of American expansionism. More pointedly, the St. Louis fair enthusiastically made the case for empire within a racial framework of Anglo-Saxon supremacy. As Robert Rydell has described it, the fair in St. Louis resulted from the "overarching effort by local and national elites to issue a manifesto of racial and material progress and national harmony . . . the Louisiana Purchase Exposition gave a utopian dimension to American imperialism."[52] Wilson, as one of the chief organizers of the exposition, helped provide a blueprint for that utopia.

At the Louisiana Purchase Exposition, Americans got their first chance to inspect the fruits of their imperial conquest, and Wilson had been put in charge of organizing the Philippine display. He had taken a leave of absence from the museum in 1903, at the request of Philippine governor William Howard Taft, to prepare the St. Louis exhibit.[53] While Wilson wanted to demonstrate the commercial possibilities for American business all over the globe, after 1898 the Philippines occupied a special place in the American imagination and, consequently, a special place among the nations Wilson put on display. In many ways, educating Americans about the Philippines became Wilson's most significant assignment in the early years of the twentieth century. In his speeches Wilson might remain committed to a peaceful conception of commercial expansion, but his work at the St. Louis Exposition demonstrated how seamlessly genuine imperialism could be incorporated into that conception.

His selection to take charge of the Philippine display in St. Louis surely resulted from his cordial relationship with members of the Republican administration, but it also reflects the prevailing assumption that empire for the Americans remained a commercial venture. Wilson had done more than any other American to display the possibilities of foreign commerce to an American audience, so who better to present the possibilities of the Philippines to the millions who came to St. Louis? His work did not disappoint. Corresponding with Taft throughout 1903, Wilson wrote to him describing the progress of the Philippine exhibit: "On the whole we are going to have a magnificent exhibit, and it will be ten times the largest single exhibit anywhere in the Fair."[54]

In designing the Philippine exhibit, Wilson tried to defuse the racial anxiety that characterized some of the American opposition to empire. Both sides of the debate over American imperialism shared essentially the same views about Anglo-Saxon supremacy. For some, like former Secretary of State Richard Olney, that view led to aggressive posturing. Speaking at the museum's 1897 dedication he bellowed: "The Anglo-Saxon in America has lost none of the qualities which for centuries made the race predominant in the history of the world's trade and commerce. . . . He wants to conduct his foreign trade in American bottoms under the American flag."[55] For those like Olney, the equation between racial supremacy and national destiny was easy and obvious. For others, racialist ideas led in the direction of isolationism. Andrew Carnegie articulated this point of view emphatically: "The Philippines have about seven and a half millions of people, composed of races bitterly hostile to one another, alien races, ignorant of our language and institutions. Americans cannot be grown there."[56]

Wilson's task, then, was to present the Philippines in such a way as to answer the objections of both groups. In addition to objects, Wilson brought over 1,200 Filipinos to St. Louis and displayed them on a "reservation." These living objects, according to Rydell, were the most popular exhibit at the fair.[57] Wilson's exhibit made it clear for fair visitors that the United States now controlled the resources, the markets, and even the inhabitants of the Philippines. The Philippine exhibit, like all museum displays from this era, purported to function as a synecdoche. Objects, including in this case people themselves, stood for the totality of the islands. All Americans needed to understand about the Philippines could be gleaned from the exhibits assembled by Wilson. In this synecdochic way, the Philippines had been conquered again. Visitors to the St. Louis fair could see through Wilson's exhibit, that the whole of the Philippines, in every sense, had been tamed. The 1904 world's fair in St. Louis, quite literally, brought empire home. Perhaps not surprisingly, the election of that same year "marked the last time in which anti-imperialism would be a really active and vital force on a broad national scale."[58]

Americans may have felt ambivalent about assuming control over an "alien race," but the prospects of commercial expansion into Asia excited almost everyone. Using an almost grotesque metaphor, suited to the excess of the Gilded Age, Frank Carpenter described prospects in the Philippines for readers of the *Saturday Evening Post:* "Within a year conditions should have become settled, and then the big, fat oyster of the Philippines will be ready for any one who is big enough and brave enough to attempt to open it."[59] Theodore Noyes, writing for the *Washington Evening Star,* saw Manila as America's "Oriental Capital," from which American businessmen could stage their drive into the Chinese market. Already, Noyes told his readers, "the beginnings of a wonderful trade with this people have been made." He described this trade in a way familiar to anyone who had seen the Commercial Museum's exhibits from Africa: "They are fast learning, for instance, to use our flour and our cotton goods. Southern cotton and western wheat, after passing through American mills, find here entrance to an unlimited market." [60]

Americans might debate between "expansionism" and "imperialism," but the debate really turned on a question of degree. Some Americans might be reluctant to annex territory and peoples, but by the late 1890s most agreed that America's economic future lay overseas. As Walter LaFeber has written, the imperialist versus anti-imperialist struggle can best be viewed as "a narrow and limited debate on the question of which tactical means the nation should use to obtain commonly desired objectives." [61] Wilson and his museum embodied both sides of this narrow debate. The epistemology of expansion developed and displayed at the museum put commerce at the center of progressive civilization. The museum tried to demonstrate that commerce could flourish without empire. In the face of the kind of military conquest he thought unnecessary for American commercial expansion, Wilson simultaneously tried to show Americans that they could comfortably be colonialists while reminding them that commerce, not imperial acquisition, should be the nation's primary objective.

After the Louisiana Purchase Exposition closed, many objects came back with Wilson to Philadelphia. The Philippine material, though, was the prize. Wilson wrote in the museum's 1905 Annual Report: "The Philippine collection is a great museum of itself, illustrating the entire range of ethnology, industry, commerce, production and transportation in those islands." [62] In addition to the initial collection, the museum received occasional loans from the Philippines, as in 1913 when "a large exhibit of industrial work from the Philippine schools was loaned to the museum for a short time by the Philippine Bureau of Education." [63] In 1909, Wilson described what visitors to the museum could see from the Philippines: "Rice, sugar, piña, tobacco, bamboo, tropical cabinet woods, ores, coal, and other natural products are shown in great variety as well as life-sized figures of civilized and savage people, clothing, tools, weapons, musical instruments, pottery, baskets, houses and a variety of other exhibits which illustrate the people of the Philippines." [64] This collection from the Philippines was a microcosm of the larger efforts of the museum. In the exhibit, Wilson combined raw materials, finished goods, and items illustrating the ethnology of both "civilized" and "savage" people. Wilson clearly believed in the differences between "civilized" people and "savages," defined again as those who engaged in commerce and those who did not. Unlike some who insisted that Filipino savages would never be compatible with Americans, his exhibit demonstrated that there were both kinds in the Philippines, and, moreover, it underscored that savages could be civilized through participation in commerce. With the Philippine exhibit, Wilson tried to demonstrate not simply that American business could profit from the islands but that, through commerce, American business could play the role of civilizer to people desperately in the need of it. Wilson thus reasserted, through this exhibit, the museum's central intellectual assumption. By making such a point of including exhibits to illustrate the people of the islands, along with their commercial and natural products, Wilson wanted to help Americans grow more comfortable with their new colonial charges and with their new role in the world.

The Sun Sets on the Commercial Museum

At the conclusion of the First World War, the Commercial Museum could look back on twenty-five years of extraordinary activity. Wilson had created a wonder of the American continent, and the future seemed just as promising. After the First World War, the museum became even more ambitious in the extension of its educational usefulness through the establishment of satellite museums. The *Annual Report* for the years 1918–20 announced: "Another new project is being slowly developed which should prove to be of great benefit to the schools of Pennsylvania. This is the establishment of branch museums in many cities and towns."[65] Yet in writing this report, Wilson either did not acknowledge or did not recognize that the Commercial Museum's role had shifted, and its place as the primary institutional proponent of commerce had been usurped. As quickly as Wilson's museum had grown and flourished, by the end of World War I the Commercial Museum had already enjoyed it greatest triumphs.

The Great War did not have the devastating impact on the United States that it did on Europe, but the European cataclysm did have significant, if indirect, effects over here. Several of those would have profound meaning for the Commercial Museum. Still committed to the notion that commerce created peace, the museum sent delegates to the Conference of the League to Enforce Peace in 1916, a year before the United States officially entered the conflict. With the declaration of war in 1917, however, the Commercial Museum resolutely did its part. That year the University of Pennsylvania established a branch of the Reserve Officers Training Corps. Having done so, Penn found that it did not have the facilities in which the Corps could drill and asked the Commercial Museum for the use of its hall. In addition, because the museum abutted train tracks, the Army asked to use museum buildings as a storage depot for war material. The board agreed to this request, which meant dismantling many of the museum's exhibits.[66]

These disruptions lasted for only a matter of months. More significantly, the First World War proved to many Americans that George Washington had been right after all when he warned Americans against entangling alliances. The Senate's defeat of the Treaty of Versailles, and of President Wilson as well, signaled a growing suspicion of overseas involvements. Congress then enthusiastically passed sharp restrictions on immigration in the early 1920s in an attempt to literally keep Europeans on their side of the ocean. The prospects for overseas adventuring that had seemed so inviting to Americans at the turn of century now seemed more treacherous and threatening. Certainly American businessmen still desired to sell their products in foreign markets, but by the 1920s the excitement with which Americans approached the challenge was dampened. Calvin Coolidge was no Teddy Roosevelt.

Along with this, Americans in the 1920s discovered that their domestic market could absorb far more consumer goods than previously imagined. If it seemed imperative at the turn of the century to develop overseas markets for American products, then after World War I professional economists suggested that this equation might be more complicated. In his research E. Dana Durand concluded that, by the mid-1920s, "this country has not become more dependent on the outside world either for its consumption or its markets." Indeed, Durand believed that the assumption that foreign markets would be good for the domestic economy ought to be reversed. It is more correct, he wrote "to say that our favorable prospects for progress at home hold promise of growing foreign trade."[67] As a new consuming society ripened in the 1920s, the relationship between the domestic and foreign markets proved more complicated than Wilson and the Commercial Museum had supposed.

Of greatest importance perhaps for the Commercial Museum, the First World War presented a troubling paradox. On the one hand, the Great War shook the Western world's faith in progress itself. Most educated Americans did not experience the nihilism that permeated European intellectual and artistic circles after the armistice. But the war put the very principle of the Commercial Museum to the test, and that principle failed. It is no coincidence that the great age of world's fairs, which had given birth to the Commercial Museum in the first place, ended with World War I. There would be famous fairs in the 1930s, of course, but they did not revel in a contentedness about the present. Instead, they created technological fantasies about the cities of the future and worlds of tomorrow.

Commerce and economic connections had not prevented war, as Wilson said they would. In his 1901 speech at Buffalo's Pan-American Exposition, he had assured his audience that "the influence of commerce on the whole, has been steadily in the direction of peace and prosperity, until to-day it has become the one great factor in the prevention of war." Events proved him wrong. The Europeans tore themselves apart, in some measure, precisely over access to colonial possessions, and therefore over markets and resources. Commerce had not prevented American involvement in a terrible war; in the aftermath of that war, the link between civilization, progress, and commerce seemed more problematic than it had been when Wilson opened his museum.

On the other hand, the war was clearly a boon to American commerce. The value of foreign trade had risen from approximately $4.25 billion in 1914 to over $7.3 billion in 1919. Needless to say, most of this growth was rooted in war.[68] Americans did now play a more active role on the stage of international commerce, but not precisely in the way Wilson had envisioned.

Finally, World War I changed the nature of foreign trade because it forced the federal government to become involved in an unprecedented way. Much of the trade carried on with Europe during the war, for example, came because of $8.5 billion of credit that Congress extended to the Allies.[69] After the war, many professional economists and businessmen called for an expanded federal role in promoting foreign trade. As a result, the Commercial Museum found itself with a formidable competitor in the federal Department of Commerce, brought to life under these circumstances in the 1920s by Herbert Hoover.[70]

The Department of Commerce had opened for business on July 1, 1903, with George Cortelyou as its secretary. Though it would eventually take on the promotion of business and trade as its chief mission, initially it oversaw such mundane operations as the Geodetic Survey, Fisheries, and Steamboat Inspection. Ten years later, the department's Bureau of Foreign and Domestic Commerce received only $60,000 from a stingy Congress.[71] Shortly after assuming his office, Secretary Cortelyou came to Philadelphia to speak about the new department. He made a special point, early in his talk, of congratulating the work of the Commercial Museum. Wilson and his colleagues at the museum, the secretary announced, "deserve the thanks of this community and the recognition . . .

for what they have contributed to the fund of our information upon commercial topics." "Some day," Cortelyou predicted, "the new Department of Commerce and Labor may find it advisable to have closer relations with these museums."[72]

That cooperation, apparently, never happened. After the war, both the Department of Commerce and the State Department expanded in ways that suspiciously resembled the Commercial Museum's Bureau of Information. Without acknowledging the years of work done at the Commercial Museum, University of Pennsylvania economist Harry Collings announced: "It is the business of the United States Government . . . to provide American exporters and importers with information on general changes in market conditions abroad." He went on to list the kind of information the government should make available to business: "price movements, foreign production and costs, import and export statistics, changes in tariff policies . . . and a thousand other similar and vital changes in foreign market conditions."[73] According to Raymond Bye, "one of the chief duties of our consuls in foreign lands is to supply information regarding opportunities for the sale of American products in the countries where they are stationed." By the mid-1920s, the federal government had taken responsibility for stimulating foreign trade, and the world of international commerce left the Commercial Museum behind.

The First World War, the event that caused so many to question fundamental assumptions of the Victorian era, did not, however, change the thinking of William P. Wilson or the direction of his museum. In describing the service the Commercial Museum provided to its businessmen clients, Wilson repeated yet again his belief in the inextricable connection between commerce, civilization, and progress. In the *Annual Report* for the years 1922–23—it might as well have been any year—he reiterated the museum's primary purpose: "To collect and display the raw and natural products from every quarter of the globe, to study them with reference to their commercial, economic and scientific value or their usefulness in the civilized world. In other words, the Commercial Museum is designed to search the world for new products which may be made available in the arts, the sciences, in manufactures and in agriculture."[74]

The 1924 *Annual Report* mentions the Department of Commerce for the first time, and the almost defensive tone of the report makes it clear that those at the Philadelphia museum viewed the federal department as a threat. Touting the Commercial Museum's own accomplishments, the report noted: "Eight years prior to the organization of the Federal Department of Commerce, the Commercial Museum sent out its own investigators to China and Japan, to India, to Africa, to Australia and New Zealand; also throughout the different countries of Latin America." [75] A history of the museum written by F. M. Huntington Wilson in 1931 reminded readers of the trailblazing role of the Commercial Museum. Huntington Wilson told his readers that "the Foreign Trade Bureau was established before the Department of Commerce at Washington, and indeed served as a model for the latter." [76] But though the Commercial Museum served as a model for the Department of Commerce, it could not compete with the resources available to a federal agency. Having pioneered ways to help American businessmen conquer foreign markets, the Philadelphia Commercial Museum was made redundant by the house that Hoover built.

The usurpation of the Commercial Museum's function by the Department of Commerce signaled a larger change in the way in which commerce and trade would be understood in the modern world. Wilson had seen the need for both a museum and a Bureau of Information. The former provided the object lessons essential to conquer foreign markets. After the First World War, the need for such displays of objects disappeared. As with natural science and anthropology, the creation of knowledge about commerce became the province of academic professionals, located largely in university departments of economics. This shift from the museum to the university had been foreshadowed at the museum's International Commercial Congress in 1899. Among the many sessions, Columbia University president Seth Low presided over one considering "Commercial Education." The most forceful statement about the need for commercial education came from panelist Charles Eliot, Low's counterpart at Harvard. In his talk, Eliot listed a bewildering variety of subjects that a successful business person needed to master, including languages, statistics, banking, commercial geography, maritime legislation, and on and on. [77] Wilson predicated his museum on the idea that this kind of information would complement the object lessons provided by the museum's exhibits. By the 1920s, however, the Commercial Museum's objects had ceased to teach, and the information American businessmen required, embodied in charts, graphs, and tables rather than in objects, could more efficiently be produced by the federal government in conjunction with academic professionals. In 1926 the American Academy of Political and Social Science, ironically located at the time down the street in Philadelphia from the Commercial Museum, devoted a whole volume of its *Annals* to the consideration of "Markets of the United States." [78] Contributors to the volume included economics professors and statisticians. Not an ex-botanist in the bunch. A great museum of commerce, placing objects at the center of how commerce would be understood, became unnecessary to the museum's original and primary constituency.

The *Annual Report* of 1926 marked an important milestone in the museum's history. The museum had begun in 1893 with a donation of material from Chicago. Since 1926 saw the Sesquicentennial Exposition held in Philadelphia, the museum naturally saw another opportunity to expand its collection: "The Sesqui-Centennial Exposition brought to Philadelphia a considerable number of interesting and valuable exhibits. . . . Official application was made . . . for the transfer of such collections for permanent exhibition in the Commercial Museum." But the Sesquicentennial failed to capture the popular imagination the way previous fairs had. The nation had grown tired of world's fairs as snapshots of the current state of technological and commercial progress. If the Centennial had the Corliss engine as its symbolic exhibit, then the most popular exhibit in 1926 was a recreated colonial-era "High Street." Americans visiting the Sesquicentennial seemed as excited to look to the past as their grandparents in 1876 had been to admire the present.

The tired tone of the 1926 *Annual Report* reflects some of the malaise that plagued the Sesquicentennial. Though the museum was able to claim that 1926 had been the "most successful year from the standpoint of volume and character of service rendered," it also had to acknowledge that its "Library of Commerce" had become second "to that of the Department of Commerce at Washington." [79] More than any of this, however, the 1926 *Annual Report* began with an obituary for William P. Wilson, the Commercial Museum's founder. He had served as the museum's director and been its driving force for over thirty years. His death in May 1927 signaled the end of the museum's dynamic period. Though it would continue its educational activities even into the 1990s, the museum sank increasingly into obscurity. [80]

Not surprisingly then, by 1928 several people including Ernest Trigg, now president of the Board of Trustees, had drafted a formal proposal to turn the site of the Commercial Museum into a "Convention and Exhibition Hall." In his statement at a meeting convened by Mayor Harry Mackey, Albert Greenfield, the proposal's primary author, stressed "the necessity of providing necessary facilities for trade and educational exhibitions held alone or in connection with conventions." Greenfield de-

14 William Powell Wilson, botanist by training, left the University of Pennsylvania to found and direct the Philadelphia Commercial Museum. His vision for the museum largely died with him in 1926. (Courtesy of the City Archives of Philadelphia)

scribed how Philadelphia missed out on trade shows because no facility existed to accommodate them. More galling, Greenfield reminded the meeting that Philadelphia had lost these shows to Cleveland, which had recently completed a convention complex. For his part, Ernest Trigg seemed resigned to the idea of transforming the Commercial Museum into a place to hold conventions. He told the mayor: "The Trustees of the Commercial Museum have for some time been willing to have the property in their custody developed by the erection of a building designed to provide needed facilities for important exhibitions and conventions." He went on to acknowledge that "such a plan has been discussed . . . from time to time at meetings held during several years past." Trigg's statement suggests that, by the end of 1920s, the museum had lost the energy of its original purpose.

Despite the founder's faith, after 1918 the museum's role had clearly begun to shift. The board seems to have spent an increasing amount of its time considering requests for the use of museum space. The Flower Show, the Automobile Association, and the Knitting Arts Exhibition made annual use of the museum through the 1920s. Where once the museum had tried to teach Americans how to gaze over the oceans in search of commercial opportunities, now it looked only as far as Lancaster, Cleveland, and Topeka.

Having been founded to promote American business expansion overseas, the Commercial Museum scaled back its ambitions throughout the 1920s. With William P. Wilson's death the museum lost more than its founder and tireless promoter. It lost as well its sense of possibilities and the principle that commerce could be understood and promoted through the collection, arrangement, and display of objects. Without these, the Commercial Museum seemed content to shift its focus from shaping the natural science of international commerce toward simply providing a place for trade groups and others to meet.[81] The museum which tried to create a permanent world's fair now played host to temporary exhibitions like the Dairy and Ice Cream Machinery and Supplies Association, which did not bear an even a pale resemblance to the great fairs of Chicago and St. Louis. The system of collecting artifacts and information that Wilson had developed, and the worldview that it represented, had now devolved into a convention center.

FIVE

~

Objects and American History:
The Museums of Henry Mercer and Henry Ford

America did not realize what a great Country it was to be,
and therefore did not perceive the wisdom of preserving the
early relics of our Country.

SUSAN WHITNEY TIMOCK

History is bunk.

HENRY FORD

When a new generation of historians professionalized themselves in the last quarter of the nineteenth century, they had little interest in objects. Their's was to be a textual science, based on German methods of analysis. These new professionals, with beach-heads at universities newly focused on research, fought on two fronts. On one hand, they rejected what they saw as the romantic fictions that passed for historical writing in the nineteenth century. On the other, in their quest for a new kind of historical objectivity, they rejected an object-based history and refined instead historical methodologies rooted in the retrieval and critical analysis of documents.[1]

This proved to have two consequences in the late nineteenth and early twentieth centuries. First, research based on documents precluded much study of ordinary people who left no such documentary residue. Most American historians chose to focus instead on great men and pivotal events. The second consequence was to ensure that professional history would not be located in museums. George Brown Goode anticipated that history museums would be part of his encyclopedia set, but according to Gary Kulik, even "in Goode's Smithsonian, history had become a residual category, the repository for collections that did not fit the elaborate natural-science model that Goode championed." As a result, in Kulik's view, the Smithsonian's role in the development of history "was limited and insignificant."[2]

Yet there were those who believed that history could be understood through objects and could be displayed in museums. Henry Mercer and Henry Ford were perhaps the most ambitious of these during the period under consideration here. Neither man was trained or credentialed in the study of history, but each developed a vision both of what American history ought to be and of how it ought to be studied. In creating their museums, they believed that the history of ordinary Americans, as embodied in the ordinary objects they made and used, could be presented to a wide public. Their experiments stood as alternatives to the more narrowly focused, and less accessible, academic history that would ultimately triumph.

"An Engineer's Vision of History"

The ironies are almost too rich at the Henry Ford Museum and Greenfield Village.[3]

Built by the richest man in America, the museum and village pay homage to America's simple folk. Erected as a memorial to America's preindustrial past and its "village" life, they were originally squeezed in between the tracks of the Michigan Central on one side, Ford Motors Engineering buildings on another, and the Henry Ford Airport on a third. Conceived as a way of rescuing a disappearing past, the objects and buildings were collected by the man whose automobiles and factories, perhaps more than anything else, caused that past to vanish. As he himself recognized, "improvements have been coming so quickly that the past is being lost to the rising generation."[4] Envisioned as the largest, most comprehensive museum of American history, the museum and village were the child of a man whose most famous utterance was to declare history "bunk."

Amidst the irony, one is struck as well by the extraordinary, almost poignant, sentimentality of the place. Doubtless aware of his role in creating the modern industrial world, Ford reached back to retrieve his own past. Here, in the village, is the one-room schoolhouse that Ford attended; over there is a replica of his first factory. Nearby is the cabin in which McGuffy—author of the McGuffy Readers Ford read as a child

15   Henry Ford built a history museum in two parts. At the bottom of this map, behind the re-created version of Independence Hall, are the galleries displaying a variety of objects. The Village itself, however, can also be seen as collection of architectural objects on a grand scale. (Courtesy of the Collections of Henry Ford Museum Greenfield Village)

and admired so much as an adult—was born. Through the buildings he accumulated for the village, Ford joined his own history to that of the Americans he most admired—a small Illinois courtroom where the young Abe Lincoln argued cases, Noah Webster's New Hampshire house, and, most importantly, Thomas Edison's complex all now share space in Henry Ford's ersatz neighborhood.

Comprised of dozens of buildings, all uprooted from their original sites and moved to Dearborn, Greenfield Village is a fiction in two senses. Most obviously, Greenfield Village never existed as such. The village is at one level a reservation onto which these otherwise incongruous buildings have been herded. At another level, of course, the past which Ford created with these buildings—a pleasant, pastoral, harmonious past—never existed either. Both the village and the past which it purports to represent sprang from the sentimental longings of an aging industrial giant.

This much historians and others have observed, and quite rightly. Serious historians snicker at the ironies and the sentimentality, or sneer at the way in which, in the view of many, Henry Ford whitewashed American history. Condescending or contemptuous, American historians would largely agree that while a stroll through Greenfield Village might well be fun, it does not pass academic muster. The tens of thousands of visitors who take that stroll are not, we would all agree, being presented with an accurate representation of the American past but rather with the idiosyncratic nostalgia of a very rich man.

But to look beyond the contradictions and the nostalgia is to see that Henry Ford did believe that his museum and village would tell the story of American history more thoroughly and more accurately than any textbook or work of scholarship. What is perhaps most significant here is not the particulars of Ford's historical fictions, but the way he tried to tell the story—not the product but the method. The principle of his historical enterprise was that objects more powerfully conveyed historical meaning than words. Objects were direct and tangible links with the past, unmediated, he believed, in any way, and they could communicate far more effectively with the great American public. In this sense, Ford relied on his own version of an object-based epistemology to understand American history, just as others had relied on objects to understand anthropology or natural science.

More so, perhaps, than natural science or anthropology, history fell victim to the subjective interpretations of writers. Ford relied on objects to create an "objective" history instead. When Henry Haigh visited in 1925 he wrote of Ford's collections as "true history. These relics of days that are gone tell only truthful tales. They cannot lie." Henry Ford's museum and his village stand as the most ambitious (and well-funded) attempt to tell the story of American history through objects. As Haigh put it, succinctly summarizing the whole foundation of an object-based epistemology, Ford's historical objects "are mute, but they are eloquent."[5]

Collecting the Past

Ford began his collecting of American history in 1919, in the wake of his embarrassing lawsuit against the *Chicago Tribune* for slander. When he learned that his family homestead would be torn down—fittingly enough to make room for a new road—Ford stepped in, moved the farm buildings out of the bulldozer's path, and restored them. After this experience Ford embarked on an astonishing career of collecting objects and buildings. By the time he purchased the Red Lion Tavern and had it moved from Massachusetts to Michigan in 1923, he had become the largest buyer of Americana in the country.

Ford's buying attracted enough national attention that in 1924 representatives from Williamsburg offered the town to him for five million dollars, if would promise to restore it.[6] Ford turned them down, preferring instead to build his own monument. As he continued to buy artifacts at a furious rate through the 1920s, Ford's plans for what to do with it all also took shape. In a letter written by Ford's assistant secretary Frank Campsall, he explained that "Mr. Ford has been developing the idea of an educational museum for a number of years. It has been the real purpose behind his tireless work as a Collector of Americana of every kind."[7]

Ford's historical vision had two parts. Greenfield Village would consist of actual buildings brought from around the country and rearranged along streets and around a village green. The thousands of objects Ford had collected would reside in the long galleries of the museum, whose facade would be a replica of Philadelphia's Independence Hall. Construction of the museum began in 1927. The following year, Ford hit upon the idea of buying all the buildings associated with Thomas Edison's "invention factory" in Menlo Park, New Jersey and making them a centerpiece of Greenfield Village. A year after that, on October 21, 1929, as the nation spiralled into the darkness of depression, President Herbert Hoover gave Greenfield Village its official dedication, an event designed to honor Edison and to mark the fiftieth anniversary of his invention of the electric light. Though it received its dedication in 1929, and though Ford had allowed as many as four hundred visitors a day to tour the village, it was not officially opened to the public until June, 1932. The museum, still not complete but nearly so, was similarly opened two weeks later.

Because Ford put his almost limitless fortune at the disposal of his collecting zeal, it is easy to believe that accumulation was his only guiding principle. But there was a method to Ford's actions. Ford believed, ahead of many academic historians, that American history was the history of its ordinary people, not of politicians or of wars. And he believed that the best way to tell that history was through the objects those people used, made, and with which they otherwise surrounded themselves. He did not collect antiques as such, he claimed, meaning that he did not buy items purely because of their perceived aesthetic or monetary value. Instead, he stated: "I am collecting the history of our people as written into the things their hands made and used." The *New York Times* described this "engineer's vision of history": "It is a view in which the Missouri Compromise, the Mexican War, the firing on Sumter, those thousand events that make up the whole web and woof of our story as the schoolboy learns it, are noticed, if at all, only as incidental interruptions of the main advance of national life—the progress in general conditions of living, in invention and efficiency, in comfort and taste. It is a view, moreover, in which a pewter bowl from the humblest kitchen in the Colonies would be of equal interest with one from that of George Washington."[8] Ford had indeed said that history was "bunk," but he also insisted that he had been misunderstood. He clarified himself later by making an essential distinction between textual history and an object-based history: "History as sometimes written is mostly bunk. But history that you can see is of great value."[9]

Ford drew sharp distinction between a history based in texts and one rooted in objects. "The historian," Ford said, "tries to put together a true story of the past, but he is working in words and ideas that do not include the whole of history." He believed that "the real history of a people was not expressed in wars, but in the way they lived and worked. . . . The history of America wasn't written in Washington, it was written in the grass roots."[10] And for Ford, history was not written in language but in objects. His museum, therefore, was an attempt to present this "grass roots" history: "When we are through we shall have reproduced American life, and that is, I think, the best way of preserving at least part of our history and our tradition. For by looking at the things that people used and the way they lived, a better and truer impression can be gained in an hour than could be had from a month of reading."[11] Providing his own summary of an object-based epistemology, Ford explained why objects did a more effective job transmitting historical knowledge: "You can read in every one of them what the man who made them was thinking—what he was aiming at. A piece of machinery or anything that is made is like a book, if you can read it. It is part of the record of man's spirit."[12] The *New York Times* made a more straightforward point by noting that the estimated one million annual visitors to the complex would be "an audience far beyond that of the best-seller." Democratic history, made democratically accessible through museum objects.

Like the museum builders of an earlier generation, Ford strove for an encyclopedic completeness and for an orderly system of display for the objects he assembled. As his assistant secretary Campsall explained, "the accumulations are vast and approximately complete." He also boasted: "No phase of American domestic, industrial or agricultural life has been neglected." [13] More specifically, J. G. de Roulhac Hamilton, writing in the *American Historical Review,* enumerated the categories into which the Museum's objects had been classed: "agriculture, mines and metallurgy, house and accessories, home industries and customs, recreation and amusements, communication and record of ideas, lighting, spinning, weaving, sewing, trade and commerce, timekeeping, medicine and surgery, music, photography, science and education, schools, taverns and inns, peddlers and chapmen, maps and pictures, fire prevention, forestry and woodworking, horticulture, machine tools and shop practice." [14] Just as natural-history specimens and anthropological artifacts were arranged in museums to illustrate the principle of progressive evolution, so too, Ford arranged his engines, farm equipment, and lamps to impress upon the visitor technological progress. Ford's unsurpassed collection of engines, for example, permitted visitors to "follow the development of every important application of power during the past two centuries," illustrated by "actual original specimen engines arranged in perfect chronological order." As Frank Campsall put it more succinctly, all the objects had been "arranged in an ascending series, [and] present a vivid and authentic record of American progress." [15] Henry Ford did not lament the passing of a preindustrial America; he saw it as inevitable. The exhibits at the museum persuaded that what began with the horse-drawn cart ended logically with the Model T.

Ford designed his museum to be an object-based, scientifically arranged presentation of American technological progress, and in so doing he borrowed the object-centered museum techniques of the late nineteenth century. He built long, well-lit galleries crowded with glass cases displaying objects without too many visual distractions. If the museum forced visitors into the contemplation of the historical object, then he intended his village to be the other side of a coin. Ford wanted to use the buildings in his village as the context into which to set his objects and to give them life. At the village, visitors could see the tools in operation, the lamps lit, the carts being drawn by horses. The village would be a "living history" museum, not of a specific time and place, as most living history museums are, but of all of American history across time and space. In its scope, Ford conceived of the village as the companion to the Museum—the two would complement each other to give visitors the most complete sense of the American past. Campsall explained: "Thus, articles from the Collections of the Museum will be shown in actual use in the Village. Mr. Ford dislikes mere 'dead' exhibitions of things; he wishes to see them in action in their proper setting. Hence the Village."

By viewing the village and the museum as the two linked parts of a single enterprise, we can also reevaluate the anachronistic nature of the village. At one level, the juxtaposition of the buildings makes all of them seem hopelessly out of place—a Cape Cod windmill within a stone's throw from a Georgian plantation house. As we have mentioned, Greenfield Village as a representation of any actual American small town is a multi-levelled fiction. But those are not perhaps the terms with which to evaluate what Ford tried to accomplish. Instead, we should see that in his attempt to portray the history of ordinary Americans, Ford saw buildings both as settings for the other objects he collected and as objects in and of themselves. He used the buildings of the village to give context to his blacksmith's tools and farm equipment, but he also wanted to collect these contexts in the same encyclopedic way. Just as he had collected a complete set of engines, so too he tried to assemble a complete set of American buildings—workshops, barns, churches, school houses, simple frontier cabins, elegant New England houses, slave quarters. Each building thus stands in its specificity and as representative. Ford did not intend that his village would actually represent the life of a specific historical place. Rather he conceived of the village in toto as a museum, and the buildings that make it up as specimens. Like the stuffed bird and butterflies taken from their natural context and put behind glass, like the anthropological objects taken from their cultural context and put in cases, Ford has turned the buildings of Greenfield Village into enormous museum objects and thus created a new context for them.

~

According to the recollections of Fred Smith, who worked for Ford assembling the museum, Ford sent his son Edsel on a tour of American museums—"Mr. Edsel Ford went down all through the museums down east, you know." Ford senior, though he "didn't want anything from any other museums," apparently wanted to get some sense of the extent of other museum collections and of how those museums presented their material. When Edsel returned from this tour, "he came back and set down and talked with his father in my presence about it. He told Mr. Ford right out then. He said, 'There's nothing that can compare with what we have here, father.' He said, 'Williamsburg will never be a drip in the bucket to what we have here.'"[16]

Mr. Smith's remembrances, as with all memories, are both right and not quite right. They accurately reflect that Ford's historical ambition had no equal in the 1920s—no historical museum could match the scope or the sheer size of the Henry Ford Museum and Greenfield Village. And Edsel's alleged mention of Williamsburg is interesting as well. On the one hand, it might simply have been an affirmation that Ford had made the right decision not to buy Williamsburg and instead to pursue his own vision.

At another level, the swipe at Williamsburg underscored that the two places had different agendas. At Williamsburg, the goal had been to use archaeology and other kinds of sciences to recreate a specific place at a specific moment in time. Ford wanted his museum to have a much broader sweep, nothing less than a comprehensive record of America's preindustrial past. Though it too is heavy with its own historical fictions, Williamsburg stands as a monument to the techniques of scientific and historical recreation in a way that Greenfield Village does not. And while Williamsburg now serves as the setting for an important center for academic research about early America, Greenfield Village is largely a tourist attraction for vacationing families and school groups.

Ford's museum and village did not point the way to the future of historical study, in the way that Williamsburg did. Rather, Ford built his museum upon the object-based foundations of earlier museums, and with that observation we add the final qualification to Fred Smith's memories. When he recounted that Ford "didn't want anything from any other museums," he had forgotten or was unaware that Ford had indeed been inspired by another museum of American history, one that emphasized the eloquence of objects even more than Ford's.

In July 1922, Dr. R. D. McClure, a staff member at the Henry Ford Hospital in Detroit, wrote to Dr. Henry Mercer of Doylestown, Pennsylvania, just north of Philadelphia in Bucks County. Mercer, nearing the end of his life, had built his own museum of American history, filled with precisely the same kinds of objects Ford wanted to collect—appleparers, cobbler's tools, candle-molds, etc. Ostensibly, McClure wanted to ask Mercer some questions about an old threshing machine. McClure took the opportunity, however, to suggest that Ford might come to inspect Mercer's museum. In September 1923, just as his collecting career had moved into high-gear, Ford made the trip to Doylestown to see

Mercer and his collection. After his tour he announced: "This is the only museum I've ever been sufficiently interested in to visit. Some day I expect to have a museum which will rival it." [17]

It is impossible to quantify or even adequately describe the extent to which Henry Mercer shaped the thinking of Henry Ford. Ford left Doylestown impressed enough with Mercer's Museum to have the *Dearborn Independent,* his personal forum, run an enthusiastic article about it early in 1924. The article's author told readers that this "one-man museum which tells probably more about the living history of the human race than any other institution in the world," would successfully "bring within reach of all a knowledge of things now confined to scholars." [18]

Although Ford and Mercer were importantly different from each other, it also seems clear that the two shared certain sympathies. Each elevated the ordinary and the commonplace as a way to explore what he considered the essential nature of American history and tradition. More importantly, each man viewed objects as the key with which to unlock that tradition. By his own admission, Ford found in Mercer's museum the only model upon which to base his own, and so now we will consider this earlier attempt to tell the history of the American people through the objects they made.

Mercer Finds History

In an essay written for a Harvard class sometime in the 1870s, Mercer recalled an "excavation" he undertook when he was a boy. During a childhood summer, Mercer had hoped to find an ancient camping ground of the Lenni Lenape, which was supposed to have been located near Mercer's house along the Delaware river. He wrote: "Thus far every exploration had turned out a mere wild-goose chase, [still] I often thought of mysterious amulets, and murderous tomahawks buried, no one knew where, and could fancy myself in the act of unearthing the sacred bones and war paraphernalia, of some renowned sachem—any perhaps; but it all came to nothing until one day in August." Out fishing at a favorite spot after some high water on the river on that fateful day in August, Mercer spotted several arrowheads revealed by erosion. He continued: "I had not yet given up all hopes of the Indian camp—I [left the place and] soon returned with a shovel from a farm house; and, there, in that ground, so often trodden by me, in profane unconsciousness, I began to dig. Then came to light arrowheads, by the dozen, broken, but precious, fragments of rude vessels, and savage implements of war, and the chase, that had

16   The effect of Henry Mercer's museum is of a carefully classified confusion. Here, in the central court, objects are jammed, literally, to the concrete rafters. (Collection of the Spruance Library, Bucks County Historical Society)

lain hidden there since the red man bade farewell to the spot. It took a week of digging to exhaust the relics; but after that I was satisfied; I had found the Indian camp." [19] Written—not very well—for a college composition class, the essay reveals some of the romance and sense of discovery that made archaeology so appealing for so many in the late Victorian era. It also suggests Mercer's later preoccupation with the rediscovery of a lost people through their material remains—remains that brought Mercer out of "unconsciousness." Perhaps because it foreshadowed so much of his later concerns, Mercer kept this hand-written essay until he died.

In a life which began just before the Civil War (1856), and ended at the beginning of the Depression (1930), Mercer's pursuits were remarkably wide ranging. After early abandoning a career in the law, Mercer became an important archaeologist of the New World in the 1880s and 1890s. Toward the end of that decade, he began to collect the tools and technology of colonial and early Federal America. He eventually housed these artifacts in a museum of his own extraordinary design that he built for the Bucks County Historical Society (BCHS) in 1916. At the turn of the century, Mercer began experimenting with pottery production by trying to resurrect an eighteenth-century Pennsylvania-German technique for ceramic manufacture. As a result of his experiments, he established the Moravian Tile Works near his home in Doylestown. The tiles he produced there have been installed in buildings as far-flung as the State Capitol in Harrisburg, PA, the Isabella Stewart Gardner Museum in Boston, and the Casino in Monte Carlo.

Though Mercer pursued a variety of fascinations, this fascinating individual never considered himself primarily an archaeologist, a collector, or a ceramicist. Nor was he simply a "Renaissance man" who had the means to dabble widely. Instead, Mercer thought of himself primarily as an historian, and his pursuit of history through objects gave coherence to all of his activities. He wanted nothing less than to create a kind of historiography which would tell the story of ordinary Americans in a new and "objective" way.

This desire to create a new way to study history lay beneath all Mercer's activities, but it manifested itself most dramatically at the Mercer Museum. Walking into the central courtyard for the first time, visitors are without exception stunned and amused as they look to the concrete ceiling five stories up and see the clutter of carriages, sleighs, and baby cradles suspended by metal hooks. But there is method to this museum madness. Here Mercer was able to combine science, architecture, and history to put his ideas about the historical value of objects on display. Perhaps more than any other museum in this study, Mercer in his museum took farthest the faith Americans had during this period in the ability of objects to convey meaning.

~

When Mercer graduated from Harvard in 1879, his well-to-do Bucks County family expected him to pursue a career in the law, and to that end he studied at the University of Pennsylvania Law School. Law, apparently, did not hold much appeal, and Mercer spent a great deal of the early 1880s touring Europe with friends and relatives.

In between his travels and his law study, Mercer participated in the founding of the Bucks County Historical Society in 1880, and he read his first paper there in 1884. In 1885, Mercer, expanding on his childhood interest in Native American culture, published his first book: *The Lenape Stone, or the Indian and the Mammoth.* This book is a detailed consideration of what was then a controversial archaeological discovery, and it marked Mercer's professional entry into the field of archaeology. It is instructive here because it hints at the issues that would concern Mercer throughout his career and at how he would attempt to solve them.

The stone itself was a gorget with Indian figures and a mammoth incised on one face. The central question about the stone was its authenticity. If it were genuine, it would demonstrate that Native Americans existed contemporaneously with extinct megafauna. This, in turn, would establish an antiquity for Native Americans which was significantly older than that which was then accepted. Mercer concluded, after exhaustive analysis, that the gorget's age could not be proven one way or the other. It could not, therefore, answer the question about human antiquity in the New World definitively, as many archaeologists hoped it would. With this book, Mercer established himself as a careful, deliberate, and scientific archaeologist.

The book also demonstrated the concern Mercer would have throughout the rest of his life with the significance of objects. In the nearly 100 pages of the book, Mercer considered things as minute as the depth and shape of the stone's incision marks, but he was clearly more interested in broader issues. In the book, he developed an idea that the stone might illustrate the creation story of the Lenni Lenape. As he would go on to do repeatedly, Mercer used a single object to tell a much larger story.

In 1890, Mercer became a member of the newly formed Archaeological Association of the University of Pennsylvania. This association developed into the University Museum, and in 1891 Mercer was named one of ten managers of the new museum. Using the University Museum as his institutional base, Mercer pursued the question of Native American antiquity with remarkable energy.

In his writing and in his research, Mercer insisted that the only way to prove that the continent had been populated before the last Ice Age was to find stone tools in incontrovertible association with extinct animals.[20] In Europe, human antiquity had been established by the discovery in caves of human tools in association with extinct megafauna. Mercer undertook to make similar discoveries in America. In 1892–93, he traveled to Europe to investigate paleolithic cave sites in France and Spain.[21] Between 1891 and 1898, Mercer excavated cave and mound sites in Maine, West Virginia, Tennessee, Louisiana, Texas, and the Yucatan in addition to local sites in Eastern Pennsylvania and along the Delaware River. In 1894, Mercer was appointed Curator of American and Prehistoric Archaeology at the University Museum. A year earlier, in 1893, Mercer began as Assistant Editor for the Department of Archaeology and Ethnology for *The American Naturalist,* a prestigious scientific journal. He held this position until 1898. In addition to his field work and to his museum and editorial duties, Mercer was also publishing prodigiously.[22]

As we discussed briefly in chapter three, archaeological enterprises flourished in the Old World at the end of the nineteenth century, while the study of ancient Americans languished. Work going on in other parts of the world—in Egypt and the Near East particularly—received far more public attention and much more money. John Wesley Powell lamented this situation in 1890, in an almost Emersonian way: "Our archaeological institutes, our universities, and our scholars are threshing again the straw of the Orient for the stray grains that may be beaten out, while the sheaves of anthropology are stacked all over this continent; and they have no care for the grain which wastes while they journey beyond the seas." [23] If one were to grope among the dry bones of the past, Powell insisted, they ought at least to be bones buried in American soil.

Mercer echoed Powell's concerns in a speech delivered some time during the 1890s. In it Mercer asked, "Is American Archaeology Interesting?" Like Powell, Mercer urged his audience not to neglect the archaeology of their own land. After all, Mercer reminded his listeners, the story of the taming and settlement of the Western Hemisphere constituted one of the great events of human history. Archaeology, Mercer insisted, told that story. As he put it, archaeology revealed the history of the conquest of "the continent of the great forest."[24] Just as in *The Lenape Stone,* where Mercer used a single object to tell the story of a whole people, in this lecture Mercer told his audience that the study of stone tools might convey the epic story of the whole hemisphere.

Mercer's involvement with the questions of American archaeology was intense, but it was brief. Frustrated perhaps by his inability to solve the question of Native American antiquity, and strained by his chronic bad health, Mercer retired from the archaeological field some time in the late 1890s. He had by then decided to shift his focus in order to study the history of "the continent of the great forest" from a new perspective.

Archaeological History

Archaeology, then as now, exerted an extraordinary pull on the imagination of Americans. Archaeological developments were reported widely in the press, discussed in public lectures, and otherwise watched by a broad audience. The discoveries of past civilizations in Italy, Greece, Egypt, the Near East, and especially those made by Heinrich Schliemann at Troy, gave archaeology a mystique and an authority virtually unmatched by any other humanist discipline. It is surely no accident then that when Sigmund Freud used archaeology as a metaphor to describe his new psychoanalysis, he did so in part to describe a method through which the subconscious would be "excavated." But he also did so to allude to the public authority archaeology commanded, hoping that it would lend legitimacy to his new brand of science.[25] The metaphoric and methodological allusions continue to the present. In searching for a name to give a new method of conceiving intellectual history, Michel Foucault described an "archaeology of knowledge."

When Mercer entered the archaeological field, it was seen as the most dramatic and "objective" method to recover the past. The objects unearthed by archaeologists provided a tangible connection with the past in a way that texts and documents could not. Yet even while Mercer worked at the University Museum, he began to turn his attention away from the artifacts of the most ancient Americans to those of just a few generations previous. In an address to the BCHS, Mercer recalled the beginnings of his collecting this way:

> It was probably one day in February or March of the spring of 1897 that I went to the premises of one of our fellow-citizens, who had been

17 The young Henry Mercer on site. Before he embarked on his own historical and museological pursuits, Mercer was an active archeologist, concerned particularly with questions of human antiquity in the new world. (Collection of the Spruance Library, Bucks County Historical Society)

in the habit of going to country sales and at the last moment buying what they called "penny lots," that is to say valueless masses of obsolete utensils or objects which were regarded as useless. . . . The particular object of the visit above mentioned, was to buy a pair of tongs for an old fashioned fireplace, but when I came to hunt out the tongs from the midst of a disordered pile of old wagons, gum-tree saltboxes, flax-brakes, straw beehives, tin dinner horns, rope-machines and spinning wheels . . . I was seized with a new enthusiasm and hurried over the county, rummaging the bake-ovens, wagon-houses, cellars, hay-lofts, smoke-houses, garrets, and chimney-corners, on this side of the Delaware valley.[26]

Having been struck with this "new enthusiasm," Mercer pursued it with a characteristic vengeance. Mercer hoped to assemble a complete collection of every conceivable implement used by European-Americans before about 1820. The laundry-list of items quoted above, upon which Mercer serendipitously stumbled on that late-winter day, gives a good inventory of the kinds of things he would go on to collect. Initially housed in the BCHS's one room in the County Courthouse, the collection quickly outgrew these quarters, and Mercer was forced to display many of the tools in his own house. To replace these temporary quarters, Mercer broke ground for a new museum in the spring of 1913. Three years later, on June 17, 1916, Mercer presented the museum—a bizarre seven-story pile of his own design and made entirely from reinforced concrete—and its collection to the BCHS. By the time Mercer died in 1930, the museum housed something over 25,000 items—from apple-parers to a gallows, from cobblers' tools to a whaling boat.

This shift from the study of paleolithic Americans to the collection of Colonial American tools appears an abrupt change of direction. In fact, though, Mercer saw his new passion as entirely consistent with his old. Mercer's Museum stands as a monument to his attempt to create an archaeological study of American history. True, the only digging Mercer did now would be in country attics and rural barns, but his archaeological history, like his study of American prehistory, remained based in objects, and it relied on archaeological models of classification and display.

As a prehistoric archaeologist, Mercer was primarily concerned with the study of stone tools; stone tools, after all, are the only things which can survive ten or twelve thousand years virtually unchanged. In his new collecting, Mercer's central focus remained on tools. Describing his museum, Mercer told a newspaper reporter that "every object here shown may be said to be a tool." [27] Tools, and the work to which they were set, made human progress—the taming of the continent of the great forest, in his words—possible. By changing his temporal focus, however, he was able to study tools made out of perishable material like iron and wood. Mercer also retained an archaeologist's fanaticism for classification and categorization. He even painted white identification numbers on each tool he collected, as is common practice with archaeological finds.

More than that, Mercer conceptualized his new work as archaeology, but archaeology done from the other end of the chronological continuum. By collecting the artifacts used by people in the recent past, Mercer and his museum would move backward in time, from the nineteenth century backward, rather than from prehistory forward. In 1907, Mercer described this shift of focus: "This therefore is archaeology turned upside down, reversed, revolutionized." In 1924, Mercer more succinctly described the revelation that struck him on that fateful spring day in 1897: "Then suddenly it occurred to me that archaeologists had been working from the wrong end." [28] Mercer had not abandoned archaeology; he simply wanted to do it differently.

This changed relationship to traditional archaeology was accompanied by a more profound change in the way Mercer viewed the history of Euro-America. In studying the history of ancient Americans, Mercer had, of necessity, to rely on objects. If this was sound methodology through which to recover the ancient past, why not focus on the study of objects produced more recently to study the more recent past? Again, this new notion came to him in 1897 while he was staring at the "penny lots." Marveling at "things that I had heard of but never collectively saw before," Mercer recognized that "the history of Pennsylvania was here profusely illustrated and from a new point of view." [29] From this new point of view, Mercer saw that tools and implements, which were in a very tangible sense responsible for settling the continent and building the nation, could present the everyday history of ordinary people far more effectively than anything written by academic historians in their dry textbooks. By turning archaeology upside down, Mercer felt he had made history more accessible.

Mercer staked out this position at the moment when the historical profession had begun to coalesce. Both Mercer and Ford a generation later set their object-based museum projects against a textually based academic history, although it is probably fair to say that Ford's exposure to academic history was limited, while Mercer, with his university connections, found himself in the thick of such discussions. Academic history, using colleges and universities as its institutional power base, was well established by the time Ford began shipping box-car loads of objects to Dearborn, but it was less so when Mercer began to rummage among the penny lots. Mercer's should thus be seen as one voice among several debating the most effective way of recovering the past.

Among those with whom Mercer argued was George Bancroft, who had died in 1891. Bancroft's multi-volume history of America focused on political and military history proper, on the heroes of the Revolution and of the Constitution. Although his volumes belonged to an earlier era, his was still a looming presence, and Mercer explained to the BCHS how his way of presenting American history was different. "Mr. Bancroft," Mercer said, "wrote the history of the United States and dwelt with great vividness upon the Revolutionary War." But, according to Mercer, Bancroft had missed the heart of the issue: "no history can show as these things [Mercer's collection] show, that during the war a hundred thousand hands armed with these sickles were reaping wheat and rye so as to make any kind of war possible." He continued: "You may go down into Independence Hall in Philadelphia, and stand in the room in which the Declaration of Independence was signed and there look upon the portraits of the signers. But do you think you are any nearer the essence of the matter there than you are here when you realize that ten hundred thousand arms, seizing upon axes of this type, with an immense amount of labor and effort made it worth while to have a Declaration of Independence by cutting down one of the greatest forests in the North Temperate Zone ?" [30] Mercer was unhappy with the focus of most contemporary museums of history and archaeology because they seemed to take their lead from Bancroft. Addressing the BCHS in 1897, Mercer stated that he "deplored the fact that almost all museums have devoted themselves entirely to the Revolutionary War and the Civil War, and as far as old implements are concerned, they do not exist anywhere." [31]

Mercer's complaints with other historians were not simply retrospective. In the late nineteenth century he was institutionally situated so as to be surrounded by some of the most dynamic figures in the new historical field. When he was a student at Harvard, the history faculty included Justin Winsor, Henry Cabot Lodge, and Charles Eliot Norton. [32] Mercer certainly knew and may have studied with Winsor, one of the preeminent converts to the new "scientific history," recently arrived in America from Germany. Scientific historians wanted to inject "realism" into previously "romantic" historical writing. Above all, these historians demanded documentary evidence, and they were critical and studious in their evaluation of it. This approach emphasized detail over values, facts over ultimate meanings. Winsor described the task of the historian with a photographic metaphor. The camera, Winsor wrote, "catches everything, however trivial." [33] The historian, he felt, should do the same.

When Mercer took up work at the University of Pennsylvania, he found himself again at an important center for competing schools of history. Henry Lea, the university's medievalist, was an exemplary scientific historian, while John Bach McMaster, the pioneer social historian, was at Penn during these same years. McMaster, described by a contemporary as having "burst into the historiographical firmament as a star of the first magnitude," [34] opened up the study of American history beyond the political and the military to include economics and the daily lives of people. Though James Harvey Robinson had moved to Columbia by the time he published his most famous book, *The New History,* he was one of the people associated with McMaster at Penn during the 1890s. Drawing on the work of social historians like McMaster, New Historians reacted against the arcane and too particular focus of the scientists. Robinson and his colleagues sought to make history more democratic, and they insisted that the study of history should serve primarily to answer contemporary questions. It is not clear if Henry Mercer had contact with these historians while they were all on the same campus, but certainly for anyone interested in the problems of history—how one can know the past, and how to understand the relationship between past and present—Penn was a heady place to be.

Mercer's ideas about history were drawn from all these schools. He retained the scientism he learned from archaeology, and he was wholly interested in the issues put forth by McMaster's social history. Mercer's "new point of view" echoes especially the concerns of the emergent New History that history should tell the stories of common people and that it should provide easily accessible insights into the present. To add to this, Mercer put work at the center of his historical understanding. The story of ordinary labor, and the way that labor shaped the nation, was, in his view, the most important historical narrative. Finally, his decision to work out his historical theories in a museum context reminds us that, just as in natural science, anthropology, and the study of commerce, museums were still seen as legitimate places for historical inquiry.

By foregrounding work and labor as the motive force in American history, Mercer was convinced that the tools he collected provided tangible evidence of a Turnerian view of American development. In 1893, Frederick Jackson Turner powerfully observed that the Western frontier made Americans out of Europeans, and thus made the American nation out of a vast wilderness. "It was this nationalizing tendency of the West," he told the American Historical Association in that famous address, "that transformed the democracy of Jefferson into the national republicanism of Monroe and the democracy of Jackson." He continued: "But the most important effect of the frontier has been in the promotion of democracy here and in Europe."[35] Turner had identified and described the great process of American historical change, and he located it on the frontier. Mercer's tools provided the tangible evidence that demonstrated how that process was carried out by individuals, for they were the very implements by which the frontier was mastered. Having hit upon this historical recipe, Mercer returned to these themes throughout his career.

In the fall of 1897 Mercer put this new point of view on display. He entitled this first public exhibition of 761 objects "Tools of the Nation Maker." The title of the exhibit is significant. With it, Mercer announced that more so than politics or war, these simple tools, and the people who once used them, were responsible for creating the nation. "The historian," Mercer wrote in the exhibition catalogue, "has overlooked [these objects]. The antiquary has forgotten them." Nor did Mercer feel these tools to be of simply local interest. Again we find him moving from the consideration of particular objects to the consideration of the whole country: "in the largest sense the story of Eastern Pennsylvania and of its Bucks county is that of the whole nation. As often the founders of Indiana, Kansas and Missouri have returned to the shore of the Delaware to look with affectionate curiosity upon the birthplace of their ancestors." [36]

With the "Tools of the Nation Maker" exhibit, Mercer gave material form to Turner. In the postscript to the "Nation Maker" catalogue, Mercer wrote in virtually Turnerian tones: "The American pioneer, thrown for a time upon his own resources, turns back to conditions more primitive than those left behind in the Old World. Contenting himself with such makeshifts as the wooden plow, the hay drag formed of a branch, or the house of logs, which in his hands do not strictly represent stages in the general development of human culture, his wits are quickened by necessity, until suddenly, towards the beginning of the present century, he casts aside the old tools and equips himself with machines." [37]

Likewise, in *The New History,* James Harvey Robinson asked historians to study "the real sources of historical knowledge," and he listed architecture, tools, ornaments, and clothing in addition to written records as among these sources. He went on to say that "the history of man begins with his industries; and I am not sure that his industries, in a broad sense of the term, have not always constituted as good a single test of his general civilization and as satisfactory a clue to its vicissitudes as can be found." [38] Mercer anticipated Robinson by fifteen years; had it not been written in 1912, Mercer could have used this passage in the exhibit catalogue of "Tools of the Nation Maker." Mercer's collection, first exhibited as "Tools of the Nation Maker," was not an attempt simply to preserve the past. Rather, Mercer used these tools to present American history in a way that had not been done before. At a time when historians debated the best way to tell the story of America, Mercer believed he had found it.

To exhibit his new view of history, Mercer tried to refashion the way in which historical objects should be presented to the public. Mercer, and Ford a generation later, had no patience for museums that exhibited objects only because of some chance association with an historical event or person. He was confident that, after visiting his museum, "everybody will see that such a thing as a pebble labeled 'found on the beach at Ticonderoga' or a cane 'made from the doorsill of Penn's Brewhouse' will have no scientific value whatever."[39] In a small essay written about Charles Willson Peale's Museum, Mercer pointed out that Peale designed it to be a scientific display, not "a show of wonders and souvenirs." Mercer especially appreciated that Peale refused the donation of Washington's horse for his collection because it had no real scientific merit.[40] Welding the archaeological method of treating objects together with the scientific historians' reliance only on historical fact, Mercer constructed the meaning of the objects on display in his museum.

Because he insisted that each of his objects had meaning, Mercer designed his exhibits to assert the primacy of the object. His objects are not displayed in contextual recreations; rather, he displayed all tools of similar type together. Instead of creating a diorama to illustrate a cobbler's shop, for example, Mercer put all the tools related to the task together, even if that meant displaying a dozen hammers on the same shelf. The objects are thus removed from a context and displayed so that the visitor can focus attention on each type of tool, and by extension, the work represented by those tools, and yet further, the way work shaped the history of the nation. In this way, Mercer shaped his museum around an object-based epistemology, and each object in it, like the specimens in a natural history museum, served as a metonym for different aspects of American history. He explained his method to the BCHS: "We have found that history may be written from the standpoint of objects rather than from laws, legislatures, and the proceedings of public assemblies."[41] In order to augment his collection he hoped "to call in laborers, mechanics, artisans and farmers of the older generations, who can look back upon their youth and give us descriptions of what these things mean, and get those descriptions on record."[42] In calling upon members of the "older generations" to help solve his historical problems, Mercer's choice of words here is significant: members of the "older generations" would not explain what these objects were used for, but rather, what they *meant*.

Building this archaeological history of America around objects, Mercer believed that he could illustrate the processes of historical change by charting what he saw as the evolution of tools. In notes he made to himself about the changes brought about by the industrial revolution, Mercer again demonstrates the importance of objects in explaining how his history worked. In these notes, Mercer divides civilization into what he regarded as its fundamental components: Shelter; Food; Clothing; Transport; Amusement; Religion; Government; and Art. (And note again that war, diplomacy, campaigns and elections, and the other staples of most history are absent from this list). He then considers each in a schematic diagram. Under the main heading "Raw Material," the left-hand column lists objects in their "Stationary," or original, condition. The middle-column lists those same objects "Altered," and in the final column, "Transformed" by human innovation.[43] History, Mercer believed, could be systematized and ordered through objects, like the natural world, human cultures, and commerce. Mercer probably borrowed again from his experiences as an archaeologist. This schematic removes historical change from the frameworks and mechanics of political, military, or other kinds of chronology. In this sense, Mercer has applied an anthropological model of cultural change to the process of American historical change.

Viewing historical change this way, it was easy for Mercer to view the importance of his collection, ultimately, in international terms. Initially Mercer collected locally, though we have seen that, as early as the "Tools of the Nation Maker" exhibit, Mercer believed that the history of Bucks County and Eastern Pennsylvania held special significance for America generally. Eventually, the focus of the collection broadened to include tools from around the country. But as he wrote in a 1918 draft to a new museum guide, this national focus "still seemed too narrow since many of the objects belonged in type, not to one but to many nations." Picking up themes in his industrial revolution notes, he continued: "These tools show that along the great pathways of human necessity—Food, Clothing, Shelter, Transport—many men from many lands, who have come to our shores have lived, toiled and struggled with the same Nature in the same way. Shall not therefore the Traveller before he sets out, come here first so that his whole journey may be illuminated with the knowledge of God's universal way with man, the inspiring sight of familiar things which break through the barriers of language and distance and transform the stranger into a Companion and a Brother." [44] In Mercer's conception, historical change might vary in its specifics from place to place, but it was ultimately governed by the processes of tools and work. Just as William P. Wilson had put commerce at the center of human development, Mercer elevated work to center stage. He hoped that by reorienting the writing of history so that it told the story of common people from the point of view of the tools they used, he could demonstrate a shared heritage of people all over the world. To that final end, Mercer sponsored expeditions to Africa to study and collect tools, and in 1921 he commissioned Rudolf Hommel to go to China for the same purpose. In 1937, seven years after Mercer's death, Hommel published *China at Work*, a painstaking study of Chinese tools arranged with the same archaeological care and precision with which Mercer had organized his museum.[45]

Mercer reiterated his ideas about history through objects many times. He titled his 1918 revision of the Museum Guide, for example, *The Scope and Meaning of the Collection of Objects at the Museum*. But nowhere did he express these ideas more emphatically than in a lecture entitled "History in Implements." Through most of this lecture Mercer explored the history of specific objects. In the introduction, however, Mercer made a grand allusion to Emerson in describing all that was wrong with academic history, and how it might be fixed. Echoing Emerson's invocations in the "American Scholar" that the scholar not become "the parrot of other men's thought," Mercer began his lecture by announcing that the scholar was faced with a choice: stay in the library and read "books full of other men's thoughts," or "come out into the fresh air and work out our own thoughts." This choice, Mercer told his audience, was "the essence of the thing that we have come here to advise upon. How shall you get a scholar to drop the book and investigate for himself?" Emerson had told the Harvard graduating class of 1837 that each age "must write its own books. . . . The books of an older period will not fit this." Mercer picked up on the theme:

> The writer of history has kept too much in the library. That is the charge that can be made against him in the last 1800 years. When he writes a new book he shuffles the thoughts of other books into a new combination. That's about all. 100 sciences have cropped up in the last 50 years, and one of them is anthropology—that tells him that in his attempt to vary the story of man's relationship to nature he has got out of touch with the living man himself and left out some of the most important parts. Why don't he leave his books and step out into the fresh air and ask questions of [what] he sees—What's that you've got in your hand? Where did it come from? How did you make it? How is it that this chinaman has one like it? and so forth. In other words,

why don't he write an original history with a little less about politics
and constitution in it and a little more about the [common] man?[46]

In this speech, Mercer makes it clear that he is searching for a more
inclusive way to write American history. Rooted in the objects that made
American progress possible, and rooted in the observations of contemporary life, Mercer believed his history would prove to be, in the most
literal sense, objective.

The writer of an editorial, which appeared shortly after Mercer's new
museum opened, understood Mercer's intentions. The writer noted that
history, as usually written, is full of mistakes. In contrast, "one sort of
historical record cannot be questioned, and that is the sort that comes
to us in the form of tangible objects made and used by people tho long
removed from the possibility of writing or speaking of their times and
trend, thus tell much of what they were and what they did. And because
this is the only absolutely reliable form of history, a collection such as
that just given to the Bucks County Historical Society by Dr. Henry Chapman Mercer of Doylestown, must be ranked as a notable contribution to
the history of the nation."[47] Having so resoundingly resolved the conun-
drums of writing an "objective" history, Mercer confidently announced
that, in the future, students of American history "will not go to Washington, Boston, New York, Chicago, or anywhere else in the country to study
American history from this fresh point of view, but will be compelled to
come to Doylestown."[48]

Finding a Relationship with the Past

Mercer described the difference between his museum and other museums of history and archaeology this way: "The archaeology of the
museums of Europe and America begin at the past, present us with
the remains of man thousands of years old, and pretend to lead us to the
present. Generally speaking you might say that they put the cart before
the horse. But here on the other hand we look from the present backward to the past. Beginning at the doorstep of our grandfathers we go
back to the Roman and Egyptian times. . . . What seems obscure and dark
in the museums which we have visited is here rendered plain."[49] Here
again is Mercer's notion of turning archaeology around, beginning with
the recent and moving backward. But this description also reveals another aspect of Mercer's ambition. What disappointed him about other
museums was that they treated the past as something distant and dead,

18   The Mercer Museum is a bizarre, wonderful pile. Seven stories high, and everything, down to the window mullions, made from poured concrete. (Courtesy of the Spruance Library, Bucks County Historical Society)

not as something with a vital connection to the present—they "pretend to lead us to the present." His museum, by starting with the present, would illustrate the connection between the present and the past much more clearly. The relationship between past and present, which in other museums "seems dark and obscure," is what Mercer hoped to illuminate.

Ford also had this in mind with his museum, and both he and Mercer took their desire to link the past and the present one step beyond the museum. Ford opened a technical institute associated with Greenfield Village where students would be trained in the arts and crafts of the nineteenth century. By the fall of 1897, with the "Tools of the Nation Maker" exhibit barely dismantled, Mercer had decided to revive a dying Pennsylvania German pottery tradition. Working with David Herstine, a local potter, Mercer experimented, rather unsuccessfully, with ceramic bowls, plates, and cups. Mercer then met William De Morgan, an important British tile manufacturer, in 1898, and De Morgan persuaded Mercer to produce ceramic tiles, which were then coming back into fashion, especially to decorate fireplaces. After enlisting the help of Englishman John

Briddes to design a kiln, Mercer's Moravian Tile Works opened for business on September 1, 1899.

This venture into ceramic production connects Mercer to another group who found themselves looking to the past to find inspiration for the present. The Arts and Crafts movement—more properly a loosely affiliated set of projects sharing a desire to resurrect the traditions of the preindustrial past—was active in this country from the mid 1890s until the First World War, precisely when Mercer was assembling his collections and building his museum. If Mercer's connections to the world of professional history were less than tenuous, then he seems at least at one level to have shared in common a set of concerns with the Arts and Crafters.[50]

There are good reasons to consider Mercer as part of the Arts and Crafts Movement. In America, the movement had several centers. The Boston Society of Arts and Crafts, founded in 1897, "provided the model for the majority of local groups around the country."[51] Intellectuals and professionals established other major groups in Chicago, Philadelphia, and Syracuse. The first president of the influential Boston Society was Mercer's old professor, Charles Eliot Norton; among the society's founders were his friends Arthur Carey and J. Templeman Coolidge, from the Harvard class of 1879. In June 1900, they helped elect Mercer to membership in the society in recognition of his tile production. A central function of Arts and Crafts Societies was to sponsor juried exhibitions, and Mercer exhibited his work in a number of Arts and Crafts shows. His exhibition triumph came in 1904 at the St. Louis World's Fair, where he displayed his tiles in an Arts and Crafts exhibit organized by the Boston Society. Mercer won a Grand Prize for his work.

In addition to the Boston Society, Mercer had significant contact with the Arts and Crafts community of Rose Valley, Pennsylvania. Rose Valley, located just south of Philadelphia, was perhaps the most ambitious of any of the Arts and Crafts experiments. Led by the charismatic and visionary architect Will Price, the members of the Rose Valley community—the "Rose Valley folk" as they called themselves—set up workshops and studios in renovated mill buildings. Price designed houses for several of the people who moved from the city to the valley.[52]

In building houses for Rose Valley, Will Price adhered to Ruskinian notions of the integrity of materials. In the Arts and Crafts magazine *The Craftsman,* published by Gustav Stickley, Price issued "A Plea for True Democracy in the Domestic Architecture of America." He wrote: "There are few materials that are not fit to build with. It is in the misuse of them that disaster comes. When you use wood treat it as wood even though it be painted. Stop using silly cut stone details and stone construction when you are building in other materials. Use stone, plaster, brick, concrete, tile, anything you will, but use them for what they are, and let their qualities be shown forth as well as their purpose, and above all keep ornament out, unless you can get real artsmen to put it in, and even then it must tell some story of purpose or interests." [53] The last thought is particularly significant, because when Price decided to ornament his Rose Valley buildings, he chose to use Mercer's tiles.

Beyond these professional and business associations, Mercer did subscribe to some of the Arts and Crafts ideology, though the definition of that ideology is somewhat slippery. All the Arts and Crafts Societies in America paid homage to the movement's founder, William Morris. Like Ruskin, Morris was distressed by what industrialization had done to both art and labor—Morris's movement, a combination of Ruskin and Marx, aimed to redeem both. [54] In America, however, Morris's social revolution became watered-down reform, and more often than not, simple aesthetic reform, not political or economic transformation. "Rather than creating a new ideal of labor," Eileen Boris writes, "they [American Arts and Crafters] developed a new aesthetic." [55] The notion of Arts and Crafts "reform" was expansive enough, or inconsistent enough, to accommodate such diverse figures as Charles Eliot Norton, Jane Addams, and Elbert Hubbard, a huckstering soap salesman from Buffalo. T. J. Jackson Lears, in his consideration of the Arts and Crafts Movement, characterizes its muddled ideology this way: "it was meanspirited and largehearted, suffused with upper-class forebodings and utopian aspirations." [56]

In the midst of this confusion was a belief shared among all the Arts and Crafts Societies that the industrial age had degraded both labor and art. The rejuvenation of each would come from the production of handmade things, which would simultaneously ennoble labor and allow for the blossoming of individual artistic creativity stifled by the machine. Like many in the Arts and Crafts Movement, Mercer did express concern about the impact of mechanization upon art. He stated bluntly, "The place of a machine is not in the field of art." [57] Discussing how the machine had effected tile production, he said, "A blight had . . . fallen upon the modern European tile maker's craft. . . . Their defects arose, not because the designs were bad . . . but because the tiles were products of machines and not men." [58] Such a statement resonated with many made by Arts and Crafts ideologues. [59]

Many Arts and Crafts theorists, taking their cues from Ruskin and Morris, looked to medieval Europe to find aesthetic (and in some cases spiritual) inspiration. Mercer too turned to the Middle Ages to find sources for his tile designs. In a lecture about pottery delivered in Norristown, Mercer told his audience how his appropriation of the spirit of the medieval period distinguished his ceramics from other contemporary production. "Our stores and houses are full of a lot of flashy pottery," he complained; "people pay huge sums and admire it—it is very slick, has tremendous glitter and lots of color, but it is dead." His pottery, on the other hand was alive because "it refers to the great church art of the middle ages." He advised his audience on how to proceed: "I would say first turn away from the modern pottery and for three or four years study the craftsmen of the middle ages. Copy their work faithfully, reproduce it again and again till you begin to learn to express your ideas as they expressed theirs. Then cease copying. Take the things of today and [translate] them into art."[60] Here Mercer describes his belief, shared with other Arts and Crafts colleagues, that the past—especially the medieval past—can serve as a useful teacher in an industrial age, and further that there needs to be a living, spontaneous connection between the past and the present.

Despite connections of friendship and professional association, and despite statements like those quoted above, however, Mercer's sense of the meanings of history and of the uses to which history should be applied in the present was ultimately different from that of the Arts and Crafters. He did not participate in the polemical debates that characterized so much of the Arts and Crafts Movement and that filled the pages of its journals. Price clearly admired Mercer's tile, but Mercer was never part of the Rose Valley community. He filed his correspondence with Price with his other business letters, not his personal letters, suggesting that he regarded his work for Price as he regarded his other business transactions. Mercer's tile production itself certainly did not conform to the craft ideal. Initially, Mercer wanted to resurrect an old tilemaking process, but he found this to be too expensive. Mercer reduced his costs by inventing a new technique, which produced "handmade tiles, cheap enough to sell and artistic enough to rival the old ones." Mercer's tiles were (and still are) efficiently stamped out of the clay in molds. Mercer's tiles appealed because each one had the look of being handmade. No tile, however, received the individual attention of a craftsman. Mercer operated his Tile Works on a strict quota system. At full stride, pairs of workers stamped out 4,000 tiles a day.[61]

The Arts and Crafts Movement had as its initial impulse the desire to reform art and labor and to create a handcraft aesthetic. These were not Mercer's primary goals in producing ceramic tile. Unlike Mercer, the lessons Arts and Crafters drew from the past were aesthetic and moral. Mercer was not interested in the aesthetics of his flax-brakes and leather awls; he was interested in what they could tell him about the process of American history. In a note written next to his diagram charting historical change through the evolution of objects, Mercer wrote: "In this estimate only consider facts *not moral effect.*"[62] Academic historians approached the past too detached from it, thus asking the wrong questions and answering them with the wrong method. Arts and Crafters sentimentally looked to the past as a refuge from the present, as a source of therapy, perhaps for the whole society, perhaps just for themselves. Mercer's concerns were different from both groups, and those concerns manifested themselves in his tile works.

The reason Mercer began to produce tiles lies in his ideas about history. His tile manufacturing can be considered in three parts. Initially, he produced "conventional," or regularly shaped tiles patterned after medieval tiles he had seen on his trips to Europe, after his own collection of Pennsylvania-German stove plates, and after other folk designs. He then began to produce what he called "mosaic" tiles. These were not tiles, strictly speaking, but ceramic puzzle pieces which, when set together, created quite elaborate pictures. Finally, he made "brocade" tiles, each one of which was a small picture element. A group of these would be set directly into wet concrete to produce a more complex scene.

The evolution of his tilemaking technique made it easier for Mercer to use them to tell stories. Writing to William Hagerman Graves in 1925, Mercer explained his ideas about what he called the "literary" side of his tiles: "Yet to me, this so called 'literary' side of the craft, this story telling, which I understand has been said to 'contaminate' painting, has been my primary impulse or inspiration. . . . If tiles could tell no story, inspire or teach nobody, and only serve to produce aesthetic thrills, I would have stopped making them long ago."[63] In this letter, Mercer clearly distinguishes his own work from the work of the Arts and Crafts aesthetic thrill-seekers.

Mercer told many stories with his tiles. He decorated fireplaces with the story of Bluebeard, with scenes from Wagner, and with the History of Firefighting. Whether it was the legend of Rip Van Winkle, or the story of Columbus's discovery of the New World, however, Mercer used his tiles most often to convey American history. In 1903, Mercer was commissioned to decorate the floor of the new State Capitol Building in Harrisburg. The preface Mercer wrote for the accompanying guidebook sums up the history illustrated by his tiles. "It is the life of the people that is sought to be expressed; the building of a commonwealth economically great, by the individual work of thousands of hands, rather than by wars and legislatures. . . . Historical events are not omitted, but rather take a minor place."[64] Mercer's use of his tiles was simply an extension in clay of his ideas about history, about how it should be told, and upon what it should focus. Convinced that history could be "written from the standpoint of objects," Mercer took this one step further. Rather than simply collecting objects he might find, Mercer found he could tell historical tales with objects he manufactured himself.

Mercer even told his own history in ceramic tile. In a pattern designed to decorate a fireplace, Mercer pictured the folktale "The Arkansas Traveler." The traveler, a city slicker, loses his way in the backwoods. After wandering about, he stumbles upon a farmer fiddling a traditional tune. The farmer, however, can only remember the first part of the song. The traveler from the city is able to teach the farmer the rest of it, and the grateful farmer offers his new teacher and friend shelter for the night. The next day he directs the traveler back to the city. As Mercer designed the tiles to illustrate this story, he represented himself and his mission: Mercer was the educated city man who ventured out to preserve the history and traditions of the country folk, and who hoped to teach that history and those traditions to those who had forgotten them.

Like other Arts and Crafters, Mercer looked to the past in part because he was ambivalent about the present. But he insisted that his gaze backward was neither romantic nor nostalgic, that it maintained some measure of scientific distance. Certainly we can see Mercer's tiles as part of the phenomenon we call the Arts and Crafts Movement. But just as clearly he pursued this craft for different reasons than did his colleagues. Mercer did not participate in their debates about art and labor, nor was he chiefly interested in developing a craft aesthetic. Instead, he could manipulate his tiles to tell his history most directly. He did this most dramatically in the State Capitol in Harrisburg, but the "literary" uses of his tiles were his primary concern in all of his commissions.

The financial success of the Moravian Tile Works finally separates Mercer from other Arts and Crafts producers. Despite the reforming passion that many of these crafters put into their work, most had gone bankrupt by the First World War. The Tile Works, however, continued to be profitable even after Mercer's death. In 1924 he chuckled: "All goes well at the pottery. We have more than held our own all these years. Most of our artistic rivals are gone in the sheriff's hands. . . . We have stirred up things pretty well in the tile world over here."[65]

The Modern and the Past

The stories Mercer told with his tiles, his admonition to study the ceramics of the middle ages, indeed, his entire collecting enterprise, reveal a man looking backward. Behind his whole collection, after all, was the irony that the modern world made the tools he collected obsolete and was simultaneously destroying their meanings. T. J. Jackson Lears considers the Arts and Crafters to have been a part of the "antimodern" phenomenon which transformed American culture between 1880 and 1920. Faced with a brave new world, these upper-middle-class intellectuals and aesthetes retreated into an idealized and romantic conception of the past. Ultimately, the critique of the modern world articulated as the craft ideal became little more than a therapeutic exercise.[66] To this extent, an "antimodern" impulse did propel Mercer's activities.

It would be unfair, however, to see Mercer—or Ford for that matter—simply as nostalgic antimoderns. Mercer and Ford's fascination with history was doubtless suffused with a wistfulness and sentimentality. That sense is palpable even today when visiting their museums. But Mercer probably more so than Ford believed that he pursued his collecting with scientific detachment, not with the romantic nostalgia that motivated Arts and Crafts enthusiasts. His collection stopped with objects circa 1820, he claimed, not because he was disdainful of the products of an increasingly industrialized world, but because after 1820 the Patent Office began maintaining accurate records. To collect objects after 1820 would therefore have been redundant and scientifically unnecessary.[67]

Rather than using historical objects as an escape to the past, Mercer and Ford wanted to make historical objects significant to the present, to demonstrate a seamlessness between past and present. Ford, after all, saw no contradiction in putting his museum history right next to the facility where new cars were designed. Engraved over the entrance to the Ford Engineering Laboratory one reads: "Mankind passes from the old to the new over a human bridge formed by those who labor in the three principal arts—Agriculture, Manufacture, and Transportation."

Mercer never expressed his ideas about history and the process of historical change more eloquently.

This vision, at once both backward- and forward-looking, is manifest as well in the buildings Mercer built for himself. Fonthill, his home, and the museum which houses his precious collection make fanciful architectural reference to medieval buildings—indirectly perhaps to German castles. Both are built entirely of reinforced concrete, which at the time was a revolutionary and modern building technique. Concrete, after all, was building the world from which the antimoderns recoiled. The *Architectural Record* found Mercer's buildings noteworthy enough for their modernity to discuss them. W. T. Taylor, writing in 1913, said of Fonthill: "In many points it flies defiantly in the face of all precedent, but in an equal number of points its growth is from stronger and better convictions than govern the greater part of our more widely accepted American architecture."[68] As Mercer himself said, his buildings "combine the poetry of the past with the convenience of the present."[69]

Mercer and Ford's ideas about the past and its relationship to the present, their love of concrete and cars, remind us of the complicated and sometimes contradictory ways history is used and misused, understood and misunderstood. Neither can be dismissed as purely "antimodern," and neither was as free from backward looking nostalgia as they believed. Ford and Mercer were of the same generation and their lives straddled the divide between the preindustrial past and the industrial future.

In the 1920s, however, as Mercer's museum inspired Ford to build his own, Mercer made a much younger friend. On and off through the late teens and early 1920s, the painter Charles Sheeler visited Doylestown to paint. During his stays he became friendly with Mercer. Sheeler would go on to become one of the most significant figures in American Modernism, and Mercer should be credited with helping to focus his artistic vision.

Having finished his training at the Pennsylvania Academy of the Fine Arts, and having returned from a European tour shortly after World War I, Sheeler found himself in a self-confessed professional state of confusion. After the war and through the mid-twenties, Sheeler rented an eighteenth-century farmhouse next door to Mercer in Doylestown which he used as a painting studio. During this period, Mercer functioned as something of a mentor to the young painter.[70]

It is impossible to know what the elderly Mercer and the young

Sheeler discussed during the latter's visits to Doylestown, but the correspondence they exchanged during the 1920s concerned the house Sheeler rented. Mercer wanted Sheeler to buy the old house to protect it from "some vandal," as Mercer put it to Sheeler, "or money-grubber who would either modernize it or pull it down." Sheeler never did buy the house and by 1926 Mercer had proved correct. The property was indeed sold and subdivided into small building lots, and upon learning of this news, Sheeler wrote to Mercer, "Of course the place would be ruined so far as I am concerned—with a flock of the inevitable bungalows around there." [71]

Sheeler would mature into one of this country's best known modernist painters. His most famous works are those of American industry, done in a sharp, clean, monochromatic "precisionist" style. Images like "Classic Landscape" and "Rolling Power" define this style and give Sheeler his reputation as a recorder of America's machine age. At the same time, Sheeler produced some equally provocative interior scenes, like "Williamsburg Kitchen" and "American Interior," which depict small domestic worlds inhabited by artifacts of the eighteenth and nineteenth centuries. Sheeler treated both sets of subjects similarly, and Karen Lucic has explained the unity of these subjects for Sheeler by saying: "The machine age encompassed everything within its domain." Lucic goes as far as to call Sheeler's domestic scenes "Machine age interiors." [72]

There is more, though, than an all-embracing "machine age" aesthetic that connects Sheeler's paintings of Bucks County barns and steam locomotives. Like Mercer and Ford, Sheeler perceived an essential connection between history and the present, between the past and the modern. He shared as well a fascination with objects as a way of making these connections. I do not want to suggest that Sheeler treated objects in paint the way Ford and Mercer treated them in their museums—Sheeler's concerns were those of a painter, not a historian, and the objects which found their way onto Sheeler's canvases had a primarily aesthetic purpose. But the distance may not be as great as it would first appear. As he himself explained in 1923, he wanted to achieve in his paintings "the absolute beauty we are accustomed to associate with objects in a vacuum." [73]

Constance Rourke, an astute cultural critic and Sheeler's first biographer, recognized particularly the painter's capacity for linking the past and the modern. She subtitled her 1938 biography *Artist in the American Tradition.* The central question she considered in the book was the relationship of modern painters to an ill-appreciated American painting tra-

dition. Sheeler was not to be commended for painting American subjects, Rourke argued. American painters had done that throughout the
nineteenth century. Rather, what distinguished Sheeler "was a sense of
derivations, that sense of the past from which art always springs, even
when the past is left behind."

Rourke saw architecture as the most powerful source of this "sense
of derivation." Identifying Sheeler's time in Doylestown as pivotal, she
believed Sheeler was "tapping into the main source by his use of architectural forms in Bucks County and likewise by his more or less conscious study of the handicrafts he found thereabouts." Rourke made the
case that Sheeler recognized the formal similarities between the modern
and the past. Her description of the farmhouse Sheeler rented in Doylestown might have well described a modern building: "Within were strong
beams, simple panels, deep embrasures. . . . All was clarity: the walls
were of that peculiar white which only freshly burned lime seems able
to create." In architecture, more than in any other art, Sheeler found an
essential and distinctive American artistic tradition and likewise
the inspiration for an American modernism: "In turning to architecture
Sheeler had discovered forms that were basic in American creative experience. . . . The impulse that constructed them reappeared in the New
England frame farmhouses and barns; stone cottages in Maryland are
allied to both groups as are certain one-room slave houses in Louisiana."

This last quotation reads like a partial catalogue of the buildings
Henry Ford moved to Greenfield Village. More than that, though, in discussing Charles Sheeler, Rourke summarizes how for all three history
was indeed connected to the present, how the past did inform the modern. Sheeler described his love of objects made by the Shakers by saying:
"I don't like these things because they are old, but in spite of it. I'd like
them still better if they were made yesterday because then they would
afford proof that the same kind of creative power is continuing."[74] As the
speed with which the world changed increased in the twentieth century,
causing the past to recede that much faster into the distance, Henry
Mercer, Henry Ford, and Charles Sheeler believed they could keep the
connection from disintegrating through the tangibility of objects and
buildings whose essential forms and functions would continue to influence the present.

In 1927 Henry Ford, working through the Ayer and Son company,
decided to have his massive River Rouge automobile factory photo-
graphically recorded. The photographs would serve to celebrate Ford's
industrial achievements by capturing the stark grandeur and geometric

19   Charles Sheeler, *Kitchen, Williamsburg,* 1937. Sheeler met Henry Mercer in Doylestown in the 1920s and his fascination for the kinds of objects that appear in this painting probably resulted from this friendship. Sheeler was then commissioned to take photographs of Henry Ford's River Rouge plant. These connections between the painter, the historian, and the industrialist raise interesting questions about the relationship between the modern and the past. (Fine Arts Museums of San Francisco, Gift of Mr. and Mrs. John D. Rockefeller 3rd, 1993.35.24)

beauty of his plant. Ayer chose Sheeler to take these photos. The photographs and the canvases they inspired stand as some of Sheeler's most stunning and enduring productions. Mercer was at the end of his life—perhaps it is more than coincidence that the industrialist should have chosen this painter for the job.

∼

In their conceptions of history and of how it should be studied, understood, and displayed, Mercer and Ford each believed he pointed the way to the future. Mercer told the BCHS that "in this collection called 'The Tools of the Nation Maker' we are ahead of everybody, we are original, alone and unique." [75] All that remained was for scholars to study the collection and publish their findings.

Though they clearly held similar ideas about history, it is important to note that Mercer and Ford were also importantly different. Ford's ideas about his history museum were overtly nationalistic. He explained: "We have no Egyptian mummies here, nor any relics of the Battle of Waterloo, nor do we have any curios from Pompeii, for everything we have is strictly American."[76] Mercer, as we have seen, saw connections between his collections and tools from other cultures.

Both Ford and Mercer thought that academic historians failed to make the necessary connections between the past and the present. Ford asked a reporter in 1916: "What do we care what they did five hundred or one thousand years ago?" And revealing his own Emersonian bent, he went on: "That's the trouble with the world. We're living in books and history and tradition."[77] History interested Ford only insofar as it helped improve the future; Mercer thought that the present and the past could elucidate the other. Each man turned to a history rooted in objects to achieve his end. When Ford clarified his statement about "bunk" by saying that "History as sometimes written is mostly bunk. But history that you can see is of great value," he articulated exactly the insight Mercer hoped one would have walking into the carefully classified confusion of his museum.

Yet beyond the founding of a few local historical societies, Mercer's influence, and the influence of his museum, have not been felt much beyond Bucks County.[78] Ford can be counted as his most significant disciple, but neither can claim to have won the debate over how history should be studied. In part, this may be due to the fact that Mercer provided no clear methodology to extract meaning from objects. He never quite explained what one was supposed to do in the presence of these artifacts.[79] Reading history from ordinary objects, which seemed so easy and clear to Mercer, proved more difficult and opaque for others.

In addition, at precisely the moment when institutional and professional affiliations were becoming increasingly important, Mercer burned his academic bridges. The world of professional historians, a world more and more concerned with developing the kind of rigorous methodologies Mercer never articulated, had little use for amateur generalists like him.[80] Whatever the reasons for his obscurity, the eager students Mercer expected to come to Doylestown never arrived.

Toward the end of his life, Mercer made his final attempt to tell history from the perspective of objects. His *Ancient Carpenters' Tools* is a carefully photographed and meticulously described catalogue of tools arranged in specific categories. In his Preface, he reiterates his essential themes one last time. In terse, weary paragraphs, lacking the fervor that characterized his earlier writings, Mercer tells the reader that these tools are at the foundation of civilization, that they remained largely unchanged from Roman times until the eighteenth century, and that they are virtually identical to implements used by many ancient societies. Because of all this, he tells us, these tools "are of far more extended industrial interest than the wood-working machines of today, which, despite their economic importance, have at most only been with us for about a hundred years." He continues: "To weigh the historic significance of the universal distribution of these ancient tools, is to realize that all attempts to display them in order to glorify modern machinery can only distort history."[81] These are Mercer's final words about the relationship between technology and civilization, between our society and others around the world, and between history as it is usually told, and history as it ought to be told.

By the time Mercer died in 1930, he had not succeeded in reorienting the study of American history, as he had hoped to do. History continued to be written largely about the few great men and about great intangible forces. In an era when professional historians, archaeologists, anthropologists, and folklorists were energetically trying to parse the differences between their disciplines and to establish their own institutional footholds, Mercer cut his university connections and insisted in working in all of these fields. Just as his collection was an attempt to preserve that which was being destroyed by modern society, so too his career flew in the face of the prevailing academic wind. Rather than develop his own object-based methodology for the study of history, one which might have competed with other academic disciplines, Mercer continued to believe that the objects he collected yielded their meaning without difficulty or resistance.

That the museum method of history Mercer developed and Ford admired failed to become the mainstream of professional, academic American historical understanding is only one measure of the relative isolation of their efforts. Mercer and Ford failed to inspire many museum imitators either, and this legacy, or the lack thereof, requires some explanation as well. After all, the study of natural science may have left the museums, but those museums proliferated and flourished. Mercer and Ford's museums, on the other hand, stand just as lonely in the museum world as they do in the historical world.

Let me qualify that quickly: this country is littered with historical museums, monuments, and societies. But in my estimation, the vast majority tend either to preserve exactly the kind of associative material— the George Washington, or Ulysses S. Grant, or William McKinley slept here approach—that Mercer and Ford despised, or they freeze in amber a very specific historical moment. Deerfield Village in Massachusetts, Williamsburg, Virginia, and Independence National Park in Philadelphia come to mind as examples of this type. There are very few historical museums with the kind of comprehensive ambition as Mercer's and Ford's, where the entire scope of American history has been put on display within some kind of organizing framework.

The reason for this may lie in the nature of those frameworks themselves. Mercer in particular—and Ford in a less rigorous way—tried to conceive of an evolutionary model around which to organize history, with labor operating as the force driving the process forward. In this Mercer borrowed from the museum techniques of natural history and anthropology, and in those cases the evolutionary model had provided a plausible, comprehensible, even reassuring way of understanding the natural and the cultural worlds. History, however, and the particular relationship Americans have with their history may resist this schematizing more so than plants or exotic cultures.

As we have seen, at the heart of this evolutionary model was the notion of hierarchy and progress. Never mind for a moment that most late Victorians misunderstood the implications of Darwinian natural selection; the museums they visited showed that life began as crude and simple and that it evolved forward in increasingly complex ways, culminating finally in human beings. American history could not be presented quite so neatly. Americans viewed the history of their nation—and probably still do—as a paradoxical and contradictory mix of both progress and declension, of evolution and genesis. America's best moments are always behind us, forged in the cauldrons of great crises by larger-than-life heroes, or they are ahead of us in some vague future. Never are they in the disappointing present. For a history museum to arrange its objects to demonstrate a sense of evolutionary progress would mean denying the gloriousness of our past. To revel in the triumphs of the past would mean measuring the long distance of our present decline. Facing history forces Americans to confront simultaneously what has been lost as well as what has been gained in a way that the confrontation with extinct mollusks or even lost cultures does not.

Perhaps the historian who best understood these dilemmas was Henry Adams, a man who also resided professionally on the margins of academic history. More so than any other historical writer of the period, Adams searched, with increasing desperation, for a way to reconcile the new world of Darwinian evolution, of x-rays and radium, with history.

Adams was determined to make history conform to natural laws, to give it order, rationality, and purpose. He failed, and his is surely the most spectacular failure in the history of American thought. As he descended into corrosive cynicism over his failure, he retained a caustic wit about it all. Recognizing that Darwin meant the end of design in the natural world, he could quip in his *Education:* "The progress of evolution from President Washington to President Grant was alone evidence to upset Darwin." [82]

And in that jibe is the essence of the problem of how to conceive of a history museum using the only model available in the late-nineteenth century. How was one supposed to present the "evolution" from Washington to Grant, exactly? Adams, much as it made him despair, had finally to conclude that history had no frameworks—science certainly offered no such understanding. History was ultimately a set of disconnected actions, force without purpose, power without principle. This view of history, needless to say, did not sit well with Adams's contemporaries, and it has proved nettlesome to this day. [83]

Museums do not seem to have contributed much to Henry Adams's education. He "looked at most accumulations of art in the storehouses called Art Museums," but these visits did not apparently provide him with any of the intellectual comfort he was seeking. But it is surely not coincidental that some of Adams's epiphanal moments came when he strolled through some of the great world's fairs, those temporary companions to the museums. In 1893 in Chicago Adams "found matter of study to fill a hundred years," but predictably "his education spread over chaos." The passage has become canonical in American letters but is worth considering again in our context. At the fair, where millions saw the promise of a world of objects rationally arranged, where the positivist, progressive view of the world was most gloriously displayed, Adams recoiled:

> Education ran riot at Chicago, at least for retarded minds which had never faced in concrete form so many matters of which they were ignorant. Men who know nothing whatever . . . had no choice but to sit down on the steps and brood . . . aghast at what they had said and done in all these years, and still more ashamed of the childlike ignorance and babbling futility of the society that let them say and do it. The historical mind can think only in historical processes, and probably this was the first time since historians existed, that any of them had sat down helpless before a mechanical sequence.

"Chicago," Adams believed, "asked in 1893 for the first time the question whether the American people knew where they were driving." Adams, of course, did not know.[84]

Seven years later, Adams would find himself standing before the great electric dynamos at the Paris exposition and recognize them as the amoral moral force of a world he could not understand, feeling about them "much as the early Christians felt [about] the Cross."[85] The world of objects Adams saw at these fairs only heightened his sense that he could not even comprehend the way history worked, much less master those forces.

Mercer and Ford both felt reassurance in their historical objects, and what remains intriguing about Mercer and Ford is that, like American historians today who grapple with how to give historical voice to those ordinary people silent in traditional historiography, they wrestled with many of the same questions. The difference between our struggles and theirs, of course, is that Ford and Mercer believed they had found the answer.

~

From South Kensington to the Louvre:
Art Museums and the Creation of Fine Art

> The Museum, in short, was going to be great, and in the ge-
> niality of the life to come such sacrifices, though resem-
> bling those of the funeral-pile of Sardanapalus, dwindled to
> nothing.
>
> HENRY JAMES

They came like supplicants to an altar.

In 1920 New York's Metropolitan Museum of Art celebrated its fiftieth anniversary in characteristically grand fashion. Representatives from several of this country's other major art museums, including Boston's Museum of Fine Arts and Chicago's Art Institute, journeyed to Fifth Avenue bearing messages of homage. Bringing a "tribute" from Boston, Morris Gray gushed almost sycophantically to the assembled dignitaries and socialites: "The Metropolitan is indeed the gift of New York to the country. And we Americans of other cities who have no share in the making must needs feel gratitude for the gift—proud of the giver."[1] And so it went throughout the evening.

The event, the fifty years that it marked, and the fawning of delegates from the "provinces" would surely have made the founders glad. Those members of New York's social and commercial establishment who met in the wake of the Civil War had embarked to build exactly what, fifty years later, now stood on Fifth Avenue: the most opulent museum filled with the most treasured art in the United States, a museum which would be both the standard for and the envy of every other art museum in the country, first among cultural institutions in the nation. From its founding in 1870 this had been the Metropolitan's destiny, and the museum reached it, at least in the minds of some, quite quickly. James Jackson Jarves, writing in the *New York Times* in 1882, claimed confidently, if also self-servingly, "The Metropolitan Museum in New York enjoys in Europe the reputation of being a national institution. . . . Its cosmopolitan reputation . . . overshadow[s] the other American museums."[2]

At one level there can be no argument with the assessment of those who gathered in 1920. The Metropolitan had become almost certainly the preeminent art museum in the United States. Those who founded it sought nothing less than a museum to rank with the very best in Europe, and they had achieved this with breathtaking speed. A history of the Metropolitan could quite justifiably be a chronicle of dazzling acquisitions, purchases, and accumulation, beginning from its earliest days and continuing through to the present.[3] The Metropolitan, more than any other museum, stands as the elegant child produced by the union between the vast fortunes of America's robber barons and the refined good taste of its social elite.

Occupying as it does a singular position in America's cultural hierarchy, the Metropolitan Museum of Art has "won" the debate whose terms it framed in the last quarter of the nineteenth century. The Met defines both what we consider great art and what we believe a great art museum ought to be. This history I have just glanced at is, therefore, the sort of which many historians are suspicious—the kind written by the "winners," glossing over the struggles and uncertain moments, obscuring the "losers." In this case, the struggles involved how "fine art" would be defined and what the category would encompass. Further, the debate involved a struggle over how a museum of fine art should function in American society, what values it should express, for what purpose and for whom. The "losers," in this case, were those who envisioned a different kind of art museum, one which would serve more as a school or laboratory than as a temple or refuge, a place which would be not merely a cultural antidote to the vulgar materialism of the late-nineteenth-century world, but be an uplifting part of that world.

The process of defining the art museum, and the fine art that would reside in its galleries, involved negotiations over the museum's audience, over the way it would conduct its educational mission, and over the very objects to be displayed. All three of these considerations were necessarily linked in the late nineteenth century, and the boundaries around them fluid. Only in the first quarter of the twentieth century did these issues become effectively resolved, producing the art museum as we understand it today.

The outcome of the debate helped solidify what Lawrence Levine has called the "cultural hierarchy" we live with today.[4] That art museums enjoy a greater status than other kinds of museums seems now self-evident and obvious. At the turn of the twentieth century, however, their position at the top of the hierarchy was not guaranteed. Several factors doubtless contributed to this victory, among them that art museums attracted a disproportionate number of this country's wealthiest philanthropists.[5] What I will suggest in this chapter, however, is that principal among those factors is the way in which art objects themselves function in art museums.

Art museums, as they developed in the late nineteenth and early twentieth centuries, can be seen as places of ritual, in Walter Benjamin's sense, where the objects inside continued to retain their "aura," or in some cases were invested with an aura they may not have previously had. The art museum provided the context for the objects inside to retain their authority, where authenticity could be adjudicated, and where the historical testimony of objects could be heard. More than any of the other museum objects we have examined, those objects which finally fell under the rubric of fine art were originally intended to be viewed in much the same way as they are viewed in the museum. In this sense, they retained, and continue to retain, more of their epistemological value than anthropological, historical, or commercial objects. Not coincidentally, therefore, they continue to be integral to the production of knowledge about art. Economists, anthropologists, historians, and biologists, located as they are in university departments, may no longer need the objects that filled the late-nineteenth-century museums, but most art historians still rely on actual works of art themselves to produce art historical knowledge. In this case, the university department did not so completely abandon the museum.

The art museum that sits today at the pinnacle of our cultural hierarchy did not come into being fully formed. What we will look at here is the process through which one vision of the art museum triumphed over another. These two competing visions of the art museum can be summarized, without too much distortion, as a difference between those who looked to the Louvre for their model and those who turned instead to London's South Kensington complex. In the last quarter of the nineteenth century, New York's Metropolitan Museum of Art chose the Louvre, while Philadelphia's museum chose South Kensington. During the period under consideration, the two models competed with each other. By the 1920s the Louvre stood alone.

South Kensington Comes to the United States

When the "Art Committee" of the incipient "Metropolitan Art-Museum" met at the Union League in 1869, they resolved to create "a well-planned national institution devoted to Art." A year later the "Executive Committee" drew more specifically the contours of the institution. Echoing the encyclopedic aspirations of the nineteenth century museum project, the Executive Committee announced that "the Metropolitan Museum of Art should be based on the idea of a more or less complete collection of objects illustrative of the History of Art, from the earliest beginnings to the present time." The Committee also specified a definition of "Art." In its view, Architecture, Sculpture, and Painting constituted the "three great arts," while "Pottery, Porcelain, Engravings, Mosaics, Metal Works, Textile Fabrics, etc." and all of the "Arts in relation to life, and to Manufactures" fell under the broad category of the "Subsidiary Ornamental Arts."[6]

As they defined their scope with almost casual grandeur, New York's ambitious institution builders cast about looking for European museums upon which to model their own. George Fiske Comfort, a Princeton professor involved in helping start the museum, urged George Putnam in a letter to consider, among others, the Leipzig Museum, the Amsterdam Museum, the Gotha Museum, and the 'National Museum' then under construction in Berlin.[7] But as American museologists looked to Europe, however, London's South Kensington complex stood out as the most dynamic and exciting intellectual and institutional development of the age. Just as importantly, the South Kensington museums opened themselves to the general public to a much greater extent than virtually any other European museum—across town, the British Museum remained accessible only "by appointment" until well into the nineteenth century. South Kensington's more democratic ambitions seemed better suited to the pretensions and aspirations of American museum builders. Many Americans saw in South Kensington a model of sufficient scope and ambition to suit their own projects.

South Kensington grew out of the enthusiasm generated by the 1851

Crystal Palace Exhibition. The site itself remained relatively undeveloped until the exhibition, when it was transformed by the Royal Commission responsible for the exhibition. With new roads laid out, an Underground stop added in 1864, and several more international exhibitions (1862, 1871–74, and 1883–86), South Kensington became the site of a vast complex of museums and other public institutions. The Natural History Museum and the Victoria and Albert (originally the South Kensington Museum) occupy the southern end of this complex, which then stretches for roughly half a mile along Exhibition Road. Take the walk north toward Hyde Park and you will pass the museums of geology and science, the Imperial College of Science and Technology, the Royal College of Music, and the Albert Hall. Had you taken that same walk at the end of the nineteenth century, you would also have passed a collection of British art, the national School of Design, the Department of Science and Art, public gardens, the India Museum, the collections of the Patent Office, the Royal School of Art Needlework, and the National Training School of Cooking (though one practically cringes at what might have been taught in a nineteenth century British cooking school).

Unifying this vast array of institutions was a vision that fused art and science, especially through the field of industrial design. These museums and schools would serve to raise the taste of both British producers and consumers, and the institutional complex would pursue a nationalistic project by linking elevated taste with British artistic production. Henry Cole, a driving force behind South Kensington, successfully had British painting removed from the National Gallery on Trafalgar Square and put on display in South Kensington. Through this vast "exhibitionary complex," to borrow critic Tony Bennett's phrase, South Kensington demonstrated to a nineteenth-century world uncertain about the prospect that art and science could flourish together, each nurturing the other.[8]

While South Kensington seemed to provide the most ambitious example of what a museum complex might be, those who built the Metropolitan had an equivocal relationship with South Kensington. When the founders met at the Union League in 1869, C. C. Cole represented his brother Henry's project to those assembled. Early in 1870 a subcommittee of the group reported back suggesting that the museum "should include not only collections of paintings and sculpture, but should also contain drawings, engravings, medals, photographs, architectural models, historical portraits, and specimens illustrating the application of art to manufactures."[9]

When the Metropolitan's first Central Park building opened officially in March 1880, trustee Joseph Choate reminded the dedication-day crowd that the South Kensington complex had served in England both to raise taste and business profits through improved industrial design. He hoped that the Metropolitan would have the same salutary effects in New York. South Kensington seemed so much on the minds of those interested in the success of the Metropolitan that it caused E. T. Magauran to make a revealing slip. In offering space to the Executive Committee for the first exhibition, Magauran hoped he could be of service to the "directors of the Museum of Science and Art." [10]

Whatever the appeal South Kensington had for these New Yorkers, the Metropolitan would never be a museum of "science and art." Indeed, even from the outset, South Kensington provided an imperfect model for the New Yorkers. The Executive Committee's 1870 report noted that the South Kensington Museum "being the latest, suggests itself most naturally as a model for us," but it went on to say that because of South Kensington's emphasis on "Ornamental Manufactures and the Schools of Design . . . this collection could not serve for us in all respects as a pattern." [11] Although those who shaped the Metropolitan hoped it would be of educational use to the general public, South Kensington's attempts to link the aesthetic and the functional, the artistic and the industrial, proved to be not precisely the kind of educational experiments those on Fifth Avenue wanted.

Implicit in the 1870 delineation of the fields of art was that "great" art primarily would grace the galleries of the Metropolitan. Those behind the museum proved this through an inaugural exhibition of paintings they put together in 1871. Old Masters, particularly works by Rubens and Van Dyke, excited people's attention and foreshadowed the kind of institution into which the Met would eventually grow.

J. P. Morgan's arrival at the helm of the Met in 1904 signaled the official end of "the educational ideals of the South Kensington Museum," according to the Met's biographer Calvin Tomkins. Morgan assembled on the Metropolitan's board some of the wealthiest men in America, turning the board into the richest and most exclusive "club" in the city. With money enough to match his ambitions, Morgan ended the Metropolitan's deference to European museums. Working with Roger Fry, who complained in 1905 that the Met had "as yet no Byzantine paintings, no Giotto . . . no Botticelli, no Leonardo," Morgan and the rest of the board endeavored to accumulate what Fry termed "exceptional and spectacular pieces." [12]

20   After the Centennial Exposition closed, the new Pennsylvania Museum was housed in Memorial Hall, the only major building left from the fair. Located in Philadelphia's Fairmount Park, Memorial Hall housed the museum for fifty years. (Courtesy of the Philadelphia Museum of Art)

Sir Caspur Purdon Clark's brief career in New York almost symbolically underscored the end of the Metropolitan's brief and tentative flirtation with South Kensington's ideals. Morgan hired ("bought" according to the anecdote) Sir Caspur, then director of the South Kensington Museum, to be director of the Metropolitan in 1905. He did not last long. Weakened by illness almost from the beginning (the illness was attributed at the time to New York's climate, but New York's social climate and his imperious boss J. P. Morgan probably did little for his health), Clark fled back across the Atlantic in 1909 and resigned officially in 1910. Thus the Metropolitan unceremoniously said goodbye to South Kensington.

Ninety miles to the south, however, Philadelphians involved in establishing that city's art museum saw much greater promise in South Kensington. The Metropolitan was one third of a set of museum triplets born in 1870. In Washington, banker William Wilson Corcoran established an art museum around his personal collection. In Boston, the

Museum of Fine Arts received a charter in February, though it would not exist as a place to visit until 1876. It was in that Centennial year that Philadelphia joined these other eastern cities in establishing a museum of art.

Ostensibly the Centennial Exposition, held in Philadelphia's Fairmount Park, commemorated one hundred years of the American political experiment. But the event looked less to the past than reveled in the present, and in so doing the exposition also provided Americans with the chance to compare their progress with that of European countries. "Now is the time," wrote the *Philadelphia Times,* "for us to compare the national industries of the world." [13] As a yardstick against which Americans could measure their political and industrial progress, the Centennial demonstrated that the nation had accomplished a great deal.

At the same time, the Exposition was the source of some embarrassment. American products, as compared to those exhibited by European countries, seemed artistically crude, and American fine art seemed particularly backward. [14] One newspaper reporter caustically observed: "The Fairmount Park Association needed no Ruskin to declare that art and belles lettres do not find luxuriant growth in a region busy with the whirr of multitudinous machines." [15] American industrial products performed as well as any made in Europe, but according to one industry representative, "it is only when the artistic test is applied that any one of our industrial products fails in comparison." [16] The lack of artistic or design standards irritated other observers who saw the deficiency as creating a dependence on Europe. Assessing the Centennial one year after it closed, the *Philadelphia Press* complained that the exposition "for the first time made potent the fact that we were annually paying enormous sums to other countries, not for articles of special utility, but for forms of beauty." The writer called this America's "yearly tribute to art." [17]

Those who cared about such things hoped that the Centennial would reverse this situation and do for the United States what the Crystal Palace Exhibition had done for Great Britain in 1851. After all, observers pointed out, in 1851 English industrial design had been the worst in Europe, but the Crystal Palace Exhibition served to catapult that country to the forefront in the field. Surely the Centennial could have the same effect on this country. Walter Smith, State Director for Art Education in Massachusetts, in a speech delivered in Philadelphia, expressed this hope and echoed the nationalistic impulse that lay behind the South Kensington project: "Political emancipation in one form took place in

America one hundred years ago. Suppose we now try to emancipate ourselves from another kind of bondage to foreigners, and begin to develop what we know to be in us, and thus make ourselves industrially, as well as politically, an independent nation." [18] The Centennial celebration of 1876 would announce a new declaration of industrial and aesthetic independence.

The planners recognized that the exposition itself could not accomplish this goal. They hoped that the event would awaken Americans to the need for extensive industrial education throughout the nation. Beginning with a core collection assembled and donated from the Centennial, the Pennsylvania Museum would lead the way in providing Americans with an education in industrial design. This in turn would make American products more valuable, so the planners believed. As envisioned by its founders, the Pennsylvania Museum would educate the tastes of both producers and consumers, just as the South Kensington institutions had done.

As the idea for such a project circulated, one newspaper sternly told its readers: "It is high time that the citizens of Philadelphia were awakening to the importance, from a strictly material point of view, of schools of industrial art." The writer continued by reminding readers of the intended constituency of this new institution, pointing out that Philadelphia was "the greatest manufacturing centre on the continent." If the city expected to retain this position, "we must pay attention to the artistic education of our workmen and those who are becoming workmen." [19] The museum's founders believed that eventually it "could not fail to have a most beneficial influence upon the industries of our State and City." [20] That a school and museum could provide an industrial education and thus improve the quality of America's industrial production was a theme picked up by Pennsylvania governor John Frederick Hartranft. Giving a speech in the Centennial year, he told his audience: "Museums, art galleries, and other public collections are also important forces in industrial education." [21]

Philadelphians saw a museum as an indirect way to increase the value of industrial production in the city's factories. New Yorkers too recognized the economic potential of a great museum, but in slightly different terms; many in New York saw a major art museum as a way of attracting money, or at least those who had it, to the city. If New York was to become the nation's premier "social metropolis," and no one in the city would dispute that this was New York's preordained destiny, then an art museum would serve as a magnet to draw members of

America's upper-class from all over the country to move to the city. "It is taking the low view of art," wrote one journalist in 1871, "to put it upon the ground of the material and pecuniary recompenses it is likely to bring in; but low as it is, it is still a view that is not always to be neglected." [22]

Philadelphia's Centennial planners, and those who then shaped the museum which grew out of it, modeled their efforts more explicitly on the South Kensington experiment than did their counterparts in New York. Repeatedly the museum's founders referred to the school and museum complex in South Kensington as the source of their ideas. The Provisional Committee set up to plan the new institution, chaired by William Platt Pepper (University of Pennsylvania provost William Pepper's uncle), outlined the scope of the museum and school, and made explicit its English design. Reporting on November 19, 1875, the committee announced plans: "To establish in Philadelphia, for the State of Pennsylvania, a Museum of Art in all its branches as applied to Industry, and in all its technical applications, and to provide in connection therewith, with a special view to the development of the Art Industries of the State of Pennsylvania, opportunities and means of giving instruction in Drawing, Painting, Modeling, and Designing, in their industrial applications, through Lectures, Practical Schools and Special Libraries." Concluding the report, the committee felt that Philadelphia's new museum and school should be "in all respects similar to that of the South Kensington Museum of London." [23] The following fall, as the exposition itself wound down, the museum began to emerge as a viable project. The *Philadelphia Times* told its readers that the Centennial and the South Kensington complex "were organized from the same motive precisely—that of providing opportunities for the public, in the most comprehensive way, of instruction in the principles of art, as applied to all the industries." [24] The following year, when the museum and school had scarcely begun its activities, Walter Smith of Massachusetts wrote that "the P[ennsylvania] Museum & School of Industrial Art is today the most promising scheme economically, in the United States, for a purely public purpose." [25] Implicit in this statement was that the Metropolitan had neither the same economic promise nor the same public purpose.

Philadelphia's decision to focus more thoroughly on industrial art set it apart from the Metropolitan where, as we have already seen, industrial art had been forced off the stage by the bright lights of fine art masterpieces. In the last quarter of the nineteenth century, however, New York, not Philadelphia, seemed atypical of American museums. Neil

Harris pointed out some years ago that the Boston Museum of Fine Arts, founded in the same year as the Met and opened in the Centennial year, was not originally intended to be a fine arts treasure house either. Boston's MFA rested, at least initially, on three principles: art, education, and industry.[26]

Philadelphia was thus also at the forefront of a larger enthusiasm for industrial art education. By 1880, this "movement" had grown large enough to demand attention from the federal government. J. Edward Clarke, of the Interior Department's Bureau of Education, wrote to Dalton Dorr soliciting information for a survey of art schools. He explained to Dorr: "The unprecedented interest in all matters relating to art education in the United States, arising largely from the impetus given by the Centennial Exhibition makes it especially important that those connected with all such schools and institutions should furnish full statements of their progress and development."[27] Clarke's survey suggests that the Centennial was living up to its promise to be the American answer to the Crystal Palace Exposition. Likewise, those at the museum were convinced that through industrial design education, the museum could fill a genuinely useful role in the nation's burgeoning industrial economy.

Nowhere did that economy burgeon more than in the Quaker City, and the museum's founders were well aware that improvements in industrial design might very well aid the city's multiplicitous manufacturing concerns. As the *Philadelphia Public Ledger* explained, "Philadelphia, as the great centre of manufactures, looks to industrial art to supply the instruction which shall enable it to maintain its place and even to advance to a superiority over the products of foreign countries." This, then, became another distinction between New York's museum and Philadelphia's. While each tried to define the field of art, and to define how art museums should function for the "public good," they also reflected two differing conceptions of urban destiny. Just as Philadelphia's museum reflected its factories and workshops, the *Ledger* went on to explain how the Metropolitan similarly mirrored New York City: "New York, concentrating large masses of the capital of the country, naturally attracts the incidental accompaniments of great wealth, collections of art in the houses of its rich men."[28] A working man's museum for a working man's city; a rich man's museum for a rich man's city.

The Pennsylvania Museum deliberately targeted a broad audience and advertised itself as a place for ordinary citizens, not an exclusive

and elitist palace of art. Reflecting a concern for reaching the city's working population, Dalton Dorr, secretary of the Museum's Board, reminded
readers of the 1879 *Annual Report* that while the museum enjoyed support from "that portion of the community who are able to visit similar
institutions elsewhere," the primary function of the institution was to
"benefit . . . that vast majority of our citizens, the artizans [*sic*] and
mechanics, for whom it is the only resort of the kind accessible."[29] The
Philadelphia Press echoed this sentiment, but saw the Museum as a
middle-class institution. The *Press* told its readers that "the Pennsylvania Museum is designed more for the culture of the great middle class
than the entertainment of those whose aesthetic tastes have already
been developed by study or travel."[30]

Certainly we must take Philadelphians' rhetoric of democratic accessibility with the appropriate measure of salt. At the same time though,
there do seem to have been real differences in who came to visit the two
institutions. Both museums enjoyed considerable popularity in the last
quarter of the nineteenth century. Housed in Memorial Hall, the largest
building left from the 1876 celebrations, the Pennsylvania Museum probably attracted visitors who came to Fairmount Park for a day's outing. In
1883 alone, Park Commissioners recorded an astonishing 5,000,000 pe-
destrians who strolled through the Park.[31] Even so, when the museum's
Annual Report of 1890 counted an attendance of 312,000, that figure represented 30 percent of the city's population.

Because it was a place where all city residents might mingle to contemplate art and design, and where they might learn lessons to be put
later to productive use, Pennsylvania governor John Hartranft even believed that the museum could apply a healing salve to the growing rifts
in an industrial society. In an extraordinary "message" delivered to the
Commonwealth in 1878, Governor Hartranft suggested that institutions
like the new museum could ease the tension between laborers and their
bosses by restoring a craftsman's sense of pride in workmanship. In the
governor's view, the Pennsylvania Museum could provide the means to
preserve social stability.[32]

Still, the kinds of visitors those figures represented troubled some
who ran the museum. In arguing for a new museum site, the *Annual Report* of 1885 complained that the museum was not accessible enough to
horse-drawn carriages. The park, and thus the museum too, could be
reached easily by public transportation (unlike today, alas) but not so
easily by private conveyance. This, according to the *Report* was "a chief

reason why the Museum is so seldom visited and so little known by the very class of our citizens on whom we are chiefly dependent for encouragement and support."[33] At least in its early years, for some of the Pennsylvania Museum's guardians it seems to have been too popular with the city's middle and working classes and not popular enough with its wealthy.

I do not want to make too much of these off-handed references to the Pennsylvania Museum's visitors. Among other things, they reveal a confusion, or an elision between blue collar artisans and workers and middle-class, white collar aspirants. As I have discussed in the introductory chapter, it has not been my purpose in this book to deal with the immensely complicated and important issue of audience, and quotes like these require far more interrogation before they can be used to make definitive claims. Still, the differences between Philadelphia's museum and New York's do seem to have been underscored by who came and who did not. In contrast to the statements made in the Philadelphia papers, the New York press complained repeatedly and bitterly about the Metropolitan's exclusivity through the last quarter of the nineteenth century and took up a greater accessibility as a cause. "Could any prospect be more uninviting," the *Evening Post* asked in 1879, "than that presented at present to a skilled workman in search of knowledge, when he has set foot within the precincts of our Museum of Art?"[34]

Through the 1880s, a battle raged in the press over whether the Metropolitan would open its doors on Sundays. While opponents of Sunday opening held up the sanctity of Sabbath day observations as the reason that the Met should stay closed, the press portrayed the controversy as a "classes" versus "masses" fight. The *New York Herald* blared in a 1891 headline: "Let the Poor View the Art Treasures."[35] The Met ultimately capitulated to this public pressure, and huge crowds began enjoying the art on Sundays.

The contest over what kind of people could visit the museum did not end there, however. Miffed at being forced to open on Sundays, the Board of Trustees reminded the world that "the step remains only an experiment," and carped that the move "has offended some of the Museum's best friends and supporters."[36] A few years after this, in 1897, the Met's Trustees voted to ban the wearing of overalls in the galleries. When a plumber came to the Met after work in the now-forbidden garments, he was ungraciously tossed out. The *New York Journal* brought this to the attention of its readers by asking: "Overalls in Museum? Never! Workmen in Workmen's Garb Not Fit to Gaze on Art."

Without exaggerating the differences between those who visited the two museums, however, or between those who were intended to visit, these cursory observations hint that the different conceptions of what an art museum should be, what should be displayed in it, and how it should function were also related to and perhaps helped answer the question of who was welcome to stroll the galleries and who was not.[37]

Natural History Redux: The Systematics of Art

To visit the Metropolitan Museum of Art today is to walk through a glorious agglomeration. The arrangement of objects in the museum's spaces, and those spaces themselves, verge on the chaotic, as old buildings have been incorporated into new ones and as the whole museum has expanded almost organically by growing new wings. Part of the experience of touring the Met is the unexpected and surprising pleasures found from walking through a gallery of seventeenth century French objects to a collection of objects from the South Pacific, on the way to twentieth century European paintings.

From its beginnings, the organization of the Metropolitan's collections has been shaped as much by a desire to preserve the integrity of the individual collections it has acquired, and to highlight its "masterpieces," as by the imposition of art historical categories. A major gallery reinstallation undertaken in 1906 included a main gallery "of masterpieces by artists of different countries hung to secure the greatest aesthetic satisfaction, as was done in the Louvre."[38] Often the individual collections have a recognizable art historical unity, like the Annenberg collection of Impressionist paintings. In other cases, most spectacularly with the Lehman collection, which includes art from across several centuries and countries, the unifying principle is simply the taste of the collector, and the Metropolitan has preserved that through its installations. The Met's first Central Park building highlighted its first major collection given by a single donor, the di Cesnola collection of Cypriot antiquities. To some extent the Met has always been and remains a monument both to art and to individual art collectors.

In Philadelphia, however, the objects on display were expected to function educationally and epistemologically. Not surprisingly then, the Philadelphians who ran the museum borrowed from the systematics of natural history to create a taxonomy of industrial art and design. To do this, the design qualities of utilitarian objects occupied center stage at the Pennsylvania Museum. The museum displayed objects which, in a different museum context, might be appreciated and understood for their archaeological and ethnological value. This enabled those at the museum to draw connections, through their exhibits, between contemporary ceramic production in Trenton, New Jersey, for example, and ancient pottery from the American Southwest. At the Pennsylvania Museum, however, these kinds of objects illustrated what could be learned about method and design from "producers" around the world and across time. Edward Cope described the collection from the Pacific, for example, as containing "full representations of their industrial art in textiles & wood carvings, in weapons, boat forms etc."[39] Cope saw what some would consider cultural artifacts as examples of "industrial art." In this way the exhibits at Memorial Hall gave a history and an artistic fullness to contemporary manufactured products. Though the museum did not bring an anthropological understanding of culture to the display of South Seas textiles, as the University Museum would struggle to do, its exhibits did make a utilitarian connection between foreign cultures and the industrial West. Further, the exhibits were organized precisely to suggest that the "industrial" design of those people could contribute to the artistic quality of products made in Philadelphia.

When the Pennsylvania Museum opened in 1877, visitors found the exhibits systematically arranged and classified, "grouping together, so far as practicable, objects of similar character." Arranged this way, visitors could "study" the objects "more intelligently."[40] This arrangement, however, quickly proved unsatisfactory. Coleman Sellers complained in a letter to W. W. Justice in 1879 that the organization of displays deserved the criticism that some had heaped upon it because "it presents a most incongruous appearance in many of the cases—in one Ivory Carvings Spanish—Chinese—Japanese—American." Sellers suggested a more systematic way of organizing the objects. He reminded Justice that "mere show-case effect should always be subordinate to the arrangement that would give the most information to students."

Sellers saw two possible arrangements. One would "show the history of a particular art in one country," while the other would illustrate "the progress of industrial art in periods." Sellers provided Justice with an example of his idea. "Would it not be better," he offered, "so far as possible to have the specimens illustrating the Art of Pottery in one line of cases, starting with the Archaic specimens of Graeco-Roman and Etruscan Pottery and gradually leading up to the latest achievements of Deck or Minton?" Each exhibit would terminate with examples of the finest contemporary work. This kind of exhibit would give visitors a comprehensive understanding of manufactured products. This was the kind of information Sellers thought the museum could provide its visitors, and he closed his letter by stressing this. "The best way to inform [visitors]," he wrote, "is to place in each case a brief but comprehensive account of the processes used in the manufacture of the objects therein—a short history of the arts employed."[41] By 1883, the museum claimed the "system adopted for cataloguing, classifying, and arranging the collections has been perfected,"[42] and one writer approvingly described for readers the thousands who marched through Memorial Hall: "With intelligence quickened, with interest awakened by the objects on view, many of these pleasure seekers become knowledge seekers."[43]

Science remained the ideal to which the Pennsylvania Museum aspired in the arrangement of its collections. Making the museum sound more like a laboratory, the curators explained that "it has been the aim of this Museum to secure, by patient investigation and experiment, an improvement of methods relating to classification and arrangement of exhibits."[44] New cases acquired in 1907 for the Main Gallery made possible a reorganization of the ceramic collection "according to the only scientific method."

As we have seen at other museums, however, there might be considerable confusion over what the best "scientific" arrangement was. In 1904, the museum rearranged its collection of "Oriental" ceramics so that all the pieces from this part of the world were placed in the same gallery. A geographic arrangement of the collections had been popular at the museum since the 1890s. Writing to Dalton Dorr in 1892, Robert Lamborn complained that "the value of the Museum will be greatly lessened if the objects are unscientifically affiliated in the various cases to which they are assigned." He suggested that in order to "teach . . . of the growth and character of the civilization of the countries from which they [the collections] were drawn," the museum should arrange its collections according to country of origin. Without organizing the displays this way, "the progress & vicissitudes of the arts, for instance, in the Italian peninsula could not be shown. . . . Nor could the history of art and civilization in Mexico from the period of the early migrations through the time of the Spanish colonization and the republican era down to our own time to be given in a connected series."[45]

Lamborn specifically objected to an arrangement where "all objects that happened to be of leather [were put] in one case—all unglazed ware in another, all engraved brass and copper objects in another." Yet by 1908, the "only scientific method" was to arrange objects in precisely this way. According to the *Annual Report,* "the similar [ceramics] of all countries and times are installed together under the headings of glass glazed pottery, tin enameled pottery, lead glazed pottery, salt glazed stoneware etc."[46] The museum wanted a scientific arrangement of its objects, but it had trouble deciding whether that science should be based on geography or on the intrinsic properties of various kinds of industrial products. By 1911 the museum had decided on the latter, and the museum's *Bulletin* looked back on what it saw as earlier confusion to announce:

> A systematic method has been followed, whereby the various groups of objects may now be found in their respective places, instead of being scattered throughout the building, as formerly. In 1901 the collections of pottery and porcelain, for example, occupied the four corner pavilions of the building and were installed in several places between these extremes. Today they are gathered together in the eastern end and arranged in accordance with the scientific classification, based on clays and glazes. . . . Until this work had been completed the policy of the Museum had been one of accumulation only, with no attempt at proper attribution or classification.[47]

The Pennsylvania Museum tried to construct the field of art in such a way that art objects could function epistemologically in the same way other museum objects functioned within their own fields of knowledge. Its attempts to create a systematics for its art around use and material type remind us that the art historical categories we now take for granted in art museums do not represent the only way the objects can be arranged and understood.[48] The Pennsylvania Museum's failures, however, to arrive at a satisfactorily scientific arrangement of its objects echoed the same problems other museums had creating systematics for their objects at roughly the same moment. As we shall see later in this chapter, the Pennsylvania Museum solved its organizational conundrum by redefining its definition of what constituted art, by moving away from South Kensington and toward the Louvre.

Schools versus Museums

In a newspaper interview in 1884, Metropolitan Museum of Art director Louis Palma di Cesnola sketched his vision of a large educational complex. "If I could have my way," he told the interviewer, "I would establish one great university. All the societies of art and history should combine in so far as the exhibit of collections is concerned. Such a university would in twenty years rival the South Kensington Museum."[49] What such a university might actually look like, or whether di Cesnola seriously contemplated building such an institution, we cannot say. But di Cesnola did express the more general desire felt by many involved with museums in the late nineteenth century to create or preserve a unity of knowledge in the face of increasing fragmentation.

Even in this brief quote, di Cesnola has described another version of the museum-as-encyclopedia that George Brown Goode would articulate a few years later. Di Cesnola's conversation with the journalist also revealed that while everyone in the museum world genuflected to the altar of "education," how art museums would serve that purpose remained unclear. Ultimately neither di Cesnola nor anyone else in New York turned the Metropolitan into the center of a vast institutional complex devoted to education. More to our purposes, though, the different ways in which New York and Philadelphia defined the category of "art" shaped the different ways each institution approached the task of public education.

Over these last pages I have been inexact. The institution founded in Philadelphia in the wake of the Centennial was not simply the "Pennsylvania Museum," but the "Pennsylvania Museum and School of Industrial Design." The pairing of the School of Industrial Design with the museum had been central to the very conception of the institution from the outset. It was the way in which these two entities functioned in tandem that prompted the *Philadelphia Public Ledger* to pronounce, with some self-satisfaction, "The Pennsylvania Museum and School of Industrial Art, after a good deal of experimenting, is now fairly carrying out one main purpose of its formation. . . . Its museum is probably the finest outside of Europe."[50]

While the physical location of the museum in distant Fairmount Park troubled some because it did not attract enough visitors of the right class, the location of the school, in the heart of the city, did not generate the same worries. Its purpose was more obviously to provide education for the city's artisans. The school had moved into new quarters at 1336 Spring Garden Street, near Center City, within easy reach of the city's factories and residential neighborhoods. In this location the school thrived. Indeed, it probably does not overstate the case to say that in the late nineteenth century, the school attracted more public notice and attention than did the museum.

Part of the school's perceived success may have derived from the fact that it did not charge the city's workers or their children for enrollment. In this way, the school made good on its commitment to provide an education in industrial design to the working class. Admittedly, that free admission policy lasted only a few years, and in 1880 the students had to pay for the privilege of attending the school. In response to that development, the city's Board of Public Education passed a resolution granting five scholarships for graduates of Central or Girl's High to attend. Regardless of what effect either of these actions had on the enrollment at the school, they do reflect some consensus that the school was meant to be a practical place, accessible to, rather than exclusive of, working- and middle-class citizens.

If the school made half of its promises to the city's artisans and workers, then it made the other half to Philadelphia manufacturers, to whom the museum and school had pledged improved products as a result of industrial education. Here, too, the school seemed a success. Recognizing that Philadelphia producers led the nation in textile manufacture (and no doubt drawing on the South Kensington model), the school included a course in "Art Needlework" as early as 1877. Those who ran the school seem to have chosen wisely by placing their emphasis on textile design. They reported in 1884: "Of the industries of Philadelphia, the textile industry is at present by far the most important to the student of design, not only because of the closeness with which, in all class of woven fabrics, the design depends upon the process of manufacture, but because of the very great proportions which this branch has assumed in this city."[51] The school's administrators were also well aware of the gendered implications of offering such instructions. Beyond helping the textile industry by improving public taste—that, after all, was the goal at the foundation of all the school's instruction—the importance of "Art Needlework" lay in "providing . . . a means of support [for] many women who are ready to accept the needle as their only legitimate weapon in the struggle for existence."[52]

By creating relationships between manufacturers and workers through the nexus of the school, the school enjoyed an almost worrisome success as compared to the museum. In the *Annual Report* of 1887, the trustees had begun to fret about the divided fortunes of their two-part institution. "Of late years," the *Report* admitted, "the Museum has languished, although the School has flourished and obtained a great reputation."[53] A year later, the trustees considered that one way to improve the museum's fortunes might be to move it closer to the school. "That time may be approaching," the trustees felt, "when a building of our own should be provided in some more central location, where the Museum and the School could perhaps be united." [54]

As Philadelphians pursued their version of the South Kensington educational experiment, some in New York agitated to do the same. Those associated with the Metropolitan for whom South Kensington represented a goal saw an opportunity when the museum moved into new quarters in 1880. When the new building was finished—the museum's first Central Park facility—this faction assumed that possession, at least of space, constituted nine-tenths of the battle and hung a placard in one of the empty galleries proclaiming: "This room will be devoted to the collection of industrial art."

This audacious gallery grab, however, did not conjure up such a collection. Under the leadership of Thomas Egleston of Columbia University, the museum's collection of industrial art totaled one series illustrating the process of electrotyping. When the new building was opened to the public, "industrial art" was not among those things listed for visitors to see—presumably the placard had been removed. [55] The failure of industrial art to find room in the galleries of the new museum implicitly defined a distinction between those objects belonging in an art museum proper and those reserved for some other sort of industrial collection. Philadelphians, at this same moment, tried to deny that distinction.

While those who ran the Metropolitan kept industrial art out of their Central Park palace, they did, at least in the 1880s, retain a commitment to some kind of industrial art education. Robert Hoe, chairman of the Committee on Art Schools, reminded readers of *The Mail and Express:* "It was the original idea of the projectors of the Metropolitan Museum that it should be an educational institution." Consequently, beginning in January 1880, the Museum sponsored "technical schools" through which, fitfully at first, students could learn everything from mechanical drawing to plumbing. Hoe wrote that the Met's educational mission "has perhaps been somewhat diverted . . . but it is our purpose to make it less of a place of amusement and more of an educational force." [56]

Whatever the success of these technical schools—evening classes seem to have been quite well attended, while day classes were underenrolled—they came to an abrupt end after graduation ceremonies in May 1894. The *New York Times* curtly reported that the Met's trustees had decided to give up the technical schools "perhaps wisely . . . in view of the number of good schools of art elsewhere."[57] Having been, according to Hoe, at the center of the Metropolitan's founding, the Met's attempts at industrial art education lasted less than fifteen years. The trustees may have come to this decision for myriad reasons. It seems clear that the Metropolitan never embraced the larger movement for industrial art education with much enthusiasm and that its schools, unlike their counterpart in Philadelphia, floated on the edges of the Met's concerns.

Whether for financial or administrative reasons, the closing of the Met's schools and the simultaneous success of Philadelphia's school have a deeper epistemological significance. Philadelphians tried to create a seamless institution in which both museum and school would function harmoniously. What was taught in the school was reinforced by the object lessons presented in the museum, and vice versa. Here was the joining of objects and education that other museums and universities could not effect. Treating art objects as sites of knowledge to be comprehended through careful observation and study, in the same way that other museums at the same time treated their objects, meant that students could then infuse the objects they in turn produced with that knowledge.

In New York the boundaries drawn around the category of art largely excluded industrial and manufactured objects. What the Met taught in its "technical schools" therefore had little or no relationship with the objects in the museum. The complimentarity that Philadelphians tried to achieve between the museum and the school was impossible in New York because of the very way in which art and education had been defined. The Met's "fine art" might teach object lessons, but of a very different kind than those taught through the Pennsylvania Museum. The connection between objects and functional, industrial education, between museums and schools, had been broken. As the *Times* noted in 1894, "it can hardly be said that it is the special province of a museum to have schools at all."[58]

"Uneventful" Transformations

When the Metropolitan closed its technical schools in 1894, without, it seems, much debate or contest, the museum loosened its already flaccid and unenthusiastic embrace of the South Kensington museum model. Those at the museum continued to insist that education lay at the heart

21 The installation of the Wilstach Collection in Memorial Hall signaled a shift in the museum's focus away from industrial design and toward fine art proper. (Courtesy of the Philadelphia Museum of Art)

of the museum's mission, but that mission and the way it was pursued would be different in kind from that developed at South Kensington's "exhibitionary complex."

A year earlier the Pennsylvania Museum and School of Industrial Design also underwent a similarly quiet yet significant transformation, though ironically it would not prove to be the most important event for the institution that year. The *Annual Report* of 1893 announced "the greatest event in the history of our institution." With the purchase of the former School for the Deaf and Dumb as the new home for an expanded school, the trustees triumphantly predicted that the school would have "plenty of room for . . . development . . . in all its many departments."[59]

In its new location the school fulfilled the hopes of the trustees and prospered. The school found itself in a national spotlight early in 1897 when the National Association of Manufacturers, holding its annual meeting in Philadelphia, visited the institution. With the eyes of NAM and other business interests increasingly focused on international competition, this visit helped underscore a new sense of the school's importance to the nation. The school's Women's Committee described this in the wake of NAM's visit. The committee seemed pleased that "the public mind" finally understood that "perfect protections for our manufacturers can only be reached through the production of perfect work." The women went on to remind their readers that "perfect work can only be reached (especially in the manufacture of textile goods) through perfect teachers and earnest, industrious students." [60] As the new century approached, many now saw the school as contributing vitally to the economic health not solely of the city but of the whole nation as well.

While the excited trustees successfully negotiated complicated real estate deals and arranged the relocation of their thriving school, the museum accepted the Wilstach Collection of over three hundred largely European paintings. Bequeathed in 1892, the paintings went on display the following year. Now Philadelphians could see canvases by Courbet and Murillo along with ceramics and fine furniture at Memorial Hall, and they flocked to do so. Attendance jumped nearly 60,000 to 379,000 in 1893 as people came to see the Wilstach paintings. The Metropolitan had opened itself to the world twenty years earlier with an exhibition of European Old Masters. Now, with the acquisition and display of the Wilstach Collection, Philadelphia's museum veered in this same direction.

Only a few of those involved with the institution seemed to understand the transforming effect the paintings likely would have on the museum. In March 1892 Charles Dana wrote to Dalton Dorr asking a profound question. Now that the museum had obtained the Wilstach Collection, Dana wondered: "Where will the Wilstach pictures go & if in Mem. Hall, how will they effect us?" [61] The question would prove more probing that Dana imagined. The museum and school had been conceived as complementary, but by the 1890s, and particularly with the arrival of the Wilstach Collection, the museum began to struggle with a changing identity.

As late as 1893, when the museum opened the Wilstach Collection to the public, the museum did not acknowledge that the scope of its collections had changed. The 1893 *Annual Report* felt that the museum had won the struggle to convince the public that such an institution had civic value: "Most people have at last come to see and to feel, that the Art which it is profitable for most of us to study and to encourage, is that which expresses itself in glorifying common things and in informing that work of myriads of workers rather than standing for the attainment of the very few." [62]

Having built a museum for the enjoyment and education of Philadelphia's working citizens, those at the Pennsylvania Museum could feel justifiable pride at their success. In its first twenty years, the Museum had not become a palace of the fine arts, and it did have a genuinely broad appeal.[63] Believing that they carried on the tradition of Peale's Museum one hundred years earlier, the trustees felt that they had built an institution both democratic and useful. In the 1890s, those at the museum discussed the need to move, this time because Memorial Hall could no longer accommodate the crowds.

Whoever wrote the 1893 *Annual Report*, however, seems to have missed the deep irony occurring even as the report went to press. The growing numbers of visitors who increasingly crowded Memorial Hall through the 1890s came to see the Wilstach paintings as much as anything else. Whatever the *Annual Report* said, the Wilstach paintings were decidedly not "common things." The democratic and utilitarian museum never found itself as popular as when it acquired its first legitimate collection of what could be considered "fine art"—which is to say, European oils.

Despite the trustee's assumptions about the aesthetic tastes of Philadelphia's workers and artisans, they rather enjoyed seeing fine art objects as well as examples of industrial art. (The Museum hoped to "elevate" the taste of the citizenry, but perhaps that taste was already higher than the founders realized.) Indeed, as late as 1919, with annual attendance hovering at 400,000, those who ran the museum continued to complain that it was not visited enough by Philadelphia's wealthy residents. The *Annual Report* did "not hesitate to point out" that "the richer citizens have not yet realized the opportunity and responsibility" for supporting the institution.[64] Though the question warrants more systematic investigation, it does seem that the museum's visitors may have confounded its efforts to create easy dichotomies—industrial art for industrial workers, fine art for the "finer" classes. The museum's struggles to define what constituted "art" may have been predicated on a stereotyped, and ultimately incorrect, assumption of who was interested in seeing what.

This shift in the 1890s toward concern with fine art, and away therefore from industrial art, had several significances. As we have discussed, this new focus caused confusion over the museum's purpose. William Platt Pepper saw clearly that industrial art and fine art might not be compatible within the same institution. Writing to Dalton Dorr about the museum's annual show of industrial art produced by students at the school, he expressed reservations about how the show would look with the museum's new paintings. "Our Exhibition of Industrial Art," he offered, "would not show to advantage among pictures." [65] Exhibiting "fine art" did mean a change in the museum's purpose.

More than this, the museum's expanding interests in the 1890s suggest that the lines which defined the differences between "fine art" and "industrial art" were not etched clearly. Courbet stood at one end of the spectrum certainly, and a piston casing at the other. But that left much in the middle. Should ceramics, or textiles, or fine metalwork, be considered art? Objects like these came from the industrial process, but the whole point of the school and museum was to infuse that process with an artistic sensibility. If the school and museum had succeeded in introducing art into industrial production, should the objects exhibited in Memorial Hall be considered fine art? New Yorkers had largely answered these questions, but for Philadelphians the answers were not at all clear at the turn of the century.

The museum's attempts to create a "scientific" systematics for art also became confused as the museum moved toward New York's notion of fine art. As we have seen, two organizational systems competed with each other at the museum. They both, however, allowed for an increasing emphasis on authenticity and connoisseurship. Whether the objects were arranged by geography or by materials analysis, those at the museum became more and more interested in displaying the finest examples of a given type, rather than as many examples of a type as possible. At the turn of the century, the museum began the "retirement of many of the least meritorious objects in the various departments." Doing this "greatly enhanced" the value of those objects kept on display. One museum writer explained: "By this weeding out process many imitations, reproductions and counterfeits of well-known ceramic wares, such as unavoidably creep into every collection, have been withdrawn, and these will be utilized to serve a useful purpose by being displayed together in such manner as will enable investigators to distinguish genuine from spurious wares." [66] This concern for separating the "genuine" from the "spurious" helped push the museum toward the fine arts and away from the industrial arts. Authenticity and authorship, after all, have been central to the art historical endeavor from its beginnings, but they become more complicated issues when dealing with the mass-produced objects. What can be considered an "authentic" object if thousands of identical ones have been produced? Who should be considered the creator of an object produced in a factory? By concerning itself with these questions, the museum necessarily moved toward the fine arts, where these questions had more satisfactory answers.

When they moved their glass cases around, and when they rearranged the objects inside them, the Pennsylvania Museum's curators anticipated by a generation the concerns raised by Walter Benjamin in his famous 1936 essay, "The Work of Art in the Age of Mechanical Reproduction." Intuitively, those at the museum grasped, as did Benjamin, that works of art mechanically reproduced represented something new in the Western art historical tradition. Indeed, the museum's founding intention was to blur the lines that separated art from mechanically produced objects. In a sense, and to borrow Benjamin's term, the Pennsylvania Museum filled its galleries with objects deprived of any "aura" because of their origin in industrial processes.

Benjamin groped for the liberating possibilities as the aura withered, particularly in the arts of photography and film. Art, in Benjamin's sense, no longer need depend on "historical testimony," and "for the first time in world history, mechanical reproduction emancipates the work of art from its parasitical dependence on ritual." When those at the Pennsylvania Museum boxed their "spurious" objects and sent them to the basement, they grasped in the other direction. The move toward fine art and toward recreating the museum to be the repository solely of fine art objects meant first an increasing concern for accumulating singular objects like paintings, and second a redefinition of objects like ceramics, transforming them into objects which more closely resembled the singular. The Pennsylvania Museum now made more room for paintings and sculptures, those objects already invested with aura, and at the same time, by careful discrimination, it attempted to bestow that aura on a select few mechanically reproduced objects. Mechanical reproduction might strip art of its aura in the culture at large, but aura now found its home in the art museum.[67]

The acquisition of the Wilstach Collection simply underscored that by the turn of the century the museum strained against the boundaries that defined it originally. One writer noted that the "present scope" of the collection encompassed "pictures and statuary" as well as "food-products in the collection of British India." The collection was now organized into an increasing number of departments, which by 1897 included "American Pottery; Numismatics; Textiles, Lace and Embroidery; Goldsmith Work; Jewelry and Plate." [68]

Divestment, as much as acquisition, also served to redefine the intellectual turf the museum occupied in the 1890s. Collector Maxwell Sommerville, for example, moved his eclectic collection of gemstones and anthropological items out of Memorial Hall and into storage. [69] Robert Lamborn, who had contributed a small collection "illustrating the Development of Apparatus for making, preserving and using fire," wrote to Dorr asking: "Please place all the archaeological objects that relate to American or other pre-historic archaeology in a box and send to Mrs. Stevenson at the University of Pennsylvania." [70] In 1900, Clarence Moore felt "deep regret" that the museum's mummies had been removed. "Only a month ago," he wrote to Dalton Dorr, "while accompanying strangers through the Museum I pointed out that particular case as the most interesting in the museum." Moore also reminded Dorr that "it has been my experience that nothing so attracts the attention of the general public as mummies." [71] Initially, the museum had tried to fit what could be considered archaeological artifacts into a framework which defined them as industrial art, and the fit may never have been comfortable. Certainly, however, with the opening of the University Museum, the Pennsylvania Museum no longer had to concern itself with this area. [72]

The change in the museum's direction signaled by the Wilstach acquisition also changed the dynamic between the school and the museum. In its new quarters, as we have already noted, the school continued to thrive along its original lines. According to Lee McClung, a member of a group trying to open a school of industrial design in Washington, D.C., the museum's school remained "the largest and most successful" of its kind in the country. [73] Enrollment reached 1,000 students by 1903, and the museum also continued to sponsor yearly exhibitions of the school's work. The show in 1897, for example, featured textiles, embroidery, and weaving. But these annual shows no longer occupied the central place in the museum that they had previously enjoyed. Leslie Miller, principal of the school, wrote somewhat plaintively to Dorr asking him "to see if you didn't think we could have a room, or a corner of one, to fix up a more creditable display of school work than we have now at the Hall." [74] In the 1890s, the industrial art produced by the museum's own school was being pushed into smaller corners of Memorial Hall.

In the early years of the twentieth century the school was probably in a better financial condition than the museum. The latter's *Annual Re-*

port of 1912 lamented: "Financially, we are as poor as ever." [75] Yet even at the school, the founding principles had begun to change. Writing to John McIlhenny in 1917, new museum director Langdon Warner discussed an exhibit of textiles produced by students at the school. According to Warner's letter, two representatives from the school had visited him and assured him "that the object of the school is to produce graduates capable of managing and directing textile mills and allied industries." The school stressed the "commercial value" of textile products, and therefore its products were not "particularly well suited for exhibition in the Museum devoted to the display of masterpieces of fine or applied arts." Warner went on presciently to describe the direction of the museum and its relationship to the school: "Nothing less than a masterpiece should in my opinion be shown here and it is hardly fair to demand a masterpiece from a student." [76] Gone from this description was the sense that the museum and the school would marry industry and art.

∿

While those who had been with the museum since the Centennial struggled to fit its expanding collections into its original boundaries, another group of people began to push the museum hard in the direction of becoming a fine art gallery exclusively. As was the case with the University Museum, the intellectual struggles to define what objects should and should not be displayed in the Pennsylvania Museum became nicely encapsulated architecturally.

The museum's trustees were already considering a move from Memorial Hall in response to a deteriorating physical plant and because the hall could no longer accommodate the large number of visitors. The basement storage areas bulged with collections that could not be displayed in the already crowded galleries, and those galleries strained to hold nearly 400,000 annual visitors. Some proposed raising money to renovate and build new wings onto Memorial Hall. Others, led by Peter Widener, demanded a new building entirely.

Widener was one of Philadelphia's new business titans, and he wanted the city to build a proper art gallery, and an art gallery proper. Once the Wilstach paintings went on display in Memorial Hall, Widener weighed in with his opinions. Speaking to the *Philadelphia Record,* Widener told the paper that spending any money to convert Memorial Hall into an art gallery would be a waste of funds. "Any art gallery," he told the *Record's* reporter, "must be built for that specific purpose and has to be constructed from the foundations with that object in view." To waste money renovating and expanding, Widener explained, "would mean the death of the project to build a fine art gallery."[77]

Echoing the sentiment which had motivated those who built the Metropolitan from the beginning, Widener reminded Philadelphians that without such a facility the city would lose the great collections of paintings then being accumulated, as it happened, by wealthy patrons like himself: "If we had such a building, we might have secured some of the valuable paintings in the collection of the late Henry C. Gibson and other well-known Philadelphia art patrons." Widener and others now envisioned a museum to serve primarily as the repository of wealthy connoisseurship. This had been the guiding principle of the Metropolitan since the 1870s, and Widener's vision would, in a sense, transform the Pennsylvania Museum into a Philadelphian version of the Met. Widener began his agitation in 1893. He would wait nearly thirty-five years for the museum to occupy a new home. Nonetheless, he had set the wheels inexorably in motion.[78]

Seven years after the paintings went on display, the museum finally published a catalogue of the Wilstach Collection. The introduction to the catalogue announced plans (prematurely as it would turn out) for a new art gallery to be built by the city. "Memorial Hall," the introduction pointed out "is . . . reserved more especially for the exhibition of works of industrial art." With a tone of inevitability, the introduction went on, "it was accordingly only a question of time when the Wilstach collection would require a special and more suitable building for its pictures."[79]

William Platt Pepper, stalwart of the museum's old guard, understood the confusion that the Wilstach Collection had created for the museum's mission. If the city must have a new art gallery, Pepper complained, "it would be very well to install the Wilstach Collection there, and give us the room it now takes."[80] The acquisition of the Wilstach pictures had created a momentum that began to take the Pennsylvania Museum out of its original building and into a new one. That move also took the museum away from its founding purpose and toward something new. By 1906, the emphasis of the museum's language had shifted significantly. Subtly rewriting the institution's history, the *Annual Report* of that year told readers: "It will thus be seen that the Museum was originally dedicated not only to the fine arts, but to the industrial arts, as well."[81]

Clearly, the museum did not transform itself immediately from one concerned with the industrial and practical arts into one that prominently displayed fine art objects. In 1913, objects collected by the

Shackleton Expedition to Antarctica, including rocks and stuffed penguins, filled the rotunda. But this collection stopped only briefly at Memorial Hall before being transferred to the Academy of Natural Sciences the following year. During the twenty years between the acquisition of the Wilstach paintings and the outbreak of World War I the museum stretched the definition of its original purpose as people like P. A. B. Widener demanded that more attention be paid to fine arts.

This debate shifted decisively in 1913. In March of that year, the City Council approved plans to crown the new Benjamin Franklin Parkway, a broad Parisian-style boulevard slicing through the rectilinear grid of the central city, with a new museum. Echoing the opinion of Widener, the *Philadelphia Press* reported the news: "The prediction was recalled by some at the meeting yesterday that if the city made an actual start towards the construction of the art gallery valuable private collections, equaled in only few cases, if at all, elsewhere in the nation, would be presented to the city." [82] With the approval, and eventual completion of the museum and parkway project, fine art would no longer take a back seat to industrial art. Indeed, by 1913, the seating arrangement had been reversed.

The decision finally to build a new museum was rich with symbolism. Memorial Hall, despite its cramped galleries and leaking roof, provided an appropriate home for the objects of art and industrial design the founders put on display. Designed by an engineer rather than an architect, Memorial Hall stood as a reminder of the Centennial's enthusiasm about America's industrial progress and as a monument in steel and glass and stone to industrialism's aesthetic possibilities. When the museum left Memorial Hall, it left behind its founding commitment to those possibilities.

The *Annual Report* of 1917 sadly noted the passing of Dr. Edwin AtLee Barber. Barber had been a fixture at the museum since 1892, when he assumed the post of Honorary Curator. In reporting the death of Barber, which occurred on December 12, 1916, the *Report* writer characterized the years of his tenure as "a period in the history of the Pennsylvania Museum . . . which, in many respects may be regarded as prosperous, if uneventful." [83] At some literal level this claim for the years between 1892 and the First World War was undoubtedly true. In the absence of any grand exposition or any new building, the museum continued to forge ahead along the lines set out in 1876. On another level, however, these years witnessed the quiet transformation of the museum, as it began to move away from its mission of industrial design education toward an increasing focus on fine art, which would culminate in the opening of the new museum.

The Triumph on Fairmount [84]

As early as 1877, as the Pennsylvania Museum and School of Industrial Art began to take form, Eli Kirk Price had his eyes on paintings. Coleman Sellers reported a conversation he had had with Price in February of that year: "Mr. Eli K. Price has an idea that pictures must not be excluded from the building . . . he knows of large collections . . . to be willed to the city provided they find place in Memorial Hall. He looks upon pictures as the great means of cultivating and refining the tastes of people." [85] Though his letter strikes us now as prophetic, Price did not play a significant role in shaping the museum through the end of the nineteenth century. By World War I, however, as vice president of the publicly funded but largely autonomous Fairmount Park Commission, he emerged as perhaps the most significant power broker in Philadelphia's cultural world. More than anyone else, he made possible the transformation of the Pennsylvania Museum by building its new building at the top of the new Benjamin Franklin Parkway.

Like the new museum building, the parkway project had been under consideration since the early 1890s. Modeled on the Parisian boulevards created by Baron Haussmann, the parkway when it was finally built exemplified the American City Beautiful movement of the post-World War I period. [86] The design and effect of the parkway remains dramatic even today. Starting at City Hall in the heart of Center City, the parkway cuts a wide diagonal through the famous rectilinear grid of Philadelphia's original plan. Along the boulevard sit several of the city's cultural institutions, including the Free Library, the Rodin Museum, and the Franklin Institute. The parkway terminates at a small hill at the foot of Fairmount Park, which had served as the Fairmount Reservoir. On top of this hill sits the Pennsylvania Museum. [87]

With the architectural firm of Trumbauer, Zantzinger, and Borie chosen for the job in 1915, the museum's *Bulletin* predicted the move to new quarters by 1919. [88] World War I intervened to slow down progress on the new building—construction did not begin in earnest until after the armistice—but probably not as much as Philadelphia's legendary municipal corruption did. Almost from the beginning, the project seemed doomed to take longer and cost more than anyone had anticipated. As David Brownlee has observed, the project was shaped by "a confusing

22   The new Philadelphia Museum of Art, shortly before it opened in 1928. Memorial
Hall had been designed by an engineer and had celebrated the wedding of the
industrial and the artistic. In its new building, designed by the architectural firm
of Trumbauer, Zantinger and Borie, the Philadelphia Museum of Art became the
home of fine art masterpieces. (Courtesy of the Philadelphia Museum of Art)

battle" between powerful politicos, who controlled municipal funding,
and idealistic, though essentially powerless, urban planners.[89] As these
groups struggled, actual construction on the museum proceeded at a
snail's pace. In 1923, with the building's completion still not in sight, one
newspaper writer lamented: "At the end of the Fairmount Parkway we
have a magnificent fragment that should be a monument—the Art Museum. There it stands against the twilight sky. It is a mute unfinished
symphony in stone."[90]

Squabbles and cost overruns at the construction site became the
stuff of newspaper scandal. They reached a boiling point in the winter of
1923–24. The papers reported that the museum project, originally expected to cost $3.5 million, would now cost over $13 million. Underneath
the outrage at Price's raids on the public purse lurked a sense that the
new facility, unlike the old, would cater to high-brow taste exclusively
and would become, as the Metropolitan always had been, a club for the

city's wealthy. If Memorial Hall had been designed as a place to educate the city's workers so that the city's industrial products could be improved, Price made the intentions of the new museum quite plain. Quoted in a newspaper article, he explained, "The object of a museum" should not be to facilitate the development of contemporary art, but rather to "encourage men who already have bought pictures to give them to the museum."[91]

When the new building finally opened in 1928—not in time for the 1926 Sesquicentennial, as many had desperately hoped—it achieved what its planners had anticipated. The building itself remains a stunning example of neoclassical architecture, and its location at the head of the parkway, linking the center of the city with Fairmount Park, makes it probably the most dramatically sited municipal museum in America. But the opening of the new building also signaled a final departure from the original ideals upon which the institution had been founded in 1876.

The "triumph on Fairmount" represented nothing less than the triumph of the fine arts over the industrial or practical arts. The Pennsylvania Museum was not alone in making this transition. The Museum of Fine Arts in Boston, founded along much the same lines, had also changed its focus by the first quarter of the twentieth century. Speaking in 1916, the MFA's director Morris Gray announced: "the Museum is to be what its name expresses, a Museum of Fine Arts; that its primary object is to collect and exhibit the best obtainable works of genius and skill." Separating the museum even further from its original plan, Gray went on to say "that the application of the fine arts to industry and the illustration of the fine arts by archaeology are both within its province, but that neither of these is its first object."[92]

As the title of this chapter suggests, the distance that the Pennsylvania Museum traveled between its founding and the opening of its new building can be measured by traveling from the South Kensington complex in London to the Louvre palace in Paris. We have seen how the South Kensington provided the museum and the school with its original model. Each used a major international exposition as its starting point, and both were dedicated to improving the artistic quality of industrial design. The South Kensington model emulated by the Pennsylvania Museum sought to make museum collections practical. With construction on the new museum plodding along, however, those charged with running the institution increasingly found their inspiration in Paris.

As we have already discussed, the parkway project itself represented one of the most ambitious example of Parisian city planning undertaken in America since L'Enfant's plan for Washington, D.C. Shortly before the museum opened, Albert Rosenthal responded to criticism that the new building would not display contemporary art. He reminded critics that "the Pennsylvania Academy of the Fine Arts houses the modern pieces." Rosenthal thought it was more "appropriate that the new city museum should care for that of the past." "In fact," Rosenthal concluded, "it will be to Philadelphia what the Louvre is to Paris."[93] When the new facility had its official opening on March 27, 1928, French ambassador Paul Claudel came to inspect the museum. Fifty years earlier, the distinguished European guest at the museum's inaugural had been Sir Cunliffe Owen of the South Kensington Museums.

The French association implied less concern with the practical and a greater concern with aesthetic refinement. With the Louvre in mind, those at the museum left no ambiguity that this was an Art museum. When it opened, the *Philadelphia Public Ledger* called the building the "City's Great Citadel of Art." Fiske Kimball, the first and most influential director of the museum in its new incarnation, distanced the new museum from its utilitarian past in a 1928 address: "We no longer today . . . dare take the view which governed the International Exposition of 1851 and the creation of the South Kensington Museum, that technical conditions of material and use are the primary aspect of the work of art, or the aspect we wish chiefly to emphasize."[94] In a final, symbolically laden announcement, the *Philadelphia Inquirer* reported that in his address at the opening on March 26, 1928, Fiske Kimball suggested that Memorial Hall "may be abandoned with the completion of the evacuation of its art objects for installation in the new building on the Parkway."[95]

Fiske Kimball: Fine Art Philadelphia Style

Just as Eli Kirk Price had provided the organizational muscle to build the new museum, Fiske Kimball provided the institution with an overarching vision. Trained originally as an architectural historian, Kimball made an academic reputation for himself with studies of Thomas Jefferson's architecture. This work earned him a position at New York University, from which he was lured to direct the museum in 1925. As director, he committed his considerable talents and energies to shaping the museum and to making it a place of international repute, on a par with other great fine art museums.

Kimball's plan for the museum moved it unambiguously into the realm of fine art. Under Kimball's direction the museum saw its peers in places like the Metropolitan, the Museum of Fine Arts in Boston, the Detroit Institute of Art, and the Art Institute of Chicago. Mindful to a certain extent of the Museum's fifty-year history, Kimball incorporated two innovations into the museum which teased the definition of fine art so that it included at least some of the museum's past interests. Both of Kimball's experiments represented ways to reorganize and display objects systematically.

Most dramatically, and perhaps because of his own interest in architecture, he built authentic architectural elements directly into the museum's galleries. In so doing Kimball and the museum pioneered the display of "period rooms." These rooms combined the architecture, decorative arts, and fine arts of a specific time and place to recreate the mood and feel—atmosphere, as some derisively called it—of a particular moment. Several American art museums opened period rooms during this time, including the Metropolitan in its American Wing, and the new Detroit Institute of Art, although as Kimball pointed out, only three of Detroit's period rooms were genuinely old, and in Kimball's opinion Detroit's decorator "has run away with it a bit."[96] Philadelphia's period rooms, however, were unique in their scope and in that they had been planned into the building. Even the *New York Times* enthused over Philadelphia's new period rooms.[97]

The second novelty at the new museum, which attracted much attention, was Kimball's "Main Street." Kimball envisioned walking on a "main street" through the galleries which would retrace the history of art. This "Pageant of Art" would illustrate "European art from the time of Christ onward to the most vitally modern of contemporary work, or, in Asia, from the austere beginnings in India and China down to the last flowering of the delicate art of Japan." This "Main Street of Art" would give visitors "a vivid panoramic history of the art of all ages."[98] The evolutionary metaphor, according to Kimball, stood behind this method of organization. He explained how this organization complemented the period rooms: "it seems to me that the evolutionary order, and the placing together of all products of a single civilization and art, reinforcing one another by their cumulative effect, is interesting and advantageous."[99]

Kimball also realized, however, that the museum now had two audiences to please. Consequently, he created a two-part organization for the museum's galleries. The period rooms along "Main Street" were intended for the "ordinary visitor." These rooms, "limited in number," would be filled with "a selected series of the finest things in the possession of the museum in painting, sculpture and in the crafts." The rest of the museum's holdings, "the minor objects," even the "aesthetically indifferent objects," held value for the "specialist." "Why not," Kimball asked rhetorically, "place them in a different order, the order of material, as a series of study collections aimed primarily for the needs of this different group?"[100]

As a strategy of cheerleading for his institution, Kimball always distinguished between the modern museum and the antiquated institutions of the nineteenth century. Beyond stressing the new and the now, however, the way in which Kimball saw his charge reveals that the new museum would not simply be a bigger and better version of the old, but something quite different. Kimball's arrangement and ordering of the new museum's galleries stood as an implicit criticism of how older museums in general, and Memorial Hall specifically, had been arranged. Attempting to erase the Pennsylvania Museum's first fifty years, Kimball simply lumped the institution he inherited in with other "craft-museums," and noted that "paintings and sculpture were long excluded from . . . craft-museums." Kimball observed that the contents of Memorial Hall had been "classified according to materials and technique, with segregated departments of woodwork, metal work, textiles, pottery, glass, and so on. . . . Such museums became paradises for the special student, but vastly wearisome for the general public, condemned to seek there for the masterpieces of craftsmanship to be found nowhere else."[101]

As at the University Museum, architectural design helped define the collection, at least initially. The museum *Bulletin* explained that the "principal exhibition floor" would be used to display "fine works of all the arts and crafts in association." The floor below would house "the extensive study collections of paintings, prints, ceramics, glass, metalwork, textile, ivories, enamels, furniture, and other objects of special interest to the craftsman, designer, manufacturer, amateur and student of single arts and crafts."[102]

This segregation between the top and bottom floors would have made no sense to those who founded the museum in 1876. After all, those things relegated to the bottom floor study collections had been at the center of the entire conception of the museum in the first place, and the people for whom this bottom floor was intended had originally been the museum's primary audience. The new museum separated the finest art and crafts from the "aesthetically indifferent objects" and in so doing separated one kind of audience from another. In the new facility, the core of Memorial Hall's collections wound up underneath the more dazzling displays of fine art up above.

The final distinction Kimball created in his Philadelphia temple revolved around how the objects themselves functioned in a museum. Kimball, like others who shaped museums in the 1920s, recognized that museum objects had ceased to function in the epistemological way that they had in the late nineteenth century. As a result, they demanded different installations and visual treatments to function properly in the world of the 1920s.

In this sense, the popularity of period room installations in the 1920s parallels the enthusiasm with which museum curators in natural history museums replaced their glass cases with dioramas. Period rooms, like the naturalistic dioramas, created a new context for museum objects by attempting to recreate the object's "original" context. Displays that had forced viewers to regard objects without any other visual distraction were replaced, both in art museums and in natural history museums, with visually appealing settings, busy with things to look at. Arthur Edwin Bye, curator of the Wilstach Collection, drew an analogy perfect for the 1920s: "The museum is like the stage or screen, for here old memories are made real, and dreams are visualized." [103]

This change did not go unnoticed or unchallenged. The grouchy Princeton art scholar Frank Jewett Mather complained about what he called the "antiquarian sentimentality" which led curators to install period rooms. As a "worried" museum curator constructs an artificial chapel in which to display an altarpiece, Mather sarcastically proposed, why stop there: "Why not introduce a priest, waxen or in the flesh? Why not hold a Mass, oral or phonographic?" Recognizing full well that museum objects had lost their original context, Mather believed that the purpose of the museum was not to pretend otherwise but to bring out what he termed the object's "museum values." For Mather, these values, largely aesthetic and spiritual, remained invested in the art objects even after they had been removed from their original context: "Good lighting, avoidance of obvious clashes, generous spacing, simple and neutral backgrounds—this is all that is necessary to enjoyment. . . . It really doesn't matter what is alongside or opposite the masterpiece [the visitor] is contemplating, so long as he can isolate for enjoyment." [104] The museum's job, Mather believed, was simply and only to create an environment that permitted viewers to contemplate the objects as objects.

Mather complained particularly about the Isabella Stewart Gardner

Museum in Boston—"I once wrote to her that she had invented a new decorative art the raw material of which was *chefs-d'oeuvre,* and I don't think it displeased her"—and about the Pennsylvania Museum. His complaints there centered on a public opinion survey the museum conducted that seemed to demonstrate overwhelmingly that the public preferred the period rooms to the well-ordered and visually neutral galleries Mather wanted. Mather responded to this by suggesting that it would not make wise museum policy if "the art museum [were] to join the motion-picture theatre in giving the public what it wants."

Here Mather, and other critics of period room installations, swam against the tide, not only of popular opinion but of museum practice. His complaints represented an older way of conceiving how museums should display objects. Kimball, in describing the effect created by contextualizing objects in "period rooms," reminded readers of the difference between the old and the new: "The 19th century took the view . . . that the work of art should be shown against a perfectly neutral background incapable of detracting from or, I might add, of adding to the effectiveness of the work of art itself. . . . It is not because it is easily ridiculed that I myself tend not to hold this view, but because I believe that in the works of a given period there is a harmony, under the all-powerful impress of the artistic ideals and wishes of that time."[105] He was quite right in his description. His nineteenth-century predecessors had assumed that objects would yield knowledge to observers if they were arranged systematically and displayed without visual distractions—endless glass cases, with numberless specimens. In Kimball's conception the whole would be greater than the sum of the parts, and those parts, central to the nineteenth century's object-based epistemology, found themselves demoted.

Finally, while Kimball still searched, as his predecessors had, for a way to systematize the presentation of art, he did so by replacing science with history. Kimball felt that the nineteenth century relied too much on the explanatory mechanisms of science, "even in the fields of intuition and of art." The nineteenth century, Kimball believed—with some justification—was "the epoch when it was thought that science might solve all the problems of the world" and when the "ideal . . . for a museum, even a museum of art, was fundamentally a scientific ideal."[106]

Executing a nifty transposition, Kimball made the notion of evolution synonymous with historical progress. "Main Street," after all, relied on a notion of evolution. On Main Street, however, visitors saw the evolution of art through time, rather than the biological process that concerned those at the natural history museums or even the cultural processes that provided the framework for anthropological displays. Main Street demonstrated how each innovation in fine art evolved, in some quasi-organic way, out of the one previous. For Kimball, evolution had become synonymous with history. "I see no reason," he wrote, "why the museum of art should not also minister to the love of knowledge, and first the love of historical knowledge." [107] On Main Street, objects became art not through any scientific system of industrial usefulness but because of the historical testimony they were able to give.

~

I began this chapter with the assertion that art museums as we know them today have won the contest to stand atop our cultural hierarchy. While this victory surely resulted from a confluence of factors, I suggest that part of what contributed to it is that the objects now found in them continue to function in much the way they were intended to when these museums took shape. Art museums have become the places of ritual which permit the objects in them to retain their aura, in Benjamin's sense, and thus their value. The objects which fill art museums were, for the most part, intended as objects of worship, contemplation, decoration, or some combination thereof. Though they have been removed from their original contexts—be it cathedral or country house—the art museum provides the space for those objects to function in largely the same ways. In some strange secular sense we worship art, we contemplate it, and we enjoy its decorative functions, especially in museum period rooms. And, as I also alluded to earlier, art museum objects remain central to the production of knowledge about art history, the field they continue to help define.

If the art museum, as it came to be defined at the turn of the twentieth century, permits the objects inside to retain more of their use value than do other museum objects, then this is surely related to the monetary value of those objects as well. In purely vulgar terms, it is hard to imagine that the entire collection of stuffed birds at the Academy of Natural Sciences—reputed to be among the finest in the world—would fetch anything like the price of one of the Philadelphia Museum's Cezannes on the open market. That we value or at least pay more for art than for any other kind of museum object signals as surely as anything the victory of the art museum.

New York's Metropolitan Museum of Art set itself on this course from the beginning. The Pennsylvania Museum took longer to get there, imag-

23   With the skyline of Philadelphia in the background, Rocky is removed from the top of the Art Museum steps. It was felt that he more properly belonged outside the city's sports arena. (Courtesy of Todd Buchanan/*The Philadelphia Inquirer*)

ining itself initially as a meeting place for the aesthetic and the useful. But in Philadelphia there can be no doubt about the triumph of the fine arts. Given pride of place among the city's cultural institutions, the Philadelphia Museum of Art has indeed become one of the world's great museums of art, well-known, among other things, for its exceptional collections of decorative arts, a vestige of its Memorial Hall origins. Most people in this country, and even around the world, however, know the museum neither for its paintings nor for its ceramics and furniture. Rather they know it for the great stone stairs that lead up to it—the stairs Sylvester Stallone ran up in the first installment of "Rocky," raising his fists triumphantly when he got to the top. Visit the museum on any nice day and you will see would-be Rockys attempting the same thing (though be forewarned, it is harder to do than it looks).

The symbolism of the movie is potent, and it nicely encapsulates the tensions described in this chapter. Stallone plays a quintessential Philadelphia working-class Italian. The way out for Rocky is through boxing, through the brutal use of his body. Training for his big fight, he charges up the steps to the museum and uses the great building as a backdrop for his own fantasies of triumph. Without going inside the museum (though Stallone himself, as it happens, is a major collector of contemporary art), Rocky has conquered it, if only for a moment.

Several years, and several sequels later, a bronze, larger-than-life statue of Rocky posed with his fists raised was made as a movie prop. During the filming of yet another sequel, the bronze work stood in front of the museum as a reminder of Rocky's triumph in the first film. Stallone donated the statue to the city, and many in the city wanted the statue to remain where it so obviously belonged, at the top of the art museum steps. The protectors of high culture in the city, however, felt this to be . . . inappropriate.[108] Instead, they let the statue reside on the steps temporarily, until it was placed permanently outside the sports arena deep in the heart of the Italian neighborhood of South Philly. Fine art had triumphed on Fairmount, and not even Rocky could knock it off the top of the cultural hierarchy.

SEVEN

~

1926: Of Fairs, Museums, and History

The World's Fair idea is out of date. We have completely out-grown it. There must, however, be a celebration of the 150th anniversary of the nation's birth.

MRS. BLANKENBURG

Perhaps because 150 is not as magical a number as 100. Perhaps because the word "Sesquicentennial" is too obscure and more difficult to pronounce than "Centennial." Perhaps because it rained 107 out of 184 days.

Whatever the reason, Philadelphia's celebration to mark the 150th anniversary of American independence was a colossal flop. Everything that the Centennial was, the Sesquicentennial was not. Organizers had predicted that upwards of thirty six million people would attend. Roughly six million finally did. When the Fair opened on June 1, substantial numbers of exhibits remained unfinished. Only by July 5 could Fair organizers could announce, and probably optimistically, that as many as 90 percent of the exhibits had been completed. As late as October, the *Dearborn Independent* reported "Steam Shovels Still in Evidence."

According to legend, John Wanamaker had proposed the exposition as early as 1916. Though the city had ten years to plan the event, construction crawled forward, largely because the fair became embroiled in scandal and political controversy. According to the *New York Times* the Sesquicentennial "has had as many ups and downs as a roller coaster in an amusement park. The proposal has been a football of politics. . . . Bitter internal disputes nearly wrecked the enterprise on several occasions." Originally envisioned as a $50–100 million extravaganza, plans

24   Philadelphia hoped to recapture the magic of Centennial
Exposition by staging another huge celebration of a national
birthday. It was not to be. (Courtesy of the Print and Picture
Collection, The Free Library of Philadelphia)

continually became less and less elaborate. Ultimately the event cost $20
million. John Wanamaker, no longer alive to see what a hash had been
made of his idea, doubtless turned in his grave.[1]

When it became clear that the fair would not be ready by its June 1,
1926 opening date, and some suggested that the event be postponed and
opened in 1927 (after all, no one seemed to care the World's Columbian
Exposition had celebrated the 400th anniversary of Columbus' voyage a
year late), Mayor W. Freeland Kendrick insisted that the fair would be

ready.[2] When some in the city suggested that the fair be extended beyond its original closing date, Kendrick, deciding he had enough of the
embarrassment, rejected the idea, and the fair closed as ingloriously as
it had opened. The Associated Press reported: "No ceremonies marked
the official closing of the gates. . . . The once beautiful exhibition palaces
stood tall and gaunt in their nakedness. Statues of plaster . . . stood
weatherbeaten and crumbling. . . . To-day the exposition for which Philadelphia spent more than $17,000,000 was left in the care of a lone guard
to die."[3]

As we have seen, many commentators in the late nineteenth century
worried about the transient nature of world's fairs. The fairs disappeared
after a few months, taking their usefulness with them. Yet we have also
seen that in fact these fairs did leave institutional legacies. The Centennial generated the Pennsylvania Museum, and the Columbian Exposition left not only the Commercial Museum in Philadelphia but the Field
Museum in Chicago as well. Though no one seems to have been much
troubled by it, the Sesquicentennial vanished virtually without a trace.
Much of the fair grounds became a park serving the developing neighborhood of South Philadelphia; the marble fountain donated by the Italian government sits today behind the Philadelphia Art Museum; and the
athletic stadium, the largest construction at the fair, hosted the annual
Army-Navy football game (along with big rock concerts) until it was
hastily condemned and torn down in 1990. When it was over, the Sesquicentennial celebration vanished from public memory as quickly as its
buildings were demolished.

Neither did the Sesquicentennial produce a lasting symbol—no Corliss Engine, no gleaming colonnades—of the sort that helped fix other
expositions firmly in the imagination of Americans. The most important
event at the exposition was not an object or display but a prize-fight. The
fight at the fair between heavy-weights Gene Tunney and Jack Dempsey
wonderfully captured the spirit of an age increasingly fixated on specta-
tor sporting events. Thanks to the miracle of radio, the bout in the great
athletic stadium built for the exposition came into millions of American
living rooms. In the final irony, the radio broadcast permitted people
to enjoy the fair's major spectacle without even having to leave their
homes. Modern technology, which had been at the center of world's fairs
since 1876, had by 1926 obviated the need to go to the fair in the first
place.

The 1926 event has also been virtually forgotten by historians. Robert Rydell, who has studied American world's fairs extensively, ends his

first volume with the fairs of 1915–16. He treats the Sesquicentennial more or less parenthetically. Likewise, Michael Kammen is at a loss to explain the failure of the exposition. He calls the lack of interest in the fair "puzzling."[4] The immediate post–World War I era seems to have been a hiatus for extravagant world's fairs. Not until the 1930s did they emerge again as great cultural symbols when, reconceived as playgrounds of the futuristic, they offered Americans escape from the Depression. But if the fairs before the First World War and those of the 1930s stand as great symbols of their respective cultural moments, how do we explain the failure and subsequent invisibility of the Sesquicentennial?

Without question, the fair fell victim to municipal corruption on an epic scale. Cost overruns, sweetheart contracts, kickbacks—all the things that greased the wheels of big city America—now came to national attention as the city stumbled its way toward the celebration. It remains for another historian to disentangle the various malfeasances that beset the fair. (Henry Ford's *Dearborn Independent* seemed to have it all figured out when it blamed the whole mess on Jewish land speculators.)[5] The Sesqui served only to underscore Lincoln Steffens's assessment of Philadelphians' contentment amidst their corruption, and it served to define the city's image for at least a generation. As near as I can determine, the Sesquicentennial provided the fodder for W. C. Field's jokes about Philadelphia.

Corruption may have been the easiest thing to blame for the failure of the Sesquicentennial, but it was not the only obstacle the event faced. From the outset, the fair was doomed by a lack of public interest and support, especially among Philadelphians who were asked to foot much of the bill. While everyone agreed with Mrs. Blankenburg that the Sesquicentennial needed to be commemorated in Philadelphia, many opposed the idea that a World's Fair was the best way to do that. Mayor J. Hampton Moore advocated the idea initially but withdrew his support in the face of substantial public opposition. In a town meeting called late in 1923, attended by roughly 450 citizens, the idea of an international exposition was voted down ten to one. There was even enough sustained objection to spawn an "Anti-Sesqui-Centennial Association."[6]

When Moore was succeeded in office by W. Freeland Kendrick in 1924, those who wanted a World's Fair found they had a friend in the appropriately high place, and plans went ahead. A flyer published in 1923 urged Philadelphians "Let's Get Together," and assured them in no

25   The Sesquicentennial became mired in corruption and incompetence. This fair
official surveys some of the construction that remained unfinished well after the fair
had opened. (Courtesy of the Print and Picture Collection, The Free Library of
Philadelphia)

uncertain terms "that there must and will be a fitting commemoration
of the 150th Anniversary of the signing of the Declaration of Independence."[7]

While this cabal of the mayor's office and many—though by no
means all—of the city's influential business interests might force the fair
on the city, it could not make people enthusiastic about it. When Robert
Stratton, charged with running the fundraising campaign in New Jersey,
wrote to Albert Greenfield explaining his difficulties, he pointedly told
Greenfield that "this has not been what can be termed a popular
campaign."[8]

Appeals to the populace for money and other support became increasingly desperate and guilt-provoking. Charles Shisler, president of
the Victory Arch Association whose purpose was to erect a triumphal

arch at the fair memorializing America's war dead, chided South Philadelphians for their bad "attitude" and played on their sense of neighborhood pride: "Prove that you are a South Philadelphian and above everything assume a victorious attitude." The Sesqui-Centennial Exhibition
Association produced a publicity brochure in which it recreated what
must have been an oft repeated question. "Who is responsible for this
Exhibition?" asks the ordinary citizen, "I had nothing to do with it." In
response, Chairman Trigg explains why this disgruntled resident should
still buy "Sesqui Bonds": "That may be true, but that is no reason why
you and I should allow the good name of Philadelphia to be discredited
before the world for failing to carry out its promises."[9]

In late July, when the fullness of failure had become apparent to
everyone, C. F. Rhodes drafted a frantic publicity plan to advertise the
fair and presented it to Albert Greenfield. In addition to proclaiming
"WORLD'S FAIR 100% COMPLETE" (which it was not), Rhodes suggested
that an old favorite of world's fairs be resurrected on the midway (or in
this case the "Gladway"): "Secure Indians to live in their tepees, Hawai-
ians, Mexicans and Segales to live in their tents with Wikeup and Dobe
Houses to fill the vacant spot that now is an eye-sore on the Midway,
permitting them to dispose of articles of native manufacture as souvenirs without charge."[10] A reservation of "primitive" peoples would pack
the crowds in, like it did in St. Louis in 1904, and Rhodes assured Greenfield that all this could be accomplished for $100,000.

Yet in making this desperate suggestion to save the fair, Rhodes may
have unwittingly put his finger precisely on the reason why it never lived
up to its promoters' dreams. Live Indians in tepees or no, the Sesquicentennial was an old-style world's fair, organized around the same frameworks that had shaped the Centennial, the Columbian, and the Louisiana
Purchase Expositions. Using a historical commemoration as its excuse,
the Sesqui, like previous fairs, proposed to put the current state of technological and industrial progress on display. As one publication put it,
the Sesqui "will primarily show the progress of the United States and
other nations over the past fifty years since the Centennial of 1876."
One publicity brochure even used William McKinley's famous address at
the Pan-American Exposition, to remind people that "Expositions are the
timekeepers of progress."[11]

In the consumer society of the 1920s, however, when people could
buy the latest achievements of American technological genius, this kind
of fair had become an anachronism. In a society zipping around in automobiles, tuning into radio broadcasts, and filling the darkness of movie

palaces, the Sesquicentennial had little to offer by way of excitement or thrills, in the way the older fairs did. Conversely, the fairs of the 1930s were popular because they appealed to visitors by offering futuristic fantasies about what might be. The Sesquicentennial found itself between eras.

This was not lost on many at the time. When she resigned her position from the Sesqui-Centennial Association, Mrs. Blankenburg told the press: "The World's Fair idea is out of date. We have completely outgrown it." And yet fair enthusiasts recognized a need not to be out of date. When Commerce Secretary Herbert Hoover came to Philadelphia in 1923 to bestow a federal blessing on the event, he promised guests at a dinner "a new era in expositions." Hoover told the diners that he had "long been of the opinion that the old-fashioned idea of conducting expositions is past." What Hoover proposed, instead of what he called "mushroom sites," were expositions that left "permanent or semipermanent buildings." This way, the transitory and inspirational nature of the old world's fairs would be replaced by lasting "supereducational" institutions.[12]

Despite these and other promises, what Philadelphia got was essentially more of the same. After entering the main gate of the fair grounds under an enormous reproduction of the Liberty Bell—forty eight feet high, fifty feet in diameter, weighing forty tons, and illuminated with 26,000 light-bulbs—visitors found themselves in a setting familiar to anyone who had been to Chicago in 1893 or St. Louis in 1904. Proceeding down the broad Forum of the Founders, the central axis of the fair grounds, visitors could find the Palace of Liberal Arts & Manufactures, and the Palace of Agriculture & Food Products. To the west of this main boulevard could be found the Gladway amusements and rides, and beyond these, past the two lagoons, the Chinese Village, the Alpine Haus, and, duplicating Chicago exactly, the Streets of Cairo. The fair grounds were also dotted with small buildings sponsored by states, foreign countries, and corporations. These too had been a staple of world's fairs since the Centennial, though the collection of these buildings in 1926 was an odd assortment: of the original thirteen states, Connecticut, Delaware, New Jersey, and Pennsylvania built houses, New York built two buildings, and none of the others did; Argentina, Spain, India, Persia, and Czecho-Slovakia made a showing, but England, Germany, France, Mexico, and Canada did not.

The Great Concrete Stadium sat at the southern end of the fair grounds, on the east side. Opposite the stadium, fair designers created

26   Amid an otherwise disastrous event, High Street stood out as rousing success. Here an enthusiastic crowd fill the streets lined with re-created colonial buildings. (Courtesy of the Print and Picture Collection, The Free Library of Philadelphia)

a strolling park, complete with two artificial lakes. It was here, in the northeast corner of the park, just beyond the replica of the Taj Mahal built as the Indian exhibition building and "The Home Electric—A modern residence showing the latest conveniences for the home" that the most popular exhibit at the fair could be found. Built on a straight axis amidst the park's otherwise curvaceous paths sat "High Street." [13]

High Street was the creation of the Sesqui's Women's Committee. Designed to be a recreation of Philadelphia's High Street circa 1776, the Street consisted of twenty houses, the Market Place, and the Town Hall. High Street was almost entirely a woman's domain, and each of the buildings fell under the care of a different women's organization: The Daughter's of the American Revolution tended "Washington House," while the "Little Wooden House" was the responsibility of the War Mothers. Women from the Pennsylvania School of Horticulture helped plant High Street's gardens. Though it was not advertised particularly beforehand,

High Street became recognized afterward as the fair's singular triumph and the only exhibit worth remembering.[14] High Street generated such enthusiasm that several people suggested it be permanently installed in the city's new art museum.

High Street can surely be seen as a significant piece of the broader Colonial Revival that proliferated in the United States during the 1920s. That revival drove the restoration of Williamsburg, created the American Wing at the Metropolitan Museum of Art, and dotted the suburban landscape with "stone colonial" houses, among other things. Like these others, High Street glorified the domestic virtues of the colonial era and in so doing represented a twentieth-century fantasy of what life was like in the eighteenth. While the fair itself reminded Americans of their political legacy, High Street existed to demonstrate that the domesticity of the eighteenth century was worthy of equal veneration. On High Street Philadelphia's crowded, chaotic, and filthy streets, once strolled by Benjamin Franklin, were recreated, cleaned-up, and gentrified. The hostess at the recreated Stephen Girard house explained this didactic function of High Street to a reporter: "It needs an actual street like this, reconstructed before our eyes, to reveal the fine heritage of beauty and dignity in ordinary everyday life which our ancestors have passed on to us. It proves that our beginnings were not chaotic, lawless, cheap or tawdry, but essentially noble, dignified." [15]

But High Street also underscored on a larger level the complicated relationship between the Sesquicentennial and the history it purported to celebrate. Though both the Centennial and the Sesquicentennial celebrated the same event, many wanted that historical commemoration to be a more central part of the fair in 1926 than it had been in 1876. Elizabeth Frazer told readers of the *Saturday Evening Post:* "For, boiled down, the Sesqui-Centennial is nothing more or less than a great history lesson, the flesh and blood of those past events rendered visible to our eyes." This history lesson, another of High Street's guides explained, "is the fundamental idea upon which the whole exposition is based, since it is first of all a great memorial and after that a great world's fair." [16]

Others saw that history lesson as usefully applied to a current dilemma. In the xenophobic 1920s, with recently passed immigration restrictions slowing the flow of new arrivals to a trickle, many Americans turned their attention to "Americanizing" foreign-born residents. Anna Robeson Burr explained how High Street might contribute to that project: "it is customary to speak as though the elements fused together during the Revolution had been from the start homogeneous, as if it were no

27   High Street was a women's affair. The buildings were built and staffed by different patriotic women's organizations. They put a refined, elegant, aristocratic version of the eighteenth century on display at the Sesquicentennial. (Courtesy of the Print and Picture Collection, The Free Library of Philadelphia)

great matter to bring to one mind a group of men who, some may think, naturally felt and thought alike. No greater error exists. . . . These fifty or sixty men faced a task adjudged impossible and made it possible. They were men of different races, customs and religions; they met in utter unlikeness of mind and outlook and they created one national mind. They sank their differences, they got together." [17] The message here is thinly veiled. Differences among Americans have always existed. What made the founders great was their ability to transcend those differences and create unity, and if contemporary Americans strove to emulate them, that meant rising above (or eliminating altogether) differences of religion and culture. History pointed the way to a national unity in the midst of a chaotic heterogeneity.

While the women of the Sesquicentennial tried to keep the focus of the fair on these particular lessons of 1776, the Centennial itself cast at least as large a shadow for others. A major purpose of the fair, stated in official publications repeatedly, was to demonstrate the progress made since 1876. According to one brochure the "dominant aim" of the event was to mark the signing of the Declaration of Independence, "and to interpret the spirit of progress . . . of the last half century." [18] In addition, the Sesquicentennial would give a cultural legitimacy to the fifty years of tumultuous industrial and technological change since visitors had last come to Philadelphia. A typesheet suggesting an outline for speeches at the fair reminded speakers that the "scope" of the event would stress quality not quantity, aesthetics not volume. "It will not be a vulgar display of wealth, nor a boastful showing of America's bigness," the typesheet chided, but "one designed for perfection and beauty." [19]

When dignitaries assembled in the Sesquicentennial stadium on July 4 to piously observe Independence, comparisons with the Centennial, not the Revolution, seemed to be more on people's minds. After welcoming President Coolidge and his wife, Mayor Kendrick came to the point right away. In the second line of his address before the crowd he reminded those assembled: "Fifty years ago yesterday a great concourse of people assembled in Independence Square in this great patriotic city and celebrated in a fitting manner the one hundredth anniversary of American independence."

Kendrick's speech amplified what he and the city's other boosters hoped would come from the fair. Philadelphia might be the birthplace of the American political experiment, but the Centennial loomed larger in the imagination of many as the city's defining moment. Since then, while the city continued to prosper handsomely as "The Workshop of the World," the luster of the city's prestige had somehow dimmed. The Centennial had served as a gathering of national reconciliation in the wake of the Civil War and Reconstruction. So too, Kendrick told the crowd in the stadium, "we hope the Sesqui-Centennial International Exposition will accomplish among the people of the world" a similar peacemaking, as the world picked up the pieces left from World War I. [20] In his tireless campaign to promote the fair, Kendrick reminded Philadelphians that they had "lost many opportunities in the past." [21] By seizing the opportunity provided by the Sesquicentennial, Philadelphians could restore their city to a position of greater prominence.

Grasping so desperately and so self-consciously at the past in order to rescue the future proved to be a failing strategy, and not simply because the event itself was such a fiasco. The Sesquicentennial, by looking back to the fairs of the past, relied on a way of understanding and presenting the world which had, by 1926, lost much of its resonance. World's Fairs no longer spoke to people as they had in the late nineteenth century, and the objects which those fairs displayed had lost their voice as well. The Centennial of 1876 marked a high moment for an understanding of the world based on objects, and the Sesquicentennial of 1926 marks, as conveniently as anything, the end of that kind of understanding.

~

The latter half of the 1920s marked significant watersheds for the museums examined in this study. The Academy of Natural Sciences had hired a new director with business and entertainment rather than scientific sensibilities. George Byron Gordon, the last director at the University Museum to expand the museum along its original lines, died in January 1927. The Commercial Museum's founder and guiding inspiration, William P. Wilson, and Doylestown's Henry Mercer were also dead by 1927 and 1930 respectively. By 1928, the Philadelphia Museum of Art had completed its move from Memorial Hall to the Parkway. The Field Museum, while still committed to its original vision of natural history, repackaged how it would be presented to the public. Likewise, the American Museum in New York replaced its glass cases with visually exciting "dioramas" beginning in the 1920s.

Surely that all these institutions should experience such profound transitions at the end of the 1920s is coincidental, but powerfully so. Like the Sesquicentennial Exposition itself, 1926 represented the end of an era for these museums. The Sesquicentennial serves to punctuate a fifty-year period of institution building. The great world's fairs put on between 1876 and 1926 helped shape those institutions—universities and department stores as much as museums. The failure of the Sesquicentennial to captivate Americans signaled that the intellectual and cultural frameworks which shaped both fairs and museums had been supplanted.

In trying to recapture for Philadelphia the Centennial moment, the fair's planners also tried to build upon the intellectual architecture of the late nineteenth century. That architecture, which put objects at the center of understanding, had grown rickety and by 1926 could not bear the weight. The Sesquicentennial represented Philadelphia's attempt not merely to reassert itself but also to hold on to a way of conceiving of the world where objects, systematically ordered and displayed, could make perfect sense of it. It had worked in 1876; it no longer did in 1926. Mrs. Blankenburg was more right than she knew: the idea was out of date; Americans had completely outgrown it.

The cause of this erosion may well have been a shift in the meaning

Americans attributed to the past, and the Sesquicentennial fell victim to that shift. Of all the transformations visited upon American society by industrialism and Darwinism during the period of this study, the most elusive may be the changed relationship Americans had with the past. Several historians, most notably Michael Kammen and David Lowenthal, have mused on this change. As Lowenthal has put it, "Unprecedented change radically sundered the present from even the recent past in nineteenth-century Europe and North America." Lowenthal sees this break, in part, as the result of expanding knowledge. "Far too much was now known," he writes, "by historians, anthropologists, classicists and other specialists to sustain the old view that past and present were similar, that history was exemplary." [22] What Lowenthal and other scholars have studied, one of the Colonial Dames staffing Sulgrave Manor on the Sesquicentennial's "High Street" understood intuitively. She told reporter Elizabeth Frazer: "There is, you see, a distinct cleavage, a definite and conscious contrast, between the old and the new." [23]

To differing degrees, history lay at the bottom of the intellectual foundation of the museums in this study. Museums like Ford's and Mercer's dealt directly with American history, and both tried to use museums to develop a new historical understanding of ordinary Americans at a moment when the historical profession was in considerable ferment about precisely how to do that. William Wilson's Commercial Museum used a historical framework to give legitimacy to its activities and to the world of commerce generally. Museums of natural history explored the history of the natural world, and by extension tried to lay plain the history of God's works. Anthropology museums wrestled with the relationship between human history and human culture, implicitly deciding that some of the world's peoples had a history and some did not. Finally, museums of fine art borrowed the evolutionary model and decided that history most easily gave coherence to their collections.

Turn-of-the-century museums represented the institutional manifestation of an object-based epistemology. They remain the last and most glorious product of this way of understanding the world. By 1926, however, this object-based epistemology ceased to be persuasive in a world now governed by electromagnetism, relativity, and quantum mechanics.[24] Museums between 1876 and 1926 struggled to make sense of an industrial and Darwinian world and to put it on display; they could not keep up with Einstein's universe. As a result, objects, and the museums that housed them, no longer held the same kind of explanatory power that they had had previously. Contrast the "naked eye science" that

Henry Fairfield Osborn and others wanted to pursue at the American Museum of Natural History at the turn of the twentieth century with this assessment, from 1939, as a measure of how completely a faith in an object-based epistemology had been eclipsed: "Everybody nowadays, believes in scores of assumptions for which there is good evidence, but no visual proof. And does not science demonstrate that visual proof is the weakest proof? It is being constantly revealed, as mankind studies the material world, that outward appearances are not inward reality at all."[25] What makes this quotation even more remarkable is that its source is about as distant from our concerns as could be imagined. It comes from the anonymous author of the first version of Alcoholics Anonymous' "Big Book," its guide for recovering alcoholics. By the Second World War the sense that the world was precisely *not* what it seemed to be had become that pervasive.

That the old view of objects as invested inherently with scientific meaning collided with a new view which valued objects for their contextual association became apparent in an exchange between Charles Sheeler and Henry Mercer in 1924. In that year, Mercer and Sheeler traded letters about a door latch. Mercer was something of an expert on the subject, having just published an article in the *Journal for the Society for the Preservation of New England Antiquities.* The door latch in question resided in Sheeler's rented house. Mercer proposed to remove the piece to his museum and to replace it with a duplicate made by his staff. Mercer explained his rationale to Sheeler: "I hope you realize my motive is love for the past, and desire to save things at the eleventh hour for posterity." Sheeler refused the older man's request by saying, "The chief reason for my enthusiasm for the little house is that it remains so nearly intact, even to such details as the ironwork. . . . Try to appreciate my point of view, which though the opposite of yours is also based on enthusiasm."[26] For Mercer, whose whole understanding of the past revolved around objects, the door latch was an object of scientific importance, which needed to be preserved in his museum. For Sheeler, on the other hand, the piece had value because of the context in which it was situated. Mercer proposed to strip the latch from that context so that its metonymic value could be appreciated without distraction. Sheeler, though, enjoyed the way the latch contributed to the charming quaintness of an old house. For those in Sheeler's generation, objects might create pleasant associations with the past, but they no longer gave scientific meaning to it. With the disappearance of the object-based epistemology upon which these museums were founded, a case of stuffed birds may now be nothing more than a case of stuffed birds.

Museums in the 1920s, therefore, became more concerned with their role as places of entertainment and amusement. Franz Boas had sensed the movement in this direction as early as 1907, when he published his essay on museum administration. He began it by telling his readers that "the value of the museum as a resort for popular entertainment must not be underrated, particularly in a large city. . . . The people who seek rest and recreation resent an attempt at systematic instruction while they are looking for some emotional excitement."[27] When Boas wrote this, he undoubtedly offended many in the museum world, but by the 1920s his advice seemed a commonplace. Museums during this decade attempted to become "humanized,"[28] and institutions from the Academy of Natural Sciences to the Philadelphia Art Museum tried to accommodate themselves to their visitors. These museums remained committed to education, al though this now came largely through the public schools. By the Sesquicentennial, these museums had succeeded in attracting thousands of visitors each year, and they ensconced themselves as fixtures of most children's school experience.

But if museums had been seen as the centers of intellectual vitality at the time of the Centennial, then fifty years later they had been replaced in that role by universities. The study of natural science left places like the Academy of Natural Sciences for new homes in university and medical school laboratories. Anthropology was pursued in the "field" and in the classroom. International commerce became the purview of the federal government, aided by the research and theorizing of university-affiliated economists, but not by museum builders like William Wilson. History too increasingly abandoned the public realm represented by such places as Mercer's concrete castle and became comfortable in university departments and professional associations. Art historians today certainly continue to utilize the resources of art museums, but they make their living in colleges and universities. By the Sesquicentennial, exhibiting the world was no longer the best way to study it.

∿

Those who have been counting will have noticed that of the six kinds of museums sketched by George Brown Goode in his speech to the American Historical Association, we have examined five. Museums of technology, the sixth of Goode's categories, today constitute some of the most popular museums in the country. Their proliferation, however, belongs largely to the period after this study concludes, and so I want only to glance at them by returning once more to Philadelphia.

As we have seen, in the period covered by this book Philadelphia was the only city in the country where museumgoers could see the encyclopedia set of museums Goode envisioned. Other cities, notably Chicago and New York, built bigger institutions and filled them with more spectacular objects, but Philadelphians created the widest, and for our purposes, the most intellectually interesting constellation of institutions in the country. Needless to say, Philadelphia had its museum of technology too.

Philadelphia's technology museum grew out of the city's famous Franklin Institute and took its name. According to institute lore, W. H. Keating and Samuel Vaughn Merrick, young Philadelphians, wanted to learn about the applications of science to industry and applied for membership in a "mechanic's association." They were rejected, and smarting from the sting of that slap they decided to found their own society. Thus in 1824 began the Franklin Institute, open "to all men and women of intelligence, character and ambition who are interested in science."

The institute dedicated itself to "the promotion of the mechanic arts" and distinguished itself from the city's other scientific institution, the Academy of Natural Sciences, by focusing on the physical sciences, technology, and the collection of patent literature. From the beginning the institute sponsored public lectures—looking back in 1928, institute secretary Howard McClenahan boasted that "many of the scientific marvels of the world have been first publicly described in the Hall"—and in 1825 the institute began publishing a journal. Most importantly, the institute functioned as a school where students were trained to bring science and technology together. Classes in "pure and applied science, physics, chemistry, mathematics, machine design, engineering drawing, architecture" fostered "a democracy in science"—at least that is what was claimed—and made the Franklin Institute, throughout the nineteenth century, a vital center for what might be called today "technology transfer." [29]

Through its first hundred years, the institute maintained a collection of objects only as an aid to its teaching. Yet even as the institute celebrated its centenary in 1924, those who ran it had decided to change course. Despite the undeniable success the institute had training Philadelphians in applied science, by 1924 the school had closed and plans were under way for a grand museum of technology. New York and Chicago announced plans for similar museums shortly afterwards.

On its face, the idea to build this museum seems an unqualified success. Even though fundraising began in 1930, with depression enveloping the country, Philadelphians wrote checks to the tune of $5.1 million in the first two weeks of the fundraising drive. Opened to the public on January 1, 1934, the Museum attracted in its first year nearly 260,000 visitors willing to pay the 25¢ admission.[30]

For their quarter, visitors saw a museum radically different from any other in the city. They were encouraged to participate, to "stand upon a real ship's bridge," to work the controls of Baldwin Locomotive No. 60,000 as it moved back and forth across a short track. The museum's designers proudly told people that "Do Not Touch" signs would be rare. In short, this museum helped develop the "interactive" model that museums have been refining and expanding up to the present. Entertainment and amusement now became primary goals as at the other museums, but the Franklin Institute, not as burdened with the baggage of a past museum history, it achieved these goals more successfully. One writer thought that the "keynote" of Chemistry Hall ought to be "Press the button and let chemistry do the rest!" He went on to describe: "By pushing a button, a visitor may start the process of forming oxide of iron by burning iron in oxygen. . . . He may press another button, and water will be broken up into hydrogen and oxygen, with the accompaniment of an explosive 'Bang!' "[31] Visitors were no longer to be taught through the careful, systematic presentation of objects, but they were to be dazzled instead and offered the opportunity to play with exhibits rather than study them. When the "Bakelite Travelcade" came through the institute, demonstrating the wonders of modern plastic, the advertisement might well have been used to describe the whole intent of this new museum experience: "a year's education in an hour's entertainment."[32]

In the late 1920s and early 1930s, the Franklin Institute, and museums like it, helped chart a course for the future of museums. By opening a new chapter in museum history, they necessarily closed another. In several ways, the museum of the Franklin Institute represented the end of one era as much as the beginning of a new one.

For the institute itself, building the museum ended its hundred year history of training Philadelphia's artisan mechanics. Secretary McClenahan acknowledged, "with regret" that this teaching role had been usurped by other institutions.[33] Historians have yet to adequately explore the relationship between mechanics institutes like Philadelphia's Franklin and the rise of American industrialism. I suspect that it is more than coincidental that while the Franklin Institute was training the mechanics and engineers who filled Philadelphia's factories, the city was also a world leader in innovating industrial processes, from chemical refining, to locomotive making, to radio building. Philadelphia well deserved its nickname, "The Workshop of the World." Thus it may well be more than coincidental that the institute gave up this educational role at roughly the same moment that Philadelphia's industrial leadership began to slip.

More to our point, however, by giving up its schools the Franklin Institute severed its connection to a past in which it served to promote the "mechanic arts." Visitors might now have their curiosity and interest sparked by the interactive exhibits, but the museum did not pretend to provide them with the kind of education in applied science that the institute once did. As an advertising brochure put it, "science will be made understandable, the application of invention to the affairs of life will be portrayed."[34] Portrayed yes, but developed and carried out no longer. In severing this connection, the institute also conceded that it could no longer create "democracy in science," as it once had pretensions of doing. The application of science to industry would now take place in vocational training schools and university-level engineering departments. The new museum would be a push-button affair.

More generally, the new kind of museum embodied by the Franklin Institute signaled a shift in the way objects functioned. In galleries now filled with whirring gyroscopes, exploding water molecules, and clanging train bells, objects no longer occupied the central place in the intellectual architecture of museums as they had in an earlier generation. The new exhibits relied on recreating hands-on experimentation—however half-heartedly—and not on the careful contemplation of systematically arranged specimens. Hoping to teach visitors how things worked, the Franklin Institute treated its objects as means to an end rather than the ends unto themselves.

The transformation in the way objects functioned at the Franklin Institute accompanied a change in the way in which objects were perceived to have meaning. As Secretary McClenahan explained, in a museum where visitors are encouraged to handle the objects, "originals" become less desirable than reproductions of originals: "If one exact copy can be made, another can also be made—so that there is no necessity for withdrawing it from contact with the observers—it can used until it is 'used up," then replaced by a second without irreparable loss." Museum objects in the age of mechanical reproduction, to bastardize Walter Benjamin's phrase.

McClenahan spun a telling metaphor to describe the way original objects functioned in the new museums: "The originals are like salt on food—they add flavor and give distinction. But, as in the case of salt, a little goes a long way. A few great originals are enough." [35] Since the mid-nineteenth century, American museums had been predicated on collecting, classifying, and displaying original objects. By 1928, they had been reduced by McClenahan to that which was sprinkled on top of something more substantial. What had been at the heart of the museum enterprise for roughly a century had become the most ordinary cultural condiment.

For visitors to the Franklin Institute, it is this sense of loss and of things past that first greeted them. The broad entrance stairs led up to a memorial rotunda in which sits an enormous marble statue of the institute's namesake. Smiling genially at the hundreds of thousands who file past, the statue serves to remind people that the museum turned the institute into a monument to the past.

～

This story began with a visit and it culminates in a luncheon.

Sometime in the late 1920s or early 1930s, the directors of several of Philadelphia's museums had lunch. There is nothing extraordinary in that, except that this meal had an extraordinary purpose. Over their food, the directors agreed to divide up the world. The evidence for this meeting is indirect. Indeed, it may never have actually happened, though I have heard the story from too many different archivists to doubt it. What we can say is that by the late 1920s or early 1930s, most of Philadelphia's museums had drawn clearer boundaries around their areas of interest than they had ever done before. Those lines remain fixed more or less to this day.

In 1927, John Jenks wrote to Fiske Kimball, informing him that Charles Harrison was dying. "This means," he wrote, "that a future policy for the University Museum will have to be decided." [36] Jenks realized that with the impending opening of the new art museum, both institutions would do well to establish a clear relationship. By the following year, Kimball could explain the difference between his museum and the one at the university. Writing to an inquirer, he explained: "In the division of the museum field in Philadelphia between our own Museum and the University Museum . . . we leave the whole field of ethnology to the University Museum. Our own scope is European and American art since the Christian era."[37] An internal memorandum written sometime in the early 1930s elaborated on Kimball's letter. "While there is no formal protocol," the memo states, "the policy of the two museums is based on the idea that the field of the University is archaeology and ethnology, and includes primitive and ancient civilizations including the Greek and Roman, the field of the Pennsylvania Museum is the history of art roughly from the time of Christ, Buddha, and Confucius." The memo concluded by describing the tangible results of these policy decisions: "Egyptian and Mesopotamian antiquities have already been transferred to the University Museum; Sasanian and some Mohammedan material to the Pennsylvania Museum of Art."[38] Dividing up the world meant swapping collections.

The Academy of Natural Sciences also seems to have participated in this dividing up, though the evidence for that consists primarily of acquisitions records at the University Museum listing archaeological objects on loan from the academy, sent there during this period. In any event, by 1935 the academy concentrated on natural objects, the Pennsylvania Museum on Western art from the early Christian era to the modern, and the University Museum focused on artifacts from ancient and primitive societies. (Both the University Museum and the Pennsylvania Museum continued to collect Asian objects, a reflection of the peculiar place those cultures occupy in the Western imagination.)[39]

It had taken fifty years of experimentation before those museum directors could sit down to have lunch. Rather, for fifty years, museums in America had experimented with and struggled over how to define the intellectual boundaries of their institutions. They had tried to shape and to keep up with the ways in which categories of knowledge changed in the late nineteenth century. American museums between 1876 and 1926 tried to give order to a world growing increasingly chaotic both socially and intellectually. Museums crave stasis and stability; knowledge has little respect for either. Lunch, therefore, represented the final fruition of a fifty-year process, and a final concession. The museum directors could finally agree on how to define their respective turf, but in drawing firm boundaries around their institutions, they acknowledged that they would no longer attempt to keep up with the way knowledge might change.

The museums of the late nineteenth century, no more or less than those of today, helped create categories of knowledge and depended on those categories for their intellectual authority. It has not been my purpose to suggest that these museums got those categories right or wrong. As we have already discussed, the sum of the world's knowledge might well be divided in several other ways. The walls these museums put around bodies of knowledge did not or do not represent immutable truths. Here, Foucault and others are surely right.

At the same time, we must admit that to have any knowledge at all means human beings must construct intellectual categories of some kind. In this sense, we might better see these museums instead as embodiments of truth in a Jamesian, pragmatic sense. Museum builders tried to faithfully reconstruct the world as they understood it inside their institutions, and in so doing they reinforced the truths that they tried to represent. In his most famous definition of pragmatism, James wrote: "Truth happens to an idea." Stretching James's articulation of pragmatic truth we can say that truth happened to the museums of the late nineteenth century in two mutually reinforcing ways. The ideas, represented through objects on display, became true by virtue of their being in a museum. At the same time, these museums drew authority by representing with the power of objects a coherent worldview that, at least for some and at least for a while, worked to create intellectual order. For a time, these museums—the objects they assembled and the systematic way in which they were presented—functioned quite well to explain the world to people. Under the pressure of further intellectual developments, however, the truths on display at museums began to crumble, replaced by others, more functional and equally fragile.

These museums also developed a distinctive form in the second half of the nineteenth century through which to convey their meaning. The systematic arrangement of objects and their display in glass cases allowed those objects to tell what I have earlier called narratives of evolutionary progress. As the truths of those narratives strained under new ideas about science, history, or anthropology, the forms which these museums developed changed as well. Most museums, the Smithsonian notably excepted, could not afford to simply rebuild themselves from the ground up. But within the walls of their original homes, many museums experimented with new forms through which to present new narratives. Dioramas replaced glass cases beginning in the 1920s; interactive rather than passive exhibits have become the rage more recently.

It is for another historian and another book to examine the ways in which museums changed during the twentieth century. What I want to observe here is that this dilemma of content and form has contributed in large measure to the "crisis" that museums find themselves in today. We should be quick to qualify. It has been an essential continuity of museum history that those who run the institutions perceive them always to be in crisis. But without the unifying narrative of evolutionary progress, and without the form that was developed to convey that story, museums today find themselves unsure about how best to put their collections on display, or even what to display.

Some museums, like Pittsburgh's Carnegie, retain a version of the encyclopedic ideal. Natural history, art, and science are all on display in a single complex at the Carnegie. The Smithsonian, on the other hand, governed by circumstances which make it unique, has built a new building each time it wanted to create a new subject for display. Most science museums simply have not figured out how to display much of what has gone on in twentieth century science, especially in physics and chemistry. A new computer museum in Boston hopes to create a museum space to consider this technology, but one wonders how successful it will be when, even as I write this, my computer has become outdated.

Art museums, as we have already discussed, hold on to their original form and content perhaps more than any other kind of museum because, as I have suggested, the intellectual endeavor of art history remains closer to its museum origins than is true in other fields. Though they may differ in their details, most of America's major museums of art are arranged chronologically, and they demonstrate the evolution of Western art from the classical or medieval period (depending on the scope of the museum's holdings) through to the modern. The paintings hang on walls much as they have always done, and in a few places it has recently become fashionable to preserve or restore the old Victorian gallery, high-ceilinged and sky-lit.

Interestingly, art museums, along with anthropology museums, have become the sites where some of these questions are debated most vigorously. Artifacts from "exotic" or "primitive" peoples appeared in museums first as illustrations of the scientific study of culture. Often they were and are displayed according to typologies and seriations developed by anthropologists and archaeologists. By the mid-twentieth century, these kinds of cultural objects were exhibited as part of cultural dioramas, anthropological versions of the natural history dioramas, re-creating the "natural habitat" of a particular cultural group. These reconstructed life scenes, complete with mannequins showing the ways in which the objects would be used, stressed the functional aspects of anthropological artifacts.

For a variety of reasons, both intellectual and political, displaying anthropological objects in these ways has become increasingly problematic. For some anthropologists, these kinds of exhibits incompletely and imperfectly represented what was understood about the cultures on display. Worse, they presented these cultures as static and unchanging when culture is by its very nature always changing and shifting. By freezing a particular culture at a particular moment in time, these exhibits implied that any subsequent change in that culture, especially change brought on through contact with the West, represented a deterioration.

Politically, for some both inside and outside the world of professional anthropology, these exhibits only obfuscate the complex process of Western imperial expansion, and they beg the question of how this material got into these museums in the first place. The complicated question of cultural ownership has been a vexing one ever since Lord Elgin stole the sculptures off the Parthenon and brought them to London in the early nineteenth century. During the past generation this question has taken on a new urgency. As countries in the Third World struggle with the legacies of imperialism and with the problems of nation building, they have wondered out loud why so much of their cultural patrimony should sit in Western museum galleries. In the United States, Native American groups have pushed this issue further, demanding the repatriation of cultural material—especially human remains—and with some success.

While it has become increasingly unacceptable to exhibit cultural material as pieces of scientific curiosity, some of this very same material has leapt across institutions, and thus across categories, to become part of the world of fine art. Beginning probably at the Metropolitan Museum of Art's Rockefeller Wing and more recently at places like National Museum of African Art on the Mall, objects which might once have been shown for their "cultural," and by implication "scientific" value, are now displayed as fine art objects. Placed in sharp, clean Lucite cases and lit attractively, almost erotically, these objects are now displayed with the same visual techniques as medieval reliquaries or Monet waterlilies. Even anthropology museums like the University of Pennsylvania's, which recently reinstalled its African collection in this way, have followed this lead.

This transformation of anthropological objects into fine art pieces attempts to resolve the political issues discussed above. To treat objects as anthropology is seen now as a sign of cultural disrespect. The unstated assumption is that the category of "fine art" represents the pinnacle of our cultural hierarchy. Westerners have a respect and reverence for "art" and "artists" that they simply do not have for crafts or their producers. So by designating Yoruba masks and Benin bronzes as fine art, museums like the Met and the Smithsonian pay this material the ultimate cultural compliment.[40]

This strategy may or may not prove politically acceptable, but either way it elides the intellectual question of how we are to understand these materials and how—or even if—we should convey that understanding through display. We have already discussed how anthropological exhibits in museums removed objects from an original cultural context and resituated them in a new one. That new one, heavy with the baggage of Western cultural assumptions and museum practices, reflected the prejudices of museums builders at least as much as it allegedly represented the cultures on display.

Yet we must also acknowledge that those who constructed these exhibits made some attempt, however flawed, to present objects as representative of larger cultural wholes. They hoped that visitors would come away from their museums with some sense of the worldviews of other cultures, although we might now admit the exceeding difficulty of that endeavor.

The newer strategy of display virtually denies cultural context altogether. Any sense of the cultural knowledge to be gained through objects has been replaced entirely with aesthetics. Under the Lucite, these are now objects to be considered almost exclusively for their formal beauty. Recreated now as art objects to be appreciated and understood in the same way as the Old Masters, these objects are now often tagged with labels that follow the convention of Western art history: name of the artist, date, place and school, even if the name of the artist is, more often than not, "Anonymous."

Finally, art museums have not been able to erase entirely the categories that once separated cultural artifacts from art pieces. Seattle has recently opened a gorgeous art museum, designed by the Philadelphia architect Robert Venturi. The heart of the museum's collections, in my view at any rate, is the non-Western material and especially the objects from the cultures of the Pacific Northwest. These reside on the third floor. Above on the fourth floor is the museum's modest collection of Western art.

The objects on the third floor exist in a double stasis. They are mounted attractively and arranged by cultural group. But the objects are fixed in their current positions (some are simply too big to move) and consequently neither the pieces themselves nor their interpretive arrangement will ever change. Consequently, we are left without any context or framework through which we can understand this art. Further, they are presented ahistorically—eighteenth-century objects right next to objects produced in the 1960s. Once again, people outside of time, without history. Up on the fourth floor, however, the Western art is arranged along the familiar chronological path—we begin with Egypt and Greece and we make our way to the modern. Though many of these pieces are second-rate at best, we can rely on this chronological framework to understand the narrative they tell. The pieces back on the third are left on their own to speak only in the language of aesthetics.

The problem of categories remains as troubling as it was in the late nineteenth century, and we are left not with solutions but only with ironies. Anthropology museums might have constructed views of other cultures without histories, but bestowing upon these cultural objects the status of art has not restored that history. Instead, it has merely deprived them of an art history as well. Objects that might once have been derisively labeled as "fetishes" have now become fetishes of quite a different kind. And the glass cases, reincarnated as spot-lit Lucite, are back.

At some level, we have come full circle: visitors asked to contemplate objects without distraction. But without the reassuring narratives of evolutionary progress to give them meaning, the objects now speak in barely audible voices.

～

One final set of observations, and perhaps a final irony.

In the world of America's post-industrial cities, some booming, others declining, museums and other cultural institutions continue to measure the perceived health of cities. During the past twenty-five years or so, "new" cities, especially in the Southwest, have announced their arrival as major urban centers by importing famous architects to build new museums. These extravagant facilities are intended to demonstrate that places like Phoenix or Houston should be taken seriously by the rest of the nation. The oligarchy of Dallas-Fort Worth set the standard for this kind of institution building when they hired the Philadelphia architect Louis Kahn to design the Kimball Art Museum in Fort Worth. Kahn produced a stunning building, even if the museum did not initially have much of a collection to fill his concrete vaults. Most recently, the opening of the new J. Paul Getty Center has been greeted with enthusiasm by some Angelenos not simply because it is a major cultural event but also because they feel it will recast the city's image and make serious people take the city seriously. In the words of Director John Walsh, the museum "will change the caricatured view of Los Angeles." (Entertainment mogul David Geffen was reportedly less sanguine. "This is too good for Los Angeles," he pronounced when he toured the new building.)[41] In this sense, these new museums serve one of the purposes of their predecessors of the late nineteenth century. They lend an aura of cultural legitimacy to a new class of arrivistes.

As cities in the sunbelt celebrated their prosperity by building magnificent temples of culture, however, older museums, especially in the rustbelt, became equally important symbols of urban decline. During the ongoing budget crises of the late 1980s and early 1990s, the lovely Brooklyn Museum of Art was only able to open half of its galleries at a time. The recession and subsequent losses of public funding devastated many arts organizations, even including the Los Angeles County Museum of Art, which had relied almost exclusively on public appropriations. Most dramatic and most tragic perhaps have been the struggles of the Detroit Institute of Arts. The institute symbolized the vital city that built it shortly after the First World War. It has grown to become the sixth largest art museum in the country, with major collections, especially of American art. Its troubles began to emerge in the 1970s, and the institute actually closed for a time in June 1975. By the recession of the early 1990s, the institute lost considerable state funding, which forced it to lay off 45 percent of its workforce and curtail its hours. Like the city that surrounds it, the institute seems perilously close to being abandoned. With permanent closing a real possibility, the Detroit Institute of Art may become, in the words of one observer, "the nation's largest art warehouse."[42] The museum fights desperately just to stay open, and through recent heroic efforts the institute's future seems a bit brighter.[43]

Museums and other cultural institutions have assumed a new importance as these older American cities face their post-industrial future. Cities like Philadelphia, once the centers of industrial production, no longer manufacture much beyond tourism and conventions. Museums, therefore, are now seen as economic engines driving the production of those tourists. Faneuil Hall in Boston and South Street Seaport in New York are but two examples of how cities have tried to "develop" their history and culture. In the 1980s Lowell, Massachusetts took this idea as far as it could be taken when it turned many of its empty textile mill buildings and much of its downtown into a National Park. The former textile center tried to transform itself into a tourist center highlighting the history of textile production.

Many cities now turn to their cultural institutions as economic saviors. New York's Metropolitan, in a bid for continued public appropriation, claims to have a larger economic impact on the city than all the city's sports teams combined. Since the start of his administration in 1991, Philadelphia mayor Ed Rendell has featured the "Avenue of the Arts" project as the centerpiece of his plans to expand the city's tourism industry. The Avenue project will expand the cultural resources of the city considerably by building on existing institutions like the Academy of Music and the University of the Arts and by creating new ones. The first of these new facilities opened in early 1994.[44]

In December 1993, the Philadelphia Art Museum scored a major coup when it announced that it would be the only U.S. venue for the 1996 Cezanne retrospective. Already hailed by one expert as "one of the most important art exhibitions of the second half of the 20th century," the Cezanne show was a major feather in the museum's cap.

An editorial in the *Philadelphia Inquirer* got right to the point as it explained the significance of the news. Gushing about the museum's "phenomenal achievement," the editorial stated: "Estimates are that the exhibition will bring more than $21 million to the local economy. An expected 340,000 people will troop through the museum and they'll later spend millions in restaurants, shops, night spots, hotels and on a wide range of goods and other services." In case you did not get the point, the editorial continued: "These are serious numbers, and they show why it's just plain good business to boost the city's (and the region's) many cultural attractions."[45] In fact, the exhibition drew roughly three quarters of a million people and the estimates measuring the economic ripple for the city top $60 million. The show itself did not break much new interpretive ground in helping us reckon with Cezanne's career. The major lesson it taught to Philadelphians was that culture pays.

In 1895, George Brown Goode concluded an essay about museums by stating: "THE DEGREE OF CIVILIZATION TO WHICH ANY NATION, CITY OR PROVINCE HAS ATTAINED IS BEST SHOWN BY THE CHARACTER OF ITS PUBLIC MUSEUMS AND THE LIBERALITY WITH WHICH THEY ARE MAINTAINED."[46] Writing in the midst of America's industrial expansion, Goode saw cultural institutions as the best measure of a society's well-being. One hundred years later, Philadelphia and its post-industrial sisters look to those institutions to restore their health. The museums created in the late nineteenth century by America's industrial titans now find themselves in the position to be the engines of a post-industrial economy. Now that Philadelphia's factories sit empty, culture is seen as the best hope to save the city's economic future.

Requiem

In the course of writing this book, I was invited to participate in a funeral. Perhaps that is not quite the right word. Maybe it was more like one of those doctor's consultations when they decide whether to carry out the "Do Not Resuscitate" orders on a dying patient. In any event, on a spring day in 1996 I took part in a public discussion to consider the fate of what remains of the Philadelphia Commercial Museum.

The City of Philadelphia still owns both the last building and the extant collection of the old Commercial Museum. In 1995 the city closed the building and put the collections into a storage facility. The group that convened was not a tribunal as such. We could not order a summary execution. Rather we talked about what ought to be done and what might be done feasibly. We considered issues of legal obligation and of public responsibility. We asked, in essence, when has a museum ceased to be a museum, and what should be done with the residue?

For me there were two sets of questions to consider, the institutional and the intellectual. Most of those in the conference room were concerned primarily with the former. To have summoned such a gathering in the first place, after all, meant an acknowledgment that the Commercial Museum, as a functioning institution, no longer existed. What remains are some archival material, dozens of wonderful photographs, and a tiny percentage of the once extensive collections. Should this material be kept together, or dispersed to several other institutions? Which institutions might get what? Would giving the material away constitute a gift to those other institutions from the city (and would that even be legal), or would it rather be viewed as a loan in perpetuity? All difficult questions that deserved to be asked.

But at another level, our discussion was an admission that the Commercial Museum's attempt to create and embody a certain category of knowledge was dead as well. The few objects sitting in that warehouse might have certain kinds of value, but none has the value of the museum's original purpose anymore. International commerce, as a category of museum knowledge, has evaporated, leaving the question of what happens next. What does one do when the category of knowledge embodied in a museum does not simply shift or change but disappears altogether? What does it mean to preside over the death of a museum? And how does one dispose of the remains?

Our purpose was to ask these questions, not necessarily to answer them. But one suspects, as American museums face growing political, financial, and intellectual pressures, that these are questions which will be raised increasingly in the future. In this sense it was an extraordinary event, and perhaps, in an almost macabre way, it may serve as a model for other such discussions. For it is certain that other people in other places will face similar problems. As a legal expert at our meeting put it rather bluntly: There are simply too many museums in this country, and not enough support for them all.

That American museums feel themselves to be in crisis is nothing new. I have been amused to discover in my research that museums have *always* seen themselves in crisis—underattended, underfunded, underappreciated. But now as then we discuss this crisis largely in "institutional" terms, whether it be how to attract new audiences or new sources of money. I would suggest, however, that museums need to ask the other set of questions as well. What bodies of knowledge do museums purport to display? How are they given definition and why? How can that knowledge be given objective, material form (or, indeed, can it)? By wrestling with the more fundamental questions of intellectual purpose, perhaps our museums can better address their other problems in the future.

～

I suppose that at some deep level this project started when my parents began taking me regularly to museums when I was a kid. These trips are among my earliest childhood memories and among my most pleasant. They also proved habit forming, and now that I have reached adulthood I probably go to museums even more often than I did with my family. I will admit unabashedly that I love these places, big or small, famous or obscure. They fascinate me. I seek them out whenever I am in a new place, and I visit them like old friends when I am someplace familiar.

I am not alone. Perhaps it is only a function of my memories, but it seems to me that I now share the galleries with more people than I did when I was a child. Without belittling any of the very real financial and attendance challenges American museums face, as a group they probably reach a broader audience now than they ever have.

And this too requires some explanation. Without intending to do so exactly, I have written a narrative of failed hopes and reduced expectations—the "rise and fall" story I wanted to avoid in chapter 1. Founded to organize the world with and to produce knowledge through the objects they collected, organized, and displayed, the museums I have discussed here were ultimately unable to fulfill this promise in the way they thought they could. Yet museums have survived, many have flourished, and their numbers have grown.

The only explanation I will or can offer here for that obvious observation is that, whatever else may have changed, museums still display objects, and while these objects may no longer function epistemologically, they can still function—for me at any rate—magically. There remains something extraordinary, if finally inexplicable, about the experience of being in the presence of a Cezanne, or a raven-mask from Alaska, or a fossil pterodactyl. To see the thing itself, with one's own eyes and in a public place, surrounded by other people having some version of the same experience can be enchanting. Even as prosaic a group as professional historians, most of whom do not study objects, will admit to the thrill of holding actual archival material in their hands. The letter or diary or account book exerts a power over us that the published versions of those same documents—or reproductions of paintings or ceramics—do not. Perhaps this is why museums can still be places of education, of inspiration, of amusement, reflection and wonder.

Perhaps, in the end, there are the objects.

Notes

~

Chapter One

1. "Life Stories in Dead Clay," *Philadelphia Press,* September 20, 1894.

2. Ibid.

3. William P. Wilson to Edward Everett Ayer, July 16, 1894, Field Museum Archives.

4. "Museums and Their Purposes," *The Museum News* 1, no. 8 (March 1906): 110.

5. See Terence Hawkes, *Structuralism and Semiotics* (Berkeley: University of California Press, 1977), 75–87.

6. See Svetlana Alpers, "The Museum as a Way of Seeing," in Ivan Karp and Steven Lavine, eds., *Exhibiting Cultures: The Poetics and Politics of Museum Display* (Washington, D.C.: Smithsonian Institution Press, 1991); and Eilean Hooper-Greenhill, *Museums and the Shaping of Knowledge* (London: Routledge, 1992), 45.

7. G. Stanley Hall, "Museums of Art and Teachers of History," *Art Museums and Schools* (New York: C. Scribner's Sons, 1913), 72.

8. I have borrowed the phrase from Carol Duncan, *Civilizing Rituals: Inside Public Art Museum* (London: Routledge, 1995). Though he does not talk about museums specifically, John Kasson describes the struggle over "proper" behavior at the theater, opera, and symphony in the nineteenth century. John Kasson, *Rudeness and Civility: Manners in Nineteenth-Century Urban America* (New York: Hill and Wang, 1990). Tony Bennett, writing not specifically about the American case, sees museums "as an instrument of public instruction [through] which the rough and raucous might learn to civilize themselves." Tony Bennett, *The Birth of the Museum: History, Theory, Politics* (London: Routledge, 1995), 28.

9. L. P. Gratacap, "History of the American Museum of Natural History," American Museum of Natural History Library, Special Collections, chapter 3, 26.

10. George Kubler, *The Shape of Time: Remarks on the History of Things* (New Haven: Yale University Press, 1962), Preamble.

11. Most famously, Robert Wiebe synthesized this period as a "search for order." I have borrowed this phrase from Joel Williamson, *A Rage for Order: Black-White Relations in the American South since Emancipation* (New York: Oxford University Press, 1986).

12. N. H. Winchell, "Museums and their Purposes," *Science* 18 (July 24, 1891): 43.

13. David Murray, *Museums: Their History and their Use* (Glasgow: James MacLehose and Sons, 1904), 187–88.

14. Ibid., 285.

15. Alpers, "Museum as a Way of Seeing," 31.

16. Morris Vogel, *Cultural Connections: Museums and Libraries of Philadelphia and the Delaware Valley* (Philadelphia: Temple University Press, 1991), 85. See also Michael Kammen, *Mystic Chords of Memory: The Transformation of Tradition in American Culture* (New York: Knopf, 1991).

17. Edward Drinker Cope, "The Academy of Natural Sciences," *The Penn Monthly* 7 (March 1876): 176.

18. Kammen, *Mystic Chords of Memory*, 154.

19. J. A. Udden, "Museum Building in the United States," *Science*, n.s., 36 (July 26, 1912), 110–11.

20. George Stocking, "Philanthropoids and Vanishing Cultures: Rockefeller Funding and the End of the Museum in Anglo-American Anthropology," *The Ethnographer's Magic and Other Essays in the History of Anthropology* (Madison: University of Wisconsin Press, 1992), 181.

21. "The Metropolitan Museum Rebuilds the Past," *New York Times,* September 13, 1993.

22. Neil Harris, "The Gilded Age Revisited: Boston and the Museum Movement," *American Quarterly* 14, no. 4 (1962): 546, 553, 562.

23. Tony Bennett, "The Exhibitionary Complex," in Nicholas Dirks et al., eds., *Culture/Power/History: A Reader in Contemporary Social Thought* (Princeton: Princeton University Press, 1994), 131–33; Bennett, *Birth of the Museum,* 95.

24. Hooper-Greenhill, *Museums and the Shaping of Knowledge,* 2.

25. Paul Di Maggio, "Cultural Entrepreneurship in Nineteenth-Century Boston, Part 2, *Media, Culture and Society* 4 (1982): 320.

26. Kubler, *Shape of Time,* 67; and Igor Kopytoff, "The Cultural Biography of Things: Commoditization as Process," in Arjun Appadurai, ed., *The Social Life of Things: Commodities in Social Perspective* (Cambridge: Cambridge University Press, 1986), 70.

27. Thomas Schlereth, *Victorian America: Transformations in Everyday Life, 1876–1915* (New York: Harper Collins, 1991), xiv. For more on late Victorian material culture, see Simon Bronner, ed., *Consuming Visions: Accumulation and Display of Goods in America, 1880–1920* (New York: Norton, 1989).

28. Miles Orvell, *The Real Thing: Imitation and Authenticity in American Culture, 1880–1940* (Chapel Hill: University of North Carolina Press, 1989), 49. For good discussions of the rise of American department stores, see William Leach, *Land of Desire: Merchants, Power and the Rise of a New American Culture* (New York: Vintage Books, 1993); and Leon Harris, *Merchant Princes: An Intimate History of Jewish Families Who Built Great Department Stores* (New York: Harper & Row, 1979). Neil Harris also talks about the relationship between art museums and department stores in his essay "Museums, Merchandising, and Popular Taste: The Struggle for Influence," *Cultural Excursions: Marketing Appetites and Cultural Tastes in Modern America* (Chicago: University of Chicago Press, 1990).

29. Kenneth Ames, "Meaning in Artifacts: Hall Furnishings in Victorian America," *Journal of Interdisciplinary History* 9 (Summer 1978): 21; Orvell, *The Real Thing,* 40.

30. In "Museums, Merchandising and Popular Taste," Neil Harris suggests that these three competed with each other to shape public tastes. I do not disagree with Harris, but whereas Harris stresses the differences between museums, department stores, and fairs, I am more interested in their similarities.

31. I have paraphrased these ideas from Norman Denzin and Herbert Blumer, quoted in M. Gottdiener, *Postmodern Semiotics: Material Culture and the Forms of Postmodern Life* (Oxford: Blackwell, 1995), 57.

32. Quoted in Susan Stewart, *On Longing: Narratives of the Miniature, the Gigantic, the Souvenir, the Collection* (Baltimore: The Johns Hopkins University Press, 1984), 162.

33. Jane Addams to Frederic Skiff, January 2 (?), 1902, Field Museum Archive, Historical Documents, Box 3, folder marked General Correspondence 1893–1905.

34. John Fiske, "University Reform," *Darwinism and Other Essays* (Boston: Houghton Mifflin, 1885; reprint, Kraus, 1969), 292.

35. J. A. Udden, "Museum Building in the United States," 111.

36. Orvell, *The Real Thing,* 35.

37. Edward Drinker Cope, "Academies of Science," *The Penn Monthly* 7 (August 1876): 641.

38. John Higham, *History* (Englewood Cliffs, N.J.: Prentice Hall, 1965), 8. For a discussion of the professionalization of the social sciences in particular, see Dorothy Ross, *The Origins of American Social Science* (Cambridge: Cambridge University Press, 1991).

39. Curtis Hinsley, "The Museum Origins of Harvard Anthropology," in Clark Elliott and Margaret Rossiter, eds., *Science at Harvard University: Historical Perspectives* (Bethlehem, Penn.: Lehigh University Press; Toronto: Associated University Press, 1992), 141–42.

40. See Abigail A. Van Slyck, *Free to All: Carnegie Libraries and American Culture, 1890–1920* (Chicago: University of Chicago Press, 1995), 98.

41. For the most thorough discussion of the ways in which science has been communicated (and miscommunicated) to the public, see John Burnham, *How Superstition Won and Science Lost: Popularizing Science and Health in the United States* (New Brunswick, N.J.: Rutgers University Press, 1987).

42. Anon., "The Museum and the Schools," *Museum Journal* 2, no. 3 (1911): 58.

43. David Brigham, *Public Culture in the Early Republic: Peale's Museum and Its Audience* (Washington, D.C.: Smithsonian Institution Press, 1995).

44. Orvell, *The Real Thing,* xviii.

45. Thomas Kuhn, *The Structure of Scientific Revolutions* (Chicago: University of Chicago Press, 1962), 24.

46. George Brown Goode, *The Principles of Museum Administration* (York: Coultas & Volans, Exchange Printing Works, 1895), 22.

47. George Brown Goode, "The Museums of the Future," *Report of the National Museum, 1888–89* (Washington, D.C., 1891), 427–34.

48. J. G. Wood, "The Dulness of Museums," *Nineteenth Century* 21 (1887): 384–96; F. A. Bather, "How May Museums Best Retard the Advance of Science?" *Science,* n.s., 5 (April 30, 1897): 678.

49. Bather, 678.

50. Henry Adams, *The Education of Henry Adams* (Boston: Houghton Mifflin, 1918), 486–87.

51. Stewart, *On Longing,* 162.

52. William Henry Flowers, quoted in "Museums and Their Purposes," 109–10.

53. Peter Gathercole has similarly argued that "museum artefacts are analogous to commodities, in that they have properties bestowed upon them by virtue of the museum existence." Peter Gathercole, "The Fetishism of Artefacts," in Susan Pearce, ed. *Museum Studies in Material Culture* (Washington, D.C.: Smithsonian Institution Press, 1989), 74.

54. Arjun Appadurai, "Introduction: Commodities and the Politics of Value," in Appadurai, ed., *The Social Life of Things,* 4.

55. Jean Baudrillard, "The System of Collecting," in John Elsner and Roger Cardinal, eds., *The Cultures of Collecting* (London: Reaktion Books, 1994), 8.

56. Sally Kohlstedt, "International Exchange and National Style: A View of Natural History Museums in the United States, 1850–1900," in Nathan Reingold and Marc Rothenberg, eds., *Scientific Colonialism: A Cross Cultural Comparison* (Washington, D.C.: Smithsonian Institution Press, 1987), 169.

57. Robert Young, *Darwin's Metaphor: Nature's Place in Victorian Culture* (Cambridge: Cambridge University Press, 1985), 156.

Chapter Two

1. Charles Dickens, *Hard Times* (Oxford: Oxford University Press, 1978), 1–5.

2. Smithsonian Institution, *Annual Report,* 1849, pt. 2, 16.

3. See Frederick William True, "The United States National Museum," in George Brown Goode, ed., *The Smithsonian Institution, 1846–1896* (Washington, D.C.: Smithsonian Institution Press, 1897), 333.

4. See David Brigham, *Public Culture in the Early Republic,* 113.

5. Quoted in Brigham, *Public Culture,* 5.

6. See George Daniels, *American Science in the Age of Jackson* (New York: Columbia University Press, 1968), 7. See also John Burnham, *How Superstition Won and Science Lost.* Dewey quoted in Burnham, 145.

7. For the most recent discussion of Baird's career, see E. F. Rivinus and E. M. Youssef, *Spencer Baird of the Smithsonian* (Washington D.C.: Smithsonian Institution Press, 1992).

8. True, "The United States National Museum," 313.

9. Smithsonian Institution, *Annual Report,* 1856, 31. In the mid-nineteenth

century, as Karen Wonders has noted, natural history panoramas and dioramas, which had been popular and successful displays earlier in the century, began to disappear. See Wonders, *Habitat Dioramas: Illusions of Wilderness in Museums of Natural History* (Upsala: Acta Universitatis Upsalensis, Figura Nova Series 25, 1993), 13.

10. William Leach, *Land of Desire,* 32.

11. See another handwritten note on this topic, untitled, and undated, Academy of Natural Sciences Archives (hereafter ANSP) Collection 435, 10–11.

12. "Report of the Condition of the Academy of Natural Sciences of Philadelphia on Moving into its New Edifice," 1876, ANSP Archives, 43–44.

13. W. S. W. Ruschenberger, "The Claims of the Academy of Natural Sciences to Public Favor," 1871, ANSP Archives, 17.

14. Ibid., 18.

15. "Report of the Building Fund Committee," 1874, ANSP Archives, 9.

16. Lawrence Levine, *Highbrow/lowbrow: The Emergence of Cultural Hierarchy in American Culture* (Cambridge: Harvard University Press, 1988).

17. Quoted in Paul Boller, *American Thought in Transition: The Impact of Evolutionary Naturalism 1865–1900* (Chicago: Rand McNally & Co., 1969), 13.

18. See Edward Nolan's manuscript history of the Academy of Natural Sciences, ANSP Archives, Collection 463, 423.

19. Quoted in "Report of the Building Fund Committee," ANSP Archives, 1878, 8.

20. For an account of Agassiz's visit to Philadelphia, see Elizabeth Cary Agassiz, ed., *Louis Agassiz: His Life and Correspondence* (Boston: Houghton, Mifflin and Co., 1885), 2:416–17.

21. John Michael Kennedy, "Philanthropy and Science in New York City: The American Museum of Natural History, 1868–1968" (Ph.D. diss., Yale University, 1968), 3.

22. W. S. W. Ruschenberger, "Address Delivered in Laying the Corner-Stone, October 30, 1872," reprinted in *Proceedings of the Academy of Natural Sciences* (hereafter, *Proceedings*) 23 (1872): 4.

23. Darwin to Charles Lyell, May 8, 1860; quoted in Edward Nolan, Notes on ANSP History, ANSP Archives, Collection 464.

24. Darwin to Joseph Leidy, March 4, 1860; Ibid.

25. Darwin's reception in the United States is the subject of a long historiography. See for example Cynthia Russett, *Darwin in America: The Intellectual Response* (San Francisco: W. H. Freeman, 1976), and Boller, *American Thought in Transition.*

26. See "Report of the Curators," *Proceedings* 21 (1869): 235.

27. See Edward Nolan's unpublished history of the academy, ANSP Archives, Collection 463, 540, and William Ruschenberger, "Report of the Condition of the Academy of Natural Sciences of Philadelphia on Moving into its New Edifice," 1876, ANSP Archives, 9.

28. J. S. Kingsley, "The Philadelphia Academy," *Popular Science Monthly* 20 (1881–82): 536.

29. Nathan Reingold, ed., *Science in Nineteenth Century America: A Documentary History* (New York: Hill and Wang, 1964), 239.

30. Unidentified newspaper clipping, May 12, 1891, ANSP Archives, Collection 417.

31. Reingold, *Science in Nineteenth Century America,* 236.

32. See "Dr. Joseph Leidy: Sketch of the Life of the Great Naturalist," unidentified newspaper clipping, ANSP Archives, Collection 417; for a personal recollection see "Address" by Henry Fairfield Osborn, "Proceedings of the Centenary Meeting," *Academy of Natural Sciences Journal,* 2d ser., 15 (1912). Paleontology focused more and more on heroic but enormously expensive expeditions to the American West. Cope and Marsh could afford these undertakings on their own, but Leidy simply could not. After Leidy's death in 1891, Ruschenberger offered an explanation for Leidy's "inability to generalize in his line of work." He weighed Leidy's brain and discovered that it weighed 2.5 oz. less than average. See memo to Nolan, May 2, 1891, ANSP Archives, Collection 464.

33. For a further discussion of this topic see Peter Bowler, *Fossils and Progress: Paleontology and the Idea of Progressive Evolution in the Nineteenth Century* (New York: Science History Publications, 1976), 12.

34. Ibid., 123.

35. In 1872, Cope won the first Walker Prize, given by the Boston Society of Natural History, for his essay, "The Darwinian Question and its Bearing on the Development of Animal Life."

36. Herman Bumpus, "Darwin and Zoology," *Popular Science Monthly* 54 (April 1909): 364.

37. See Nolan's History, ANSP Archives, Collection 463, 329.

38. Edward Cope, "On the Origin of GENERA," *Proceedings* 20 (1868): 242–44.

39. Edward Cope, "The Theology of Evolution," n.d., ANSP Archives, Collection 328, 18.

40. See Charles Singer, *A History of Biology* (New York: Henry Schuman, 1950), 305–6.

41. Ronald Rainger, *An Agenda for Antiquity: Henry Fairfield Osborn and Vertebrate Paleontology at the American Museum of Natural History, 1890–1935* (Tuscaloosa: University of Alabama Press, 1991), 13.

42. Peter Bowler, *The Non-Darwinian Revolution: Reinterpreting a Historical Myth* (Baltimore: The Johns Hopkins University Press, 1988), 40.

43. See Russett, *Darwin in America,* 10, and also Bowler, *Non-Darwinian Revolution,* 37.

44. Charles Rosenberg, "Science, Society, and Social Thought," *No Other Gods: On Science and American Social Thought* (Baltimore: The Johns Hopkins University Press, 1976), 4.

45. See William Berryman Scott, "Development of American Paleontology," *Proceedings of the American Philosophical Society* 66 (1927): 421.

46. For this whole discussion, see Rainger, *Agenda for Antiquity,* 3–23, and also Bowler, *Non-Darwinian Revolution,* 102.

47. See Nolan's history, ANSP Archives, Collection 463, 562.

48. Ruschenberger, handwritten memo, n.d.; ANSP Archives, Collection 567.

49. See Smithsonian Institution, *Annual Report,* 1864, 34.

50. Smithsonian Institution, *Annual Report,* 1865, 60.

51. Smithsonian Institution, *Annual Report,* 1851, 45.

52. For this discussion, I have relied on Edward Lurie, *Louis Agassiz: A Life in Science* (Chicago: University of Chicago Press, 1960), 214–32.

53. For a more complete consideration of the connection between colleges and museums, see Sally Gregory Kohlstedt, "Museums on Campus: A Tradition on Inquiry and Teaching," in Ronald Rainger, Keith Benson, and Jane Maienschein, eds., *The American Development of Biology* (Philadelphia: University of Pennsylvania Press, 1988).

54. Joel Orosz, *Curators and Culture: The Museum Movement in American, 1740–1870* (Tuscaloosa: University of Alabama Press, 1990), ch. 6.

55. For this discussion I have relied on John Michael Kennedy, "Philanthropy and Science in New York City," esp. pp. 60, 65, 92, 124.

56. Ruschenberger, "The Claims of the Academy of Natural Sciences to Public Favor," 1871, ANSP Archives, 11.

57. "Report of the Building Fund Committee," 1875, ANSP Archives, 13–14,

58. Ruschenberger, "Report of the Condition of the Academy of Natural Sciences of Philadelphia on Moving into its New Edifice," 1876, ANSP Archives, 40.

59. W. S. W. Ruschenberger, "On the Value of Original Scientific Research," *Penn Monthly* 4 (November 1873): 18–19.

60. Ruschenberger did so by drawing on the authority of the original letter from the Jessups setting up the fund: "Women are not mentioned in their letter. Therefore they are not eligible to be beneficiaries of the Jessup fund."

61. For this discussion of the Jessup Fund scholars, see two manuscripts by W. S. W. Ruschenberger, ANSP Archives, Collection 375.

62. Edward Cope, "The Academy of Natural Sciences," *Penn Monthly* 7 (March 1876): 173–180.

63. Ibid., 174, 176.

64. William Pepper to Joseph Leidy, March 19, 1884; ANSP Archives, Collection 567.

65. In his history, Edward Nolan explained the origins of Penn's biology department by saying that it arose "from the lack of means for the study of biology by women." See Nolan's history; ANSP Archives, Collection 463, 442.

66. W. S. W. Ruschenberger, "On the Invitation from the University to remove to West Philadelphia," W. S. W. Ruschenberger Memorial Volume II, n.d., ANSP Archives, Collection 435, 5–6.

67. Ibid., 9–12.

68. Ruschenberger to Dixon, January 30, 1895; ANSP Archives, Collection 241.

69. George Brown Goode, "Museums of the Future," *The Origins of Natural*

Science in America: The Essays of George Goode Brown, ed. Sally Gregory Kohl-stedt (Washington, D.C.: Smithsonian Institution Press, 1991), 337.

70. "Report of the President," *Proceedings* 30 (1880): 404–5.

71. "Report of the President," *Proceedings* 31 (1881): 477.

72. George Brown Goode, *The Beginning of American Science: The Third Century* (Washington D.C.: Presidential Address to the Biological Society, 1888), 93.

73. "Report of Committee on Instruction on disagreement with Professors on the subject of one of the Popular Lectures," 1887, ANSP Archives, Collection 289.

74. See advertising flyers, Program of Lectures, 1899–1900, ANSP Archives, Collection 289.

75. Dorothy Ross, "Historical Consciousness in 19th Century America," *American Historical Review* 89 (1984): 925.

76. For further detail on this discussion see Keith Benson, "From Museum Research to Laboratory Research: The Transformation of Natural History into Academic Biology," in Rainger, Benson and Maienschein, eds., *Development of American Biology,* 63–72. See also William Coleman, *Biology in the Nineteenth Century: Problems of Form, Function, and Transformation* (New York: John Wiley & Sons, Inc., 1971). For more on the development of German biology, see Lynn K. Nyhart, *Biology Takes Form: Animal Morphology and the German Universities, 1800–1900* (Chicago: University of Chicago Press, 1995).

77. Goode, *Origins of Natural Science in America,* 170. Coulter quoted in Burnham, *How Superstition Won and Science Lost,* 168.

78. Curators Report, *Proceedings,* 1910, 680.

79. Edwin Conklin, "The World's Debt to Darwin," rpt., *University of Chicago Magazine,* March/April 1909, 184–192.

80. "Report of the President," *Proceedings,* 1879, 434.

81. "Report of the President," *Proceedings,* 1876, 40.

82. Benjamin Smith Lyman, "Natural History Morality," *Proceedings,* 1912, 138–39.

83. See Kennedy, "Philanthropy and Science in New York City," 203–4. The very first diorama at the American Museum was probably an orang-utang display which opened in 1880. In the 1920s, however, the museum made a major commitment to developing these kinds of displays.

84. The way in which science was presented to the public and taught in the schools underwent changes in many venues in addition to museums. For the most thorough consideration of this topic see Burnham, *How Superstition Won and Science Lost.*

85. Samuel Dixon, "Address," *Academy Centenary Volume,* 1912, xiv.

86. Heye to Moore, April 15, 1929, ANSP Archives, Collection 102.

87. Clyde Goulden, ed., *Changing Scenes in Natural Sciences, 1776–1976* (Philadelphia: Academy of Natural Sciences, 1977).

88. See Anna Bramwell, *Ecology in the 20th Century: A History* (New Haven: Yale University Press, 1989), esp. ch. 3.

Chapter Three

1. Lewis Mumford, "The Marriage of Museums," *Findings and Keepings: Analects for an Autobiography* (New York: Harcourt Brace Jovanovich, 1975), 29–36.

2. George Brown Goode, "Museum-History and Museums of History," *Origins of Natural Science in America*, 311–12.

3. Ibid.

4. W. H. Holmes, "The World's Fair Congress of Anthropology," vol. 4 (October 1893): 431.

5. "Doors Wide Open," *Chicago Times*, June 3, 1894.

6. George Dorsey, "The Department of Anthropology of the Field Columbian Museum—A Review of Six Years," *American Anthropologist*, n.s. 2 (1900): 248. In 1895 the museum also included the department of "Industrial Arts, and the Columbus Memorial, and the divisions of Transportation and the Railway."

7. George Stocking, "Philanthropoids and Vanishing Cultures," 113–14. Perhaps the first scholarly consideration of the relationship between museums and anthropology can be found in Donald Collier and Harry Tschopik's article "The Role of Museums in American Anthropology," *American Anthropologist* 56 (1954): 768–79.

8. See Fred Eggan, "Ethnology and Social Anthropology," in J. O. Brew, ed., *One Hundred Years of Anthropology* (Cambridge: Harvard University Press, 1968), 119–23.

9. Quoted in David Jenkins, "Object Lessons and Ethnographic Displays: Museum Exhibitions and the Making of American Anthropology," *Comparative Studies in Society and History* 36, no. 2 (April 1994): 257.

10. I have borrowed a phrase from David Jenkins, ibid., 248.

11. F. J. V. Skiff, "The Uses of the Museum," *Chicago Times-Herald*, April 29, 1895.

12. Photocopy entitled "Department of Anthropology," Field Museum Archives, no other citation.

13. Field Museum Archives, Franz Boas Papers, 1893–1923, folder 2.

14. For a standard narrative of this history, see A. Irving Hallowell, "The Beginnings of Anthropology in America," in Frederica de Laguna, ed. *Selected Papers from the American Anthropologist, 1888–1920* (Evanston: Row, Peterson & Company, 1960).

15. Boas to Skiff, March 2, 1894, Field Museum Archives, Franz Boas Papers, 1893–1923, folder 1.

16. Boas, quoted in Ralph Dexter, "Frederic Ward Putnam and the Development of Museums of Natural History and Anthropology in the United States," *Curator* 9 (1966): 151.

17. Ralph Adams Cram, "The Work of Frank Miles Day & Brother," *Architectural Record* 15, no. 5 (1904): 411–17.

18. Harlow Higinbotham to A. B. Jones, December 14, 1904; Field Museum Archives, Historical Documents, box 1.

19. See Peter Bowler, *The Invention of Progress: The Victorians and the Past* (Oxford: Basil Blackwell, 1989), 33–34.

20. Anthropologist Alfred Kroeber, looking back on this era, believed that this separation was complete by 1917. See George Stocking, *Race, Culture and Evolution: Essays in the History of Anthropology* (New York: Free Press, 1968), 267.

21. W. J. McGee, "Fifty Years of American Science," *Atlantic Monthly* 82 (September 1898): 318.

22. John Wesley Powell, "The Three Methods of Evolution," in George Daniels, ed., *Darwinism Comes to America* (Waltham, Mass.: Blaisdell Press, 1968), 116.

23. Quoted in the *New York Times,* August 4, 1895. The *Times* article about the Field Museum was wonderfully condescending, demonstrating that the tone of the paper has not changed much in a hundred years. It began: "It is just beginning to dawn upon the people of this city [Chicago] that they have a great museum somewhere down in Jackson Park, and that it is worth going to see some day when the fish will not bite in the lake."

24. For a further discussion of Powell's views, see Jenkins, "Objects Lessons and Ethnographic Displays," 264–65.

25. See Smithsonian *Annual Report, 1888,* pt. 2 "Report of the National Museum," 26.

26. See Ralph Dexter, "The Role of F. W. Putnam in Developing Anthropology at The American Museum of Natural History," *Curator* 19 (1976): 303–10.

27. Quoted in John Michael Kennedy, "Philanthropy and Science in New York City," 163; cf. 172–74.

28. *Bulletin of the Free Museum of Science and Art,* June 1899, 71. See also the "Alumni Register," University of Pennsylvania, January 1900, 4 #4, 5, 7 for another description of the original layout of the museum.

29. See Susan Pearce, "Collecting Reconsidered," in Gaynor Kavanagh, ed. *Museum Languages: Objects and Texts* (Leicester: Leicester University Press, 1991), 148.

30. See Jenkins, "Object Lessons and Ethnographic Displays," 261–63. There is an extensive literature examining the ideas of nineteenth-century social evolution as they developed both in Britain and in the United States. For example, see Henrika Kuklick, *The Savage Within: The Social History of British Anthropology, 1885–1945* (Cambridge: Cambridge University Press, 1991), and George Stocking, *Race, Culture, and Evolution: Essays in the History of Anthropology* (New York: The Free Press, 1968).

31. Regna Darnell, "Daniel Garrison Brinton: An Intellectual Biography" (master's thesis, University of Pennsylvania, 1968), 88.

32. Daniel Brinton, "The Aims of Anthropology," *Proceedings of the American Association for the Advancement of Science* 44 (1895), 3. For a more thorough discussion of Brinton's ideas and his career see Regna Darnell, *Daniel Garrison Brinton: The "Fearless Critic" of Philadelphia* (Philadelphia: University of Pennsylvania Publications in Anthropology, no. 3, 1988), 15.

33. William Pepper, *Addresses Delivered at the Opening Ceremonies of the Exhibition of Objects Used in Worship* (Philadelphia: Printed for the University, 1892), 1.

34. The job of assembling the comprehensive collection envisioned by those at the museum required more work than could be done by field workers sent by the museum. In 1914, Gordon reported to the board of managers that "warehouses in London, Berlin and Hamburg were now full of excellent ethnological material" and he urged the board to purchase objects from European collectors. Gordon also reported on the possibilities of obtaining specimens from missionaries, and the board voted to begin correspondence with such people. Early in 1916, three cases of African ethnological material arrived from missionaries Wight and Probst. See Minutes, Board of Managers, February 20 and March 20, 1914, January 21, 1916.

35. Gordon to Harrison, September 8, 1913, University of Pennsylvania Archive, UPT 50 H319.

36. "Life Stories in Dead Clay," *Philadelphia Press,* September 20, 1894.

37. Jenkins, "Objects Lessons and Ethnographic Displays," 250–51.

38. "Life Stories in Dead Clay."

39. Through the Egyptian Exploration Fund, which hired the English archaeologist Flinders Petrie, institutions like the University Museum and the Museum of Fine Arts in Boston received artifacts commensurate with their financial contributions. These contributions supported Petrie's excavations.

40. For a consideration of Penn's contribution to Near East Studies during these years, and of the whole development of the field, see Bruce Kuklick's splendid *Puritans in Babylon: The Ancient Near East and American Intellectual Life, 1880–1930* (Princeton: Princeton University Press, 1996).

41. Sara Stevenson to Clark, June 5, 1895; Administrative Record, Director's Office, University Museum Archive, Box 3.

42. See "Report of the Board of Managers of the Department of Archaeology and Paleontology of the University of Pennsylvania, 1893" (Philadelphia, 1894). This split was not unique to the University Museum. The Field Museum in Chicago also struggled over which cultures would be the primary focus of resources and interest. New World research seems to have been taken more seriously in Chicago, but the director did report in the years 1896–97 that "the only accession representing American archaeology was a gift from Mr. Clarence B. Moore of an interesting collection of shell cups and ornaments, earthen vases, and stone implements from mounds of Georgia and Florida." Ironically, this sole acquisition came courtesy of a Philadelphian. See Dorsey, "The Department of Anthropology of the Field Columbian Museum," 255.

43. A version of this two-part arrangement was put on display in Chicago in 1893. At the exhibit of North American Indians visitors were presented with a rough chronology that began with the Colorado Cliff Dwellers, proceeded through the Aztecs, and ended with "representatives of the races found and dispossessed by Columbus." Those indigenous groups not yet "dispossessed" were arranged geographically for the visitor, beginning with the Eskimos and

ending with the "Papagos and Yakuis from the extreme southern border of the United States and Mexico." See Jenkins, "Object Lessons and Ethnographic Displays," 258.

44. Sara Stevenson to Charles Harrison, July 20, 1893, University of Pennsylvania Archives, Dept. of Archaeology, Correspondence and Papers, 1891–94, Box 3.

45. Adolf Michaelis, *A Century of Archaeological Discoveries* (London: John Murray, 1908), xiii.

46. Quoted in Curtis Hinsley, "The Museum Origins of Harvard Anthropology," 127.

47. *Christian Science Monitor,* May 16, 1913.

48. "Annual Report from the President to the Board," August 1907, University Museum Archives, Director's Files, Box 7.

49. Quoted in Karen Wonders, *Habitat Dioramas,* 142.

50. Furness to Stevenson, July 29, 1903, University Museum Archives, Director's Files, Box 6.

51. Gordon to Harrison, September 8, 1913, University of Pennsylvania Archive, UPT 50 H319.

52. Merwin Henry Childs, "On Being Civilized Too Much," *Atlantic Monthly* 79 (June 1897): 845–46.

53. Curtis Hinsley, "The World as Marketplace: Commodification of the Exotic at the World's Columbian Exposition, Chicago, 1893," in Karp and Lavine, eds., *Exhibiting Cultures,* 363.

54. *Chicago Record-Herald,* August 23, 1908.

55. *Chicago Record-Herald,* December 24, 1907. For a more thorough discussion of the connections between anthropology and imperialism, see Johannes Fabian, *Time and the Other: How Anthropology Makes its Object* (New York: Columbia University Press, 1983).

56. *New York Sun,* October 6, 1912.

57. Gordon to Houston, April 19, 1907; University Museum Archives, Director's Files, Box 7.

58. Laura Bragg, "Culture Museums and the Use of Culture Material," *Museum Work* 8, no. 3 (September/October 1924): 83.

59. Laurence Vail Coleman, *The Museum in America: A Critical Study* (Washington, D.C.: American Association of Museums, 1939), 83–84.

60. George Byron Gordon, "The Purposes of the University Museum," *Museum Journal* 7, no. 4 (1916).

61. George Byron Gordon, "Growth of the Museum," *Museum Journal* 1, no. 1 (June 1910): 3.

62. Gordon to Harrison, September 8, 1913, University of Pennsylvania Archive, UPT 50 H319.

63. Sara Stevenson appears to have tried to hire Boas for the museum in 1893. In a note, written later, attached to a letter dated November 29, 1893 , she wrote: "This closes the Boas episode & the hope of *real* anthropological and

anthropometric work at the Univ.—Boas was snapped up at once by the American Mus. of Nat. Hist. New York where he has done *superb* work." Pepper-Stevenson Correspondence, University Museum Archive, Director's Files, Box 1. See also Board of Managers Minutes, December 12, 1893.

64. George Stocking has written most extensively of the career of Franz Boas. See, for example, his introduction to Franz Boas, *The Shaping of American Anthropology, 1883–1911: A Franz Boas Reader,* ed. George Stocking (New York: Basic Books, 1974). For a consideration of Boas, anthropology, and race, see Vernon Williams, *Rethinking Race: Franz Boas and his Contemporaries* (Lexington: University of Kentucky Press, 1996). Anthropologists have also written about the significance of Boas's work. See Marvin Harris, *The Rise of Anthropological Theory: A History of Theories of Culture* (New York: Thomas W. Crowell, 1969), and Murray Leaf, *Man, Mind, and Science: A History of Anthropology* (New York: Columbia University Press, 1979).

65. George Stocking, in discussing the shift away from museums in anthropology, has stressed more institutional considerations, especially sources of funding which the museums provided initially but which became available through philanthropic entities and eventually through universities and government as well. See George Stocking, "Philanthropoids and Vanishing Cultures."

66. Curtis Hinsley, "The Museum Origins of Harvard Anthropology," 139.

67. See Regna Darnell, "Daniel Garrison Brinton" 20, and Darnell, *Daniel Garrison Brinton,* 15.

68. Quoted in Darnell, "Daniel Garrison Brinton," 71.

69. Stevenson to Brinton, n.d. (January 1894?), University Museum Archives, Director's Files, Box 3.

70. *Sara Yorke Stevenson: A Tribute from the Civic Club of Philadelphia,* 1922, 13–14.

71. University Museum Archive, Director's Files, Box 1.

72. Bruce Kuklick has discussed the Hilprecht controversy in *Puritans in Babylon.*

73. Franz Boas to Sara Stevenson, May 12, 1903, University Museum Archive, Director's Files, Box 6.

74. Regna Darnell, "The Emergence of Academic Anthropology at the University of Pennsylvania," *Journal of the History of the Behavioral Sciences* 6 (1970): 89.

75. Gordon to the Board of Managers, Curatorial Reports, University Museum Archive, January 16, 1907.

76. Minutes, Board of Managers, University Museum Archive, February 17, 1911.

77. Darnell, "The Emergence of Academic Anthropology at the University of Pennsylvania," 89.

78. Franz Boas, "Some Principles of Museum Administration," *Science* 25 (June 1907): 921–33.

79. For a consideration of Boas's ideas about museum exhibits and his

frustration with museum work, see Ira Jacknis, "Franz Boas and Exhibits: On the Limitations of the Museum Method of Anthropology," in Stocking, *Objects and Others.*

80. Quoted in Curtis Hinsley, "Parallels and Rivalries: Encounters Between Boas and Starr," *Curator* 32 (1989): 225.

81. George Byron Gordon, "The Extension of the Museum Building," *Museum Journal* 3, no. 4 (December 1912): 59–62.

82. Ibid.

83. Ibid.

84. Gordon to the Board, Minutes, Board of Managers, University Museum Archives, February 16, 1915.

85. Richard Handler, "Boasian Anthropology and the Critique of American Culture," *American Quarterly* 42 (June 1990): 254. As Handler describes it, "Much of Boas's lifework was an attack on nineteenth century social evolutionism." Boas quoted in Stocking "Anthropology as Kulturkampf: Science and Politics in the Career of Franz Boas," *The Ethnographer's Magic,* 99.

86. I am certainly not the first to notice this critical shift in the history of anthropology. As long ago as 1954 the Wenner-Gren Foundation sponsored a conference at the University of Pennsylvania Museum to consider the place of museums in the history and future of American anthropology.

87. Hinsley, "The Museum Origins of Harvard Anthropology," 121. See also Stocking, "Anthropology as Kulturkampf," 92, and "Ideas and Institutions in American Anthropology: Thoughts Toward a History of the Interwar Years," *The Ethnographer's Magic,* 127.

88. At Penn, according to Regna Darnell ("The Emergence of Academic Anthropology at the University of Pennsylvania," 89–91), as with the rest of the discipline later, cultural anthropologists opposed archaeologists, and Boas's partisans acted as a coordinated group.

89. For a more detailed discussion of Gordon's efforts to reach new audiences, see Steven Conn, "To Organize and Display: Museums and American Culture, 1876–1926" (Ph.D. diss., University of Pennsylvania, 1994), 160–74.

90. *Chicago Daily News,* October 1909 (no specific date), FMA Scrapbook.

91. For a notice of this exhibit, see Stanley Field, "Chicago's Famous Museum Marks Its 50th Year," *Townsfolk,* September 1943, 19.

Chapter Four

1. Jastrow to Pepper, May 3, 1897; Pepper Papers, Department of Special Collections, Van Pelt Library, University of Pennsylvania, vol. 8, 1571.

2. William P. Wilson, *The World's Trade and the United States' Share of It* (Philadelphia: Philadelphia Commercial Museum, 1899), 2.

3. See Edward Crapol, "Coming to Terms with Empire: The Historiography of Late-Nineteenth-Century American Foreign Relations," *Diplomatic History* 16 (Fall 1992): 573–97.

4. I am making reference to the title of Kaplan and Pease's edited volume, *Cultures of United States Imperialism* (Durham, N.C.: Duke University Press, 1993).

5. *The Philadelphia Museums, Dedication of the Museums by President Mc-Kinley, Report of the Annual Meeting of the International Advisory Board* (Philadelphia, 1897), 17.

6. Emily Rosenberg, *Spreading the American Dream: American Economic and Cultural Expansion, 1890–1945* (New York: Hill and Wang, 1982), 229.

7. On August 30, 1893 Wilson reported to Thomas Meehan, a member of Philadelphia's Fairmount Park Commissioners, that "the amount of economic material that will be left behind at the breaking up of the Columbian Exposition is simply enormous, and could not probably be directly secured for half a million dollars." When the other commissioners reported this to the City Council, the council authorized the commissioners to take the necessary steps to bring the material to Philadelphia. The commissioners, in turn, relied on Wilson to execute the task. See "The Proposed Economic Museum," (n.d.), Archive of the Museum of the Civic Center.

8. See Wilson's obituary, *Philadelphia Bulletin,* May 12, 1927.

9. Hermon C. Bumpus, in *William Powell Wilson* (Washington, D.C.: American Association of Museums, 1927), 3.

10. See David Healy, *U.S. Expansionism: The Imperialist Urge in the 1890s* (Madison: University of Wisconsin Press, 1970), 45.

11. See Rosenberg, *Spreading the American Dream,* 6–7; and Robert Rydell, "The Open (Laboratory) Door: Scientists and Mass Culture," in Rob Kroes, ed., *High Brow Meets Low Brow: American Culture as an Intellectual Concern* (Amsterdam: Free University Press, 1988), 61–74.

12. *The Philadelphia Museums,* 52. The Commercial Museum, from an early date, had its own printing press and issued a tremendous number of its own pamphlets and booklets, most written by Wilson.

13. See Ruth Hunter, *The Trade and Convention Center of Philadelphia: Its Birth and Renascence* (Philadelphia: City of Philadelphia, 1962).

14. W. E. Hoyle, "The Philadelphia Commercial Museum," *The Museums Journal* 1 (1901–02): 107.

15. As Andrew Carnegie summed it up early in 1894, "The great exhibition has come, triumphed, and passed away. . . . Our revels are ended. Prospero's wand has broken the spell." Andrew Carnegie, "Value of the World's Fairs to the American People," *The Engineering Magazine* 6 (January 1894): 417.

16. Paul Cherington, "The Philadelphia Commercial Museum," *World Today,* May 14, 1908. John Lopez, "First Aid for the Exporter: What the Philadelphia Commercial Museum is Doing for the Development of our Foreign Trade," *Harper's Weekly,* April 27, 1912, 9. Oliver Farrington, "The Museum as an Educational Institution," *Education* 17 (March 1897): 482.

17. William Leach, *Land of Desire,* 32.

18. For the most complete discussion of these issues, see Robert Rydell,

All the World's a Fair: Visions of Empire at American International Expositions, 1876–1916 (Chicago: University of Chicago Press, 1984).

19. William P. Wilson to Edward Everett Ayer, July 16, 1894, Field Museum Archive, Director's Correspondence.

20. William P. Wilson, "The Philadelphia Commercial Museum," *The Forum* 28 (September 1899): 116.

21. *The Commercial Museum: Its History and Development—Collections of the Resources of the World—Educational Work—Assistance to the Business Man* (Philadelphia: Philadelphia Museums Press, 1909), n.p. Museum secretary Wilfred Schoff elaborated the connection between commerce and the development of civilization in 1909 for the readers of the *Proceedings of the American Association of Museums.* "Commerce between different communities," he announced, "is at the beginning of all civilization, and is the compelling cause of all achievement in the arts and sciences. . . . Therefore a history of the commerce between nations is, more than any chronology of wars and dynasties, a history of the progress of peoples." Wilfred Schoff, "The History of Commerce in Museums," *Proceedings of the American Association of Museums* 3 (1909): 64.

22. Rosenberg, *Spreading the American Dream,* 9.

23. *The Philadelphia Museums,* 75.

24. *The Commercial Museum.*

25. Ibid.

26. Commercial Museum, *Annual Report,* 1907–08, 14.

27. Gustavo Niederlein provided a list in 1897 of the kinds of materials a visitor might expect to find in the monographic displays. It is an impressive list that includes "woods; tannings; dyeings; gums and resins; rubbers; guttapercha; fibers; spices, fruits and seed; cereals; starches and flour; sugar; oils and oil seeds; coffee, teas and cocoa; wools; hides and skins; silks and other animal products; mineral products, etc." (*Philadelphia Museums,* 75). Presumably these were the kinds of things American businessmen wanted to learn more about.

28. Commercial Museum, *Annual Report,* 1914, 14.

29. See *The Commercial Museum* for a description.

30. *The Commercial Museum.*

31. Ibid. The *Annual Report* from 1905 also includes "Notes on the Madagascar Collection" which had been installed in the Center Building, second floor.

32. Richard Foley, "The Philadelphia Commercial Museum," *World's Work* 2 (October 1901): 1260.

33. "Facts About the Commercial Museum," Commercial Museum, *Annual Report,* 1914, 5–9.

34. The Philadelphia Museums, Pepper Papers, Department of Special Collections, Van Pelt Library, University of Pennsylvania, vol. 6, 1094–98.

35. William P. Wilson, "The Philadelphia Commercial Museum," 118.

36. See *American Trade with Siam* (Philadelphia: Commercial Museum,

1898); Colonel George Bell, *American Trade with Australia* (Philadelphia: Commercial Museum, n.d.); and *American Trade with India* (Philadelphia: Commercial Museum, 1898).

37. William P. Wilson, *The World's Trade and the United States' Share of It*, 2.

38. Lester Langley, *The Banana Wars: An Inner History of American Empire, 1900–1934*, (Lexington: University of Kentucky Press, 1983), 3.

39. *The Philadelphia Museums*, 46.

40. Ibid., 13. President McKinley, however, had already contributed to the success of the museum in more tangible ways. According to C. A. Green, McKinley's administration had helped the Commercial Museum's Bureau of Information through the State Department. He told the crowd that "we are receiving efficient aid from the Federal government State Department, the facilities of its consular service having been placed at our disposal" (ibid., 18).

41. Ibid., 87.

42. Ibid., 89.

43. "The Commercial Congress," *New York Times*, August 21, 1899.

44. *The International Commercial Congress* (Philadelphia, 1899), n.p. See this brochure for a list of governments and trade organizations in attendance.

45. Amy Kaplan, "Left Alone with America," in Kaplan and Pease, eds., *Cultures of United States Imperialism*, 8.

46. Minute Books, Board of Trustees, Archive of the Museum of the Civic Center.

47. William P. Wilson, *Commerce as a Conservator of Peace* (Philadelphia: The Universal Peace Union, 1901), 1–4.

48. Ibid., 5.

49. In addition to the fairs, material came to the museum through exchanges with museums around the world. Wilson's assistant, Gustav Niederlein, traded duplicate specimens with a variety of institutions including Kew Gardens, the Commercial Museum in Antwerp, and the Botanical and Zoological Museums in Hamburg. See *The Philadelphia Museums*, 76.

50. In 1907, as Jamestown celebrated the tercentenary of its settlement, the museum "took an active part in making three separate exhibitions to be carried through the Exposition" (Commercial Museum, *Annual Report*, 1907–08), 8.

51. James Lamber, ed., *Pennsylvania: The Building of an Empire* (Philadelphia: The McCartney & Benesch Co., 1904).

52. Rydell, *All the World's a Fair*, 155, 183.

53. Minute Books, Board of Trustees, January 22, 1903, Archive of the Museum of the Civic Center.

54. Wilson to Taft, December 19, 1903, Taft Papers, Library of Congress.

55. *The Philadelphia Museums*, 168.

56. Andrew Carnegie, "Distant Possessions," *The Gospel of Wealth and Other Timely Essays by Andrew Carnegie*, ed. Edward Kirkland (Cambridge: Harvard University Press, Belknap Press, 1962), 127–28.

57. Rydell, *All the World's a Fair,* 19–20.

58. E. Berkeley Tompkins, *Anti-Imperialism in the United States: The Great Debate, 1890–1920* (Philadelphia: University of Pennsylvania Press, 1970), 167.

59. Frank Carpenter, "Chances in the Philippines," *Saturday Evening Post,* June 16, 1900.

60. Theodore Noyes's essays were published as the pamphlet *Problems of the Orient* (n.p., n.d.). See p. 29.

61. Walter LaFeber, *The New Empire: An Interpretation of American Expansion, 1860–1898* (Ithaca: Cornell University Press, 1963), 416.

62. Commercial Museum, *Annual Report,* 1905, 8. The Field Museum in Chicago also opened a big Philippine exhibit, but not until late in 1909. See *Chicago Tribune,* November 21, 1909.

63. Commercial Museum, *Annual Report,* 1913, 10.

64. *The Commercial Museum.*

65. Commercial Museum, *Annual Report,* 1918–20, 20.

66. Minute Books, Board of Trustees, 1917, Archive of the Museum of the Civic Center.

67. E. Dana Durand, "Tendencies in the Foreign Trade of the United States," *The Annals of the American Academy of Political and Social Science* 127 (September 1926): 12–13.

68. It is seems to be the case, as E. Dana Durand discovered, that because of the astonishing growth of the domestic market, "the relative importance of foreign markets has not increased as a result of the war." See Simon Litman, "The Foreign Trade of the United States Since the Signing of the Armistice," *The Annals of the American Academy of Political and Social Science* 94 (March 1921): 1, 17.

69. Litman, "The Foreign Trade of the United States, 5.

70. The museum felt competition from other sources as well. On October 25, 1915 the Board of Trustees discussed "the relation of the Commercial Museum to the re-organized Philadelphia Chamber of Commerce, especially as regards the Foreign Trade Bureau work of both organizations" (Minute Books, Board of Trustees, Archive of the Museum of the Civic Center).

71. Donald Whitnah, "Department of Commerce," in Donald Whitnah, ed., *Government Agencies* (Westport, Conn.: Greenwood Press, 1983).

72. George Bruce Cortelyou, "Some Agencies for the Extension of Our Domestic and Foreign Trade," *The Annals of the American Academy of Political and Social Science* 24 (1904): 2.

73. Harry Collings, "United States Government Aid to Foreign Trade," *The Annals of the American Academy of Political and Social Science* 127 (September 1926): 134.

74. Commercial Museum, *Annual Report,* 1922–23, 5.

75. Commercial Museum, *Annual Report,* 1924, 8.

76. F. M. Huntington Wilson, *The Philadelphia Commercial Museum* (Philadelphia: Commercial Museum, 1931), 7.

77. "Education for Business," *New York Times,* October 21, 1899.

78. *The Annals of the American Academy of Political and Social Science* 124 (September 1926).

79. Commercial Museum, *Annual Report,* 1926, 11,13,15.

80. The museum—renamed the Museum of the Philadelphia Civic Center—continued to run programs for school children until 1994. The city, owner of the museum, announced that the museum would close and be consolidated with other institutions. See "Hands-on museum is itself heading into history," *Philadelphia Inquirer,* February 21, 1994.

81. See *Proposal for the Erection of A Convention and Exhibition Hall on the Commercial Museum Site,* Archive of the Museum of the Civic Center.

Chapter Five

1. Peter Novick's *That Noble Dream: The Objectivity Question and the American Historical Profession* (Cambridge: Cambridge University Press, 1988) is the most useful consideration of the ways in which "objectivity" shaped the development of American academic history.

2. Gary Kulik, "Designing the Past: History-Museum Exhibitions from Peale to the Present," in Warren Leon and Roy Rosenzweig, eds., *History Museums in the United States: A Critical Assessment* (Urbana: University of Illinois Press, 1989), 10–12.

3. Originally, the complex was known as The Edison Institute and Greenfield Village.

4. Henry Ford, cited in "The Ford Museum," *American Historical Review* 36 (July 1931): 773.

5. Henry A. Haigh, "The Ford Collections at Dearborn," *Michigan History Magazine* 9 (1925): 34.

6. See *Detroit Free Press,* August 31, 1924, for a large feature article about this.

7. Frank Campsall to James Bishop, September 27, 1928. Ford Archives, Henry Ford Museum.

8. *New York Times Magazine,* April 5, 1931, 1.

9. Henry Ford, cited in "The Ford Museum," 773. See also Ford cited in William Greenleaf, *From These Beginnings: The Early Philanthropies of Henry and Edsel Ford, 1911–1936* (Detroit: Wayne State University Press, 1964).

10. Henry Ford, cited in Greenleaf, 98, 100.

11. Henry Ford, quoted in *New York Times Magazine,* April 5, 1931, 1.

12. Henry Ford, cited in Greenleaf, 97.

13. Frank Campsall to James Bishop, September 27, 1928. Ford Archives, Henry Ford Museum.

14. "The Ford Museum," 773–74.

15. See typescript entitled "Herbert F. Morton, Collector for Henry Ford," Ford Archives, Henry Ford Museum, Folder—Henry Ford Museum Interiors; and Frank Campsall to James Bishop, September 27, 1928, Ford Archives, Henry Ford Museum.

16. Transcript of interview with Fred Smith, conducted 1951. Ford Archives, Folder marked Henry Ford Museum Interiors.

17. *Doylestown Daily News,* September 10, 1923.

18. "Dr. Mercer's 'Tools of the Nation Builder,'" *Dearborn Independent,* February 2, 1924.

19. Henry Mercer, "An Incident in My Life," Mercer Papers, Bucks County Historical Society (hereafter BCHS), Series 4, fol. 12.

20. This view set Mercer against many in the archaeological community who argued that because a number of the stone tools being unearthed in America shared a similar morphology with European paleoliths, it was fair to assume that they shared a similar age. Mercer did not believe that drawing a parallel with European finds was appropriate; he wrote: "the study of American quarries and the refuse at Spiennes (Belgium) offers no analogies, makes no suggestion." See Henry Mercer, "Notes Taken in December, 1892 and March, 1893, at the Quarternary Gravel Pits of Abbeville, St. Acheul, and Chelles," *The Archaeologist* 1 (1893): 142.

21. Mercer's notebook from this trip is filled with stratigraphic drawings, notes on extinct animals, and thoughts about the racial origins of Europeans. His notes demonstrate that he was familiar with the most current research in the field. See "Archaeological Notebooks," Mercer Papers, BCHS, series 5, fol. 18.

22. It is difficult to say with certainty how many articles Mercer published during the 1890s; articles originally published in one journal might be reprinted with slight or no alteration in another journal. In any event, Mercer had six articles in *The American Naturalist* in 1897 alone. His work also appeared in *The American Anthropologist, The Antiquarian,* and *The Archaeologist.*

23. John Wesley Powell, "Problems of American Archaeology," *Smithsonian Forum* 8 (1890): 650.

24. Mercer Papers, BCHS, series 27, fol. 8.

25. See Donald Kuspit, "A Mighty Metaphor: The Analogy of Archaeology and Psychoanalysis," in Lynn Gamwell and Richard Wells, eds., *Sigmund Freud and Art* (Binghamton: State University of New York Press, 1989).

26. Henry Mercer, "Tools of the Nation Maker," *A Collection of Papers Read before the Bucks County Historical Society* (Doylestown: Published for the Society by B. F. Fackenthal, jr., 1909), 3:471.

27. "Dr. Mercer's 'Tools of the Nation Builder,'" *Dearborn Independent,* February 2, 1924.

28. Mercer, "Tools of the Nation Maker," 3:474–75; and *Dearborn Independent,* February 2, 1924.

29. Mercer, "Tools of the Nation Maker," 3:471.

30. Ibid, 471.

31. Mercer Papers, BCHS, series 21, fol. 38.

32. For this, and for other details about Mercer's biography, I have relied on Cleota Reed's *Henry Chapman Mercer and the Moravian Pottery and Tile*

Works (Philadelphia: University of Pennsylvania Press, 1987) and on Linda Dyke's annotated biography, which appeared in the *Mercer Mosaic, Journal of the Bucks County Historical Society* 6 (Spring/Summer 1989): 35–67.

33. John Higham, *History: Professional Scholarship in America* (Baltimore: The Johns Hopkins University Press, 1983 [1965]), 93.

34. William Dunning, "A Generation of American Historiography," *Annual Report of the American Historical Association,* 1917, 349.

35. Frederick Jackson Turner, *The Frontier in American History* (New York: H. Holt & Co., 1920), 29, 30.

36. Henry Mercer, *Tools of the Nation Maker* (Doylestown: Bucks County Historical Society, 1897), Introduction.

37. Ibid., Postscript.

38. James Harvey Robinson, *The New History: Essays Illustrating the Modern Historical Outlook* (1912; rpt. New York: The Free Press, 1965), 138–39, 144.

39. Mercer, "The Scope and Meaning of the Collection of Objects at the Museum of the BCHS," Mercer Papers, BCHS.

40. Mercer Papers, BCHS, "Historical Notes," fol. 31.

41. Henry Mercer, "BCHS: Its Aims and Purposes," *A Collection of Papers Read before the Bucks County Historical Society,* 4:41.

42. Ibid., 41.

43. Henry Mercer, "Notes of Industrial Revolution," Mercer Papers, BCHS, series 23, fol. 7.

44. Mercer, "The Scope and Meaning of the Collection of Objects at the Museum of the BCHS," Mercer Papers, BCHS.

45. Rudolf Hommel, *China at Work: An illustrated record of the primitive industries of China's masses, whose life is toil, and thus an account of Chinese civilization* (New York: John Day Company for the BCHS, 1937). For the best account of the significance of Hommel's work, see Peter Conn, *Pearl Buck: A Cultural Biography* (Cambridge: Cambridge University Press, 1996), 200–201.

46. Mercer, "History in Implements," Mercer Papers, BCHS.

47. Unidentified newspaper editorial, June 25, 1916, Mercer Papers, BCHS.

48. Mercer, "Tools of the Nation Maker," 3:480.

49. Ibid., 3:474–75.

50. Cleota Reed has given the Tile Works thorough scholarly attention in *Henry Chapman Mercer and the Moravian Pottery and Tile Works.* In this exhaustively researched study, she details every aspect of Mercer's tile production and she considers Mercer to have been "a major figure" in the movement.

51. Eileen Boris, *Art and Labor: Ruskin, Morris, and the Craftsman Ideal in America* (Philadelphia: Temple University Press, 1986), 33.

52. At Rose Valley, all property was held in common, and people rented their houses from the community. Beyond craft production, Rose Valley "folk" participated in poetry readings and theatrical productions. Rose Valley issued its own magazine, *The Artsman,* an obvious reference to the magazine Gustav Stickley produced and which he called *The Craftsman.* The title of the Rose

Valley magazine emphasized even further the relationship between art and craft which was at the center of the Arts and Crafts ideal. Most famous now for its furniture, the ambition of this alternative community was matched only by the brevity of its existence. Founded in the first years of this century, Rose Valley's experimental energy was largely spent by 1910.

53. Will Price, "A Plea for True Democracy in the Domestic Architecture of America," *The Craftsman* 16, no. 3:251.

54. For a consideration of the relationship between Morris and socialism, see Peter Stansky, *Redesigning the World: William Morris, the 1880s, and the Arts and Crafts* (Princeton: Princeton University Press, 1985). Stansky feels that Morris cannot be fully understood without appreciating his socialist commitments.

55. Boris, *Art and Labor,* 156.

56. T. J. Jackson Lears, *No Place of Grace: Antimodernism and the Transformation of American Culture 1880–1920* (New York: Pantheon Books, 1981), 60.

57. Mercer, cited in Reed, *Henry Chapman Mercer,* 25.

58. Ibid., 34.

59. It was, of course, Frank Lloyd Wright who attempted to bridge the distance between art and machine in his famous address "The Art and Craft of the Machine," delivered at Hull House in 1901. In this essay, Wright insisted that the machine be put to the purpose of making art, rather than relegated to the role of art's adversary. For a particularly useful discussion of Wright and "The Art and Craft of the Machine," see Peter Conn, *The Divided Mind: Ideology and Imagination in America, 1898–1917* (Cambridge: Cambridge University Press, 1983), 219–29.

60. Mercer Papers, BCHS, series 27, fol. 24.

61. See letter, Mercer to William Hagerman Graves, November 14, 1925, BCHS; and Marcia Wertine, "Henry Chapman Mercer: Nineteenth-Century Renaissance Man," *Archaeology* 31, no. 4 (July/August 1978): 44–51.

62. Mercer Papers, BCHS, series 23, folder 7.

63. Mercer to Graves, November 14, 1925, BCHS.

64. Henry Mercer, *The Tile Pavement in the Capitol of Pennsylvania,* rev. and ed. Ginger Duember (State College, Penn.: Pennsylvania Guild of Craftsmen, 1975), Preface.

65. Mercer to Hercules Read, June 23, 1924, cited in Reed, *Henry Chapman Mercer,* 75.

66. Jackson Lears, *No Place of Grace,* 96.

67. I have found two references to this point in Mercer's writings, one in a letter to Dr. R. D. McClure July 15, 1922, and the other in his essay "The Scope and Meaning of the Collection of Objects at the Museum of the BCHS," Mercer Papers, BCHS.

68. W. T. Taylor, "Personal Architecture," *Architectural Record* 33 (March 1913).

69. Mercer quoted in Taylor, "Personal Architecture," 243–44.

70. Martin Friedman, *Charles Sheeler* (New York: Watson-Guptill, 1975), 18, 20.

71. Sheeler to Mercer, March 4, 1926, Mercer Papers, BCHS, Series 1, fol. 131. In addition, Karen Davies has written a useful article about Sheeler's Doylestown connection, "Charles Sheeler in Doylestown and the Image of Rural Architecture," *Arts Magazine* 59 (March 1985).

72. Karen Lucic, *Charles Sheeler and the Cult of the Machine* (Cambridge: Harvard University Press, 1991), 68, 118.

73. Sheeler, quoted in Lucic, 65.

74. See Constance Rourke, *Charles Sheeler: Artist in the American Tradition* (New York: Harcourt, Brace & Co., 1938), 30, 58, 69–70, 77–78, 136. Joan Shelley Rubin has analyzed the connection between Sheeler and Rourke in "A Convergence of Vision: Rourke, Sheeler, and American Art," *American Quarterly* 42, no. 2 (June 1990): 191–222. Susan Fillin-Yeh has curated two exhibits of Sheeler's work, and her catalogues are quite helpful; see *Charles Sheeler, American Interiors* (New Haven: Yale University Art Gallery, 1987), and *The Technological Muse* (Katonah, N.Y.: The Museum, 1990). See also Karen Lucic, *Charles Sheeler in Doylestown* (Allentown, PA: Allentown Art Museum, 1997).

75. Mercer, *Papers of the BCHS,* 3:480.

76. Ford, quoted in James Wamsley, *American Ingenuity: The Henry Ford Museum and Greenfield Village* (New York: Abrams, 1985), 17.

77. Ford, cited in Greenleaf, *From These Beginnings,* 96.

78. Donna Gail Rosenstein considers this issue in "Historic Human Tools: Henry Chapman Mercer and His Collection 1897–1930" (master's thesis, University of Delaware, 1977).

79. In fairness to Mercer, it should be acknowledged that folklorists, archaeologists, historians, and others who deal with material culture still wrestle with the most effective way to interpret meaning from objects. See, for example, Jules David Prown, "Mind in Matter: An Introduction to Material Culture Theory and Method," *Winterthur Portfolio* 17 (1982): 2–18.

80. As far as I have been able to determine, Mercer had no connections either to those who were forming the new academic discipline of folklore. Likewise, as John Higham points out, by 1895, just when Mercer was about to set out on his museum career, the American Historical Association turned decidedly more "professional," effectively divorcing the academics and the amateurs. See Higham, *History,* 16.

81. Henry Chapman Mercer, *Ancient Carpenters' Tools* (Doylestown, 1929), Preface.

82. Henry Adams, *The Education of Henry Adams* (Boston: Houghton Mifflin Company, 1918), 266.

83. For this discussion I have relied on John Patrick Diggens, *The Promise of Pragmatism: Modernism and the Crisis of Knowledge and Authority* (Chicago: University of Chicago Press, 1994), esp. chapter 2.

84. Adams, *Education,* chapter 22.

85. Ibid., 380.

Chapter Six

1. *The Metropolitan Museum of Art: The Fiftieth Anniversary Celebration, MDCCCLXX–MCMXX* (New York, 1921), 21.

2. James Jackson Jarves, "About Museums of Art," *New York Times,* February 20, 1882, Scrapbook, Watson Library, Metropolitan Museum of Art.

3. In fact, such a history has been written. See Calvin Tomkins, *Merchants and Masterpieces: The Story of the Metropolitan Museum of Art* (New York: E. P. Dutton & Co., 1970).

4. I am taking this from Lawrence Levine's *Highbrow/lowbrow.*

5. Daniel Fox, for example, says that "American philanthropists were more concerned with art museums than with historical or scientific collections." See Fox, *Engines of Culture: Philanthropy and Art Museums* (Madison: State Historical Society of Wisconsin, 1963), 18.

6. See *A Metropolitan Art Museum in the City of New York: Proceedings of a Meeting Held at the Theatre of the Union League Club* (New York: Printed for the Committee, 1869), 5; and *Report to the Executive Committee* (New York: C. S. Wescott & Co., Union Printing House, 1870), 7–9.

7. Comfort to Putnam, November 13, 1869, quoted in Winifred Howe, *A History of the Metropolitan Museum of Art* (1913; rpt. New York: Arno Press, 1974), 119.

8. For this brief overview of South Kensington's development, I am indebted to Thomas Prasch, both for conversations at the Nineteenth Century Studies Association conference, April 1995, and for his paper, "The South Kensington Site and the Exhibitionary Complex."

9. Quoted in Howe, *History of the Metropolitan Museum of Art,* 121–22.

10. Quoted in Howe, 132.

11. *Report to the Executive Committee,* 8.

12. See Tomkins, *Merchants and Masterpieces,* 99, 106–07. Fry is also quoted in Howe, *History of the Metropolitan Museum of Art,* 58.

13. "The New Museum," *Philadelphia Times,* September 24, 1876.

14. Just for the record, it should be noted that what most scholars now regard as the most important American painting exhibited at the Centennial, Thomas Eakins's "Gross Clinic," was not even seen in the fine art exhibition but hung instead in the medical pavilion.

15. "Site and Suite of the Exposition," n.d., source unknown, PMA Archives, Scrapbook.

16. Lorin Blodget, Association of Industries of the United States, to unknown correspondent, May 10, 1880. PMA Archives, Dorr Collection, letterbook 4, letter 239.

17. "Industrial Art," *Philadelphia Press,* October 24, 1877.

18. Walter Smith, reprinted in Pennsylvania Museum, *Annual Report,* 1876–77.

19. "The Art Museum Project," n.d. (1876?), unknown source, PMA Archives, Scrapbook.

20. Ibid.

21. Hartranft, quoted in Pennsylvania Museum, *Annual Report,* 1876–77, 14.

22. January 16, 1871, unknown source; Scrapbook, Watson Library, Metropolitan Museum of Art.

23. Pennsylvania Museum, *Annual Report,* 1876–77, 2.

24. "Industrial Art," *Philadelphia Times,* October 12, 1876. This sense of connection deepened when the papers announced that the South Kensington Museum had made a significant donation of objects to the fledgling Philadelphia institution. See "The New Museum," *Philadelphia Times,* September 24, 1876. The British also donated virtually all of the Indian collection displayed at the Centennial to the Pennsylvania Museum. See PMA Archives, Dorr Collection, letterbook 2, letter 49, November 14, 1876.

25. Walter Smith to Dumont Wagner, February 21, 1877. PMA Archives, Dorr Collection, letterbook 2, letter 190.

26. See Neil Harris, "The Gilded Age Revisited: Boston and the Museum Movement," *American Quarterly* 14, no. 4 (1962): 545–66. These founding principles were printed on the museum's official letterhead, which featured three intersecting circles at the top: one for art, one for education, and one for industry.

27. Clarke to Dorr, February 17, 1880. PMA Archives, Dorr Collection, letterbook 4, letter 206.

28. "Education for Artisans," *Philadelphia Public Ledger,* February 9, 1877.

29. Pennsylvania Museum, *Annual Report,* 1879, 9.

30. "Industrial Art," *Philadelphia Press,* March 22, 1877.

31. Cited in Esther Klein, *Fairmount Park: A History and a Guidebook* (Bryn Mawr: Harcum Junior College Press, 1974), 68.

32. "Governor John Hartranft's Message for 1878," n.d., unknown source, PMA Archives, Scrapbook.

33. Pennsylvania Museum, *Annual Report,* 1885, 7.

34. "The Metropolitan Museum of Art," *Evening Post,* February 14, 1879, Scrapbook, Watson Library, Metropolitan Museum of Art.

35. "Let the Poor View the Art Treasures," *New York Herald,* May 13, 1891, Scrapbook, Watson Library, Metropolitan Museum of Art.

36. Quoted in Howe, *History of the Metropolitan Museum of Art,* 245.

37. Metropolitan director Philippe de Montebello, while by no means as heavy handed and exclusive as his predecessors of the last century, still unapologetically defends the Met as an elitist institution. See Calvin Tomkins, "The Importance of Being Elitist," *The New Yorker,* November 24, 1997, 58–69.

38. Howe, 59.

39. Cope to Norris, July 3, 1889. PMA Archives, Dorr Collection, letterbook, letter 195.

40. Pennsylvania Museum, *Annual Report,* 1876–77, 12

41. Coleman Sellers to Justice, April 2, 1879. PMA Archives, Dorr Collection, letterbook 4, letter 212.

42. Pennsylvania Museum, *Annual Report,* 1883, 9. Perfection did not last

long. At the turn of the century, the museum began "reclassifying and concentrating the various classes of exhibits." See Pennsylvania Museum, *Annual Report,* 1901, 19.

43. Pennsylvania Museum, *Annual Report,* 1890, 6.

44. Pennsylvania Museum, *Annual Report,* 1904, 18.

45. Robert Lamborn to Dalton Dorr, December 9, 1892. PMA Archives, Dorr Collection, letterbook 8, letter 125.

46. Pennsylvania Museum, *Annual Report,* 1908, 15.

47. Supplement to Pennsylvania Museum, *Bulletin* no. 34 (April 1911): 1–2.

48. In the midst of writing this, I had the extraordinary opportunity to visit the recently opened art museum in Shanghai. It is a stunning place, incorporating the very latest Western museum techniques (including tea and gift shops), but the objects were arranged quite differently than we in the West are accustomed to. The galleries were organized, much like some of the old Pennsylvania Museum galleries, around materials—jade in one section, ceramics in another.

49. "Our Public Museums," unknown source, n.d. (December 1884?), Scrapbook, Watson Library, Metropolitan Museum of Art.

50. No title, *Philadelphia Public Ledger,* June 7, 1881. The school also got off to a fast start. An advertising circular dated October 22, 1877 announced the school's first classes.

51. Pennsylvania Museum, *Annual Report,* 1884, 14. Philadelphia was not only a leading textile producer, but it was famous for producing finished textiles like carpets and lace, for which design was critical.

52. Pennsylvania Museum, *Annual Report,* 1876–77, 18–19. Textile design, though, was but one area of museum and school concern. Students could also study pottery, industrial drawing, glass, and woodworking. Members of several of the city's prominent manufacturing firms helped provide instruction for the school; for example, Joseph Celleskey of the Hope Manufacturing Company taught wood-carving.

53. Pennsylvania Museum, *Annual Report,* 1887, 29.

54. Pennsylvania Museum, *Annual Report,* 1888, 6–7.

55. See Howe, *History of the Metropolitan Museum of Art,* 201–202. A generation later, when John Cotton Dana of the Newark Museum organized a show of German industrial design in 1912, the Metropolitan refused to mount it, looking down its institutional nose at all things "commercial." As the United States entered World War I, the Metropolitan became interested in industrial design, and it held a series of such shows throughout the 1920s. These shows, however, concerned themselves less with linking the industrial with the artistic and more with defining the aesthetics of modernism through consumer products. See Christine Wallace Laidlaw, "The Metropolitan Museum of Art and Modern Design: 1917–1929," *The Journal of Decorative and Propaganda Arts* 8 (Spring 1988): 88–103.

56. "Our Technical Schools," *The Mail and Express,* October 24, 1883.

57. No title, *New York Times,* n.d. (May 1894), Scrapbook, Watson Library, Metropolitan Museum of Art.

58. Ibid.

59. Pennsylvania Museum, *Annual Report,* 1893, 9–10.

60. "Women's Committee Report," Pennsylvania Museum, *Annual Report,* 1897, 42.

61. Dana to Dorr, March 16, 1892. PMA Archives, Dorr Collection, letterbook 8, letter 99.

62. Pennsylvania Museum, *Annual Report,* 1893, 19.

63. Pennsylvania Museum, *Annual Report,* 1895, 12.

64. Pennsylvania Museum, *Annual Report,* 1919, 15.

65. Pepper to Dorr, July 2, 1892. PMA Archives, Dorr Collection, letterbook 8, letter 249.

66. Pennsylvania Museum, *Annual Report,* 1904, 19.

67. Walter Benjamin, "The Work of Art in the Age of Mechanical Reproduction," *Illuminations* (New York: Harcourt, Brace & World, Inc., 1968), 219–53.

68. Pennsylvania Museum, *Annual Report,* 1897, 1.

69. See Mrs. Weightman to Dorr, April 20, 1894. PMA Archives, Dorr Collection, letterbook 11, letter 185. Sommerville anticipated the opening of the University's Museum and thought his collection would find a more suitable home there.

70. Robert Lamborn to Dorr, January 13, 1893. PMA Archives, Dorr Collection, letterbook 9, letter 170.

71. Clarence Moore to Dorr, July 23, 1900. PMA Archives, Dorr Collection, letterbook 15, letter 198.

72. It is, however, certainly the case that objects like mummies continue to straddle this line between art and archaeology. The mummies in Philadelphia rest at Penn, but they are prominently on display at Boston's Museum of Fine Arts.

73. McClung, quoted in Pennsylvania Museum, *Annual Report,* 1912, 13.

74. L. W. Miller to Dorr, May 6, 1895. PMA Archives, Dorr Collection, letterbook 12, letter 12.

75. Pennsylvania Museum, *Annual Report,* 1912, 14.

76. Warner to McIlhenny, October 24, 1917. PMA Archives, Warner Collection.

77. Widener, quoted in "To Add Wings to Old or Build New Gallery," *Philadelphia Public Ledger,* April 5, 1900.

78. "For a Great Art Gallery," *The Record,* November 5, 1893.

79. *Catalogue of the W. P. Wilstach Collection* (Philadelphia: Commissioners of Fairmount Park, 1900), 7.

80. William Platt Pepper to Edwin AtLee Barber, December 20, 1906. PMA Archives, Barber Collection.

81. Pennsylvania Museum, *Annual Report,* 1906, 12.

82. "City Art Gallery Plans Approved," *Philadelphia Press,* March 13, 1913.

83. Pennsylvania Museum, *Annual Report,* 1917.

84. I have taken this phrase from the title of the standard institutional biography of the Museum: George Robert and Mary Robert, *Triumph on Fair-*

mount: *Fiske Kimball and the Philadelphia Museum of Art* (Philadelphia: Lippincott, 1959).

85. Coleman Sellers to Dumont Wagner, February 25, 1877. PMA Archives, Dorr Collection, letterbook 2, letter 187.

86. For the most thorough account of this movement in Philadelphia, see David Brownlee, *Building the City Beautiful: The Benjamin Franklin Parkway and the Philadelphia Museum of Art* (Philadelphia: Philadelphia Museum of Art, 1989).

87. Price was also instrumental in moving these other institutions to the Parkway. See Edward Carter, *"One Grand Pursuit:" A Brief History of the American Philosophical Society's First 250 Years, 1743–1993* (Philadelphia: American Philosophical Society, 1993), 56.

88. Peter Widener doubtless smiled when the model went on public display. The three architects had been his personal choice; they had built his own house and private art gallery just outside the city. Having complained about Memorial Hall's inadequacies for twenty-five years, he finally had what he wanted.

89. See Brownlee, *Building the City Beautiful,* 13.

90. "A Question in Stone," *Evening Ledger,* August 11, 1923.

91. "Museum Plans New Feature in Displaying Art," *Philadelphia Public Ledger,* November 11, 1926. Widener got his museum, but Philadelphia did not get his paintings. Widener found himself repeatedly on the outside of Philadelphia's inbred social elite, and so his son finally, in a final irony, sent his Old Masters to the National Gallery, where they form one of the cores of that collection. George Elkins, Philip McFadden, and John G. Johnson, however, did give their impressive collections to the new museum.

92. Quoted in Benjamin Ives Gilman, *Museum Ideals of Purpose and Method* (Cambridge, Mass.: Harvard University Press, 1923), xi.

93. "Calls the Art Museum Louvre of Philadelphia," *Evening Ledger,* January 19, 1927.

94. See *Philadelphia Public Ledger,* March 25, 1928, and Fiske Kimball, "Museum Values," address published in *American Magazine of Art* 19 (September 1928); PMA Archives, Kimball Collection, manuscript.

95. "New Museum Officially Opened By City Executives," *Philadelphia Inquirer,* March 27, 1928.

96. Kimball to Jenks, July 5, 1927. PMA Archives, Kimball Collection.

97. "Art in Philadelphia," *New York Times,* March 28, 1928.

98. See "Philadelphia's Great Art Museum," *Philadelphia Inquirer,* November 29, 1927, and "New Museum Plan is Pageant of Art," *Philadelphia Inquirer,* December 11, 1927, for descriptions of this plan.

99. Fiske Kimball, "Museum Values." The completion of Kimball's Main Street had to wait until the 1990s. For a variety of reasons, legal and otherwise, it was only then that the Philadelphia Museum could undertake a major reinstallation of its holdings to complete the walk. With its completion, Fiske Kim-

ball's dream has been realized, and the move from Memorial Hall to the Parkway, from South Kensington to the Louvre, is complete.

100. Ibid.

101. Fiske Kimball, "The Modern Museum of Art," *Architectural Record* 66 (December 1929): 563.

102. Pennsylvania Museum, *Bulletin* no. 11 (March 1928): 3.

103. A. E. B., "The Allurements of a Museum," Pennsylvania Museum, *Bulletin* no. 92 (February 1925): 92–94.

104. Frank Jewett Mather, Jr., "Atmosphere versus Art," *Atlantic Monthly* 146 (August 1930): 171–77.

105. Fiske Kimball, "Museum Values."

106. Ibid.

107. Ibid.

108. For a brief article about this controversy, see Anon., "Rocky: An Unlikely Phoenix for the Philadelphia Museum of Art," *Museum News* 69 (May/June 1990): 10–12.

Chapter Seven

1. See Arthur Dudden, "The City Embraces Normalcy," in Russell Weigley, ed. *Philadelphia: A 300-Year History* (New York: Norton, 1982), 571; and "Philadelphia Fair Appears Assured," *New York Times,* December 10, 1925.

2. See, for example, untitled manuscript, unknown source, Historical Society of Pennsylvania, MS 1959, Albert Greenfield, Box 29, Folder 17.

3. "Finish of Sesqui Written as New Year is Born," unidentified clipping, January 1, 1927, Historical Society of Pennsylvania, Wr * 6929.

4. See Robert Rydell, *World of Fairs: The Century-of-Progress Expositions* (Chicago: University of Chicago Press, 1993), and Michael Kammen, *Mystic Chords of Memory,* 494.

5. See "Philadelphia, Victim of Land Speculators, Sees Independence Fair Plans Fade Away," *Dearborn Independent,* March 10, 1923.

6. See "Town Meeting Votes Down Big Sesqui, 10 to 1," *Philadelphia Public Ledger,* December 1, 1923.

7. Historical Society of Pennsylvania, MSS 587, Elizabeth Walker.

8. Robert Stratton to Albert Greenfield, July 16, 1925, MSS 1959, Albert Greenfield.

9. MSS 1959, Albert Greenfield, and MSS 587, Elizabeth Walker.

10. C. F. Rhodes to Albert Greenfield, July 25, 1926, MSS 1959, Albert Greenfield.

11. See "Sesqui-Centennial Facts," MSS 587, Elizabeth Walker, and Philadelphia City Archives, Box A–1479, 232.22.

12. See untitled, undated clipping, MSS 587, Elizabeth Walker, and "A New Era in Expositions," *Philadelphia Public Ledger,* November 10, 1923.

13. I have been relying on the "Complimentary Official Guide Map through the grounds of the Sesqui-Centennial International Exposition at Philadelphia"

for my discussion of the Fair's layout. Philadelphia City Archives, Box A–1479, 232.22.

14. For example, *The Sesqui-Centennial International Exposition: A Record Based on Official Data and Departmental Reports* (1929) listed High Street as one of three achievements of the fair.

15. Elizabeth Frazer, "1776–1926 at the Sesqui-Centennial," *Saturday Evening Post,* September 11, 1926, 65.

16. Ibid. 50, 52.

17. Anna Robeson Burr, *The City We Visit: Old Philadelphia* (Philadelphia: J. B. Lippincott Company, 1926), 39–42.

18. See *The Sesqui-Centennial Anniversary of the Signing of the Declaration of Independence,* MSS 587, Elizabeth Walker.

19. "Sesqui-Centennial Facts," MSS 587, Elizabeth Walker.

20. See "Independence Day Celebration 150th Anniversary of American Independence," typescript, Philadelphia City Archives, Box A–1478, 232.11.

21. "A New Era in Expositions," *Philadelphia Public Ledger,* November 10, 1923.

22. David Lowenthal, *The Past is a Foreign Country* (Cambridge: Cambridge University Press, 1985), 96, 102.

23. Elizabeth Frazer, "1776–1926 at the Sesqui-Centennial," 52.

24. Cynthia Eagle Russett, *Darwin in America: The Intellectual Response, 1865–1912* (San Francisco: Freeman, 1976), 204.

25. Alcoholics Anonymous, *Alcoholics Anonymous: The Story of how over One Hundred Men have Recovered from Alcoholism* (New York: Works Publishing Company), 1939, 48. For this quotation, I am indebted to Andrew Walker, who came across it in his own research. "Naked eye science" was a phrase used often at the American Museum. See John Michael Kennedy, "Philanthropy and Science in New York City," 4.

26. Mercer-Sheeler correspondence, Bucks County Historical Society.

27. Reprint of Franz Boas, "Some Principles of Museum Administration," *Science* 25 (June 14, 1907): 1.

28. See, for example, "Art Museums Humanized," *Saturday Evening Post,* March 31, 1928.

29. For this thumbnail sketch of the Franklin Institute's history I have relied on Howard McClenahan, "Present and Proposed Activities of the Franklin Institute," *Journal of the Franklin Institute* 206, no. 6 (December 1928): 635–40. The standard volume on the institute's early years is Bruce Sinclair, *Philadelphia's Philosopher Mechanics: A History of the Franklin Institute, 1824–1865* (Baltimore: The Johns Hopkins University Press, 1974).

30. I have taken this figure from Carol Slater, "A History of The Franklin Institute: The Men and the Museum," unpublished paper, Franklin Institute.

31. "A Living Memorial," Franklin Institute, Building Records, Building Fund, 1906–1931, and William Jackson, "Exhibits at the Franklin Institute," *Dedication of the Benjamin Franklin Memorial* (1938).

32. "Bakelite Travelcade," Franklin Institute, Building Records, Building Fund, 1906–1931.

33. McClenahan, "Present and Proposed Activities of the Franklin Institute," 739.

34. "A Living Memorial."

35. McClenahan, "Present and Proposed Activities of the Franklin Institute," 750.

36. John Jenks to Fiske Kimball, July 29, 1927, PMA Archives, Kimball Collection.

37. Kimball to J. L. Montalvo Guenard, March 8, 1928, PMA Archives, Kimball Collection.

38. "Memorandum on the question of possible transfer of Model of Rome to the University Museum by exchange of loans," n.d., PMA Archives. Such swapping seems to have occurred several times in the early 1930s. The Academy of Natural Sciences sent material to Penn in 1930, and the Pennsylvania Museum and the University Museum traded pieces in 1934. See Horace Jayne to Brubaker, November 29, 1930, and Kimball to Jayne, July 26, 1934, PMA Archives, Jayne Correspondence.

39. In 1919, for example, the Pennsylvania Museum acquired an Indian temple which at least one newspaper thought belonged more properly at the university. The newspaper's editor threatened to write a "screed" against the acquisition. See letter from George Byron Gordon to Langdon Warner, September 29, 1919, PMA Archives, Warner Collection. See also Steven Conn, "Where is the East: Asian Objects in American Museums," unpublished paper.

40. Nelson Graburn has made a similar observation about the place of the non-Western "artist" in the Western imagination. See his introduction to Graburn, ed. *Ethnic and Tourist Arts: Cultural Expressions from the Fourth World* (Berkeley: University of California Press, 1976), 23.

41. Kurt Andersen, "Letter from Los Angeles: A City on a Hill," *The New Yorker,* September 29, 1997, 66–73.

42. See Vincent Carducci, "DIA in Decline," *New Art Examiner,* February/ March 1992, 29–31.

43. See, for example, Letter to the Editor, from Samuel Sachs, Director of the Detroit Institute of Arts, *New York Times,* November 20, 1993.

44. The *New York Times* noticed this phenomenon on November 18, 1997 when it ran a front-page special report, "Cities are Fostering the Arts as a Way to Save Downtown."

45. "Art and the City," *Philadelphia Inquirer,* December 12, 1993.

46. George Brown Goode, *The Principles of Museum Administration,* 73.

Index

~

Abbott, Charles, 92
Academy of Natural Sciences (Phila-
    delphia), **7,** 24, 25, 40–43, 53, 57,
    71, 83, 230, 244, 247, 248; archi-
    tecture of, 67–68; and Bicenten-
    nial, 71; Building Committee, 41,
    56, 58; and Charles Darwin, 44,
    68–70; Committee on Instruc-
    tion, 65–66; and ecology, 71–73;
    founding of, 37; and hadrosau-
    rus, 45; Jessup Scholarships, 60;
    and Morton Collection, 82; and
    "original research," 58–61; and
    Shackleton Expedition, 221;
    and University of Pennsylvania,
    62–63, 252
Adams, Henry, 3, 22, 189–91
Adams, John Quincy: and Smithson
    Bequest, 54, 63
Addams, Jane, 14, 178
Agassiz, Louis, 42, 49, 67; and Darwin-
    ian debate, 49; and Museum of
    Comparative Zoology, 43, 55; and
    Peabody Museum of American
    Archaeology and Ethnology, 76
Alpers, Svetlana, 5, 9
American Academy of Political and
    Social Science, 147
American Anthropological Associa-
    tion, 111
American Anthropologist, 77
American Association for the Ad-
    vancement of Science, 77, 82, 90,
    103

American Association of Muse-
    ums, 99
American Historical Association, 20,
    28, 75, 84, 170, 247
American Historical Review, 157
American Museum of Natural His-
    tory, 6, 9, 25, 26, 51, 57–58, 75,
    96, 109, 246; and anthropology,
    87, 102; and dioramas, 70, 244;
    founding of, 43; and Franz Boas,
    102, 107, 119; and public educa-
    tion, 112; and vertebrate paleon-
    tology, 52
American Naturalist, 164
American Philosophical Society, 82
American Races (Brinton), 83
"American Scholar" (Emerson), 174
Ames, Kenneth, 14
Amsterdam Museum, 195
Ancient Carpenter's Tools (Mercer),
    187–88
*Annals of the American Academy of Po-
    litical and Social Science*, 147–48
Annals of Natural History, 79
Annenberg Collection (Metropolitan
    Museum of Art), 10, 205
Appadurai, Arjun, 23–24
Archaeology, Old World vs. New
    World, 92–95, 164–65
Architectural Record, 83, 183
Architecture: collegiate Gothic,
    Academy of Natural Sciences,
    56; neo-classical, 121; of Univer-
    sity of Pennsylvania Museum, 83

Locators in boldface refer to illustrations.